EAGER EAGLES

The Stackpole Military History Series

THE AMERICAN CIVIL WAR

Cavalry Raids of the Civil War
Ghost, Thunderbolt, and Wizard
In the Lion's Mouth
Pickett's Charge
Witness to Gettysburg

WORLD WAR I

Doughboy War

WORLD WAR II

After D-Day
Airborne Combat
Armor Battles of the Waffen-SS, 1943–45
Armoured Guardsmen
Army of the West
Arnhem 1944
Australian Commandos
The B-24 in China
Backwater War
The Battalion
The Battle of France
The Battle of Sicily
Battle of the Bulge, Vol. 1
Battle of the Bulge, Vol. 2
Beyond the Beachhead
Beyond Stalingrad
The Black Bull
Blitzkrieg Unleashed
Blossoming Silk against the Rising Sun
Bodenplatte
The Brandenburger Commandos
The Brigade
Bringing the Thunder
The Canadian Army and the Normandy Campaign
Coast Watching in World War II
Colossal Cracks
Condor
A Dangerous Assignment
D-Day Bombers
D-Day Deception
D-Day to Berlin
Decision in the Ukraine
Destination Normandy
Dive Bomber!
A Drop Too Many
Eager Eagles
Eagles of the Third Reich
The Early Battles of Eighth Army
Eastern Front Combat
Europe in Flames
Exit Rommel
The Face of Courage
Fatal Decisions
Fist from the Sky
Flying American Combat Aircraft of World War II
For Europe
Forging the Thunderbolt
For the Homeland
Fortress France
The German Defeat in the East, 1944–45
German Order of Battle, Vol. 1
German Order of Battle, Vol. 2
German Order of Battle, Vol. 3
The Germans in Normandy
Germany's Panzer Arm in World War II
GI Ingenuity
Goodwood
The Great Ships
Grenadiers
Guns against the Reich
Hitler's Nemesis
Hold the Westwall
Infantry Aces
In the Fire of the Eastern Front
Iron Arm
Iron Knights
Japanese Army Fighter Aces
Japanese Naval Fighter Aces
JG 26 Luftwaffe Fighter Wing War Diary, Vol. 1
JG 26 Luftwaffe Fighter Wing War Diary, Vol. 2
Kampfgruppe Peiper at the Battle of the Bulge
The Key to the Bulge
Knight's Cross Panzers
Kursk
Luftwaffe Aces
Luftwaffe Fighter Ace
Luftwaffe Fighter-Bombers over Britain
Luftwaffe Fighters and Bombers
Massacre at Tobruk
Mechanized Juggernaut or Military Anachronism?
Messerschmitts over Sicily
Michael Wittmann, Vol. 1
Michael Wittmann, Vol. 2
Mission 85
Mission 376
Mountain Warriors
The Nazi Rocketeers
Night Flyer / Mosquito Pathfinder
No Holding Back
On the Canal
Operation Mercury
Packs On!
Panzer Aces
Panzer Aces II
Panzer Aces III
Panzer Commanders of the Western Front
Panzergrenadier Aces
Panzer Gunner
The Panzer Legions
Panzers in Normandy
Panzers in Winter
Panzer Wedge, Vol. 1
Panzer Wedge, Vol. 2
The Path to Blitzkrieg
Penalty Strike
Poland Betrayed
Red Road from Stalingrad
Red Star under the Baltic
Retreat to the Reich
Rommel's Desert Commanders
Rommel's Desert War
Rommel's Lieutenants
The Savage Sky
Ship-Busters
The Siege of Küstrin
The Siegfried Line
A Soldier in the Cockpit
Soviet Blitzkrieg
Spitfires and Yellow Tail Mustangs
Stalin's Keys to Victory
Surviving Bataan and Beyond
T-34 in Action
Tank Tactics
Tigers in the Mud
Triumphant Fox
The 12th SS, Vol. 1
The 12th SS, Vol. 2
Twilight of the Gods
Typhoon Attack
The War against Rommel's Supply
War in the Aegean
War of the White Death
Warsaw 1944
Winter Storm
Wolfpack Warriors
Zhukov at the Oder

THE COLD WAR / VIETNAM

Cyclops in the Jungle
Expendable Warriors
Fighting in Vietnam
Flying American Combat Aircraft: The Cold War
Here There Are Tigers
Land with No Sun
MiGs over North Vietnam
Phantom Reflections
Street without Joy
Through the Valley
Two One Pony

WARS OF AFRICA AND THE MIDDLE EAST

Never-Ending Conflict
The Rhodesian War

GENERAL MILITARY HISTORY

Carriers in Combat
Cavalry from Hoof to Track
Desert Battles
Doughboy War
Guerrilla Warfare
Ranger Dawn
Sieges
The Spartan Army

EAGER EAGLES

The U.S. Eighth Air Force in Europe, 1941–43

Martin W. Bowman

STACKPOLE
BOOKS

Published in paperback in the U.S. in 2013 by

STACKPOLE BOOKS
5067 Ritter Road
Mechanicsburg, PA 17055
www.stackpolebooks.com

First published in the United Kingdom in 2011 by Pen & Sword Aviation, an imprint of Pen & Sword Books Limited. This edition published by arrangement with Pen & Sword.

Cover design by Wendy A. Reynolds

Printed in the United States of America

10 9 8 7 6 5 4 3 2 1

Library of Congress Cataloging-in-Publication Data
Bowman, Martin W.
Eager eagles : the US Eighth Air Force in Europe, 1941–1943 / Martin W Bowman.
pages cm. — (Stackpole military history series)
Originally published under title: US Eighth Air Force in Europe. South Yorkshire : Pen and Sword Aviation, 2012.
Includes index.
ISBN 978-0-8117-1309-2
1. United States. Air Force. Air Force, 8th. 2. World War, 1939–1945—Aerial operations, American. 3. World War, 1939–1945—Campaigns—Europe. I. Title.
D790.228th .B683 2013
940.54'4973—dc23

2013025163

Contents

Prologue

'Yo, Howie! How's chow tonight?' I ask as I approach our navigator leaving the mess hall.

'Yo, Charlie. Same old stuff. Pork. Ya better eat though. We're on the battle order. Group Deputy Lead.'

'Deputy again? Who's leadin'?'

Howie replies but by this time he is too far away for me to hear him, so I push my way through the usual gang of loiterers, glance at the bulletin board while listening to their speculations.

'Probably another long haul.'

'I wouldn't be surprised. I always seem to get 'em.'

'Aw, quit your moaning. You don't hear me gripin', do you?'

'Quiet, paddlefoot, I guess you've done your share of it.'

Leaving them to their varied opinions, I thread my way into the chow house, pick up a *Stars and Stripes,* glance surreptitiously at the can marked '1 penny'. And with a mumbled general apology about not having any change and something about paying up tomorrow, I find an empty seat where I read and eat.

Hmmm. Poor feerliss Fosdick. Whut next? Well look here! The tribe is in fourth place; boys in France are opening things up a little, pretty hot back home. Shoving a hunk of cake in my mouth, I slide my chair back and go back to the barracks alternately perusing the *Stars and Stripes* and exchanging commonplaces with more tardy companions.

Re-established in the barracks, we have time for about one smoke before a raunchy GI thrusts his head through the door. 'Jeep is waiting, Sir. You're wanted at Group.

Howie and I grab our hats, straighten our ties and ride down to headquarters to look at the big picture.

The intelligence room is pretty well filled with the lead bombardiers and navigators on the field, as well as S-2 men and all are busy looking over target photos, courses, RAF maps, flak maps, etc. We stay for about an hour, after which time we feel we have had the gist of the mission pretty well in mind. Then we depart to tell the boys in the Boulton Paul hut, 'Better log some sack time, early breakfast.'

Though they know it is futile, there are always a few jokers who ask where we are going.

'Well, I'll tell you. Tomorrow we're going to Czechoslovakia via Berlin. We're going to load up with 3,100 gallons and carry 2 hand grenades and 100 leaflets.'

Howie joins in, 'No, Charlie's just kidding. Actually, we're going to take 500-pounders. About 700 miles east we're to meet a Zeppelin where we we'll refuel and go on to Tokyo.'

Gibes from the rest of the gang are directed at the red-faced questioners as Howie and I get undressed and turn in. Most of us want to sleep but for about half an hour we have to listen to a nightly sermon by a Texan in the far end of the barracks. Tonight he tells us about the big wind they had in the Panhandle, relating all the gruesome details and winding up by saying. 'I don't suppose there was anything between Texas and the North Pole but a single strand barbed wire fence and that doggoned wind had pushed all the barbs up into one little ol' corner.'

'Attention all combat crews! Attention all combat crews! Breakfast is now being served in the combat mess! Breakfast is now being served in the combat mess! That is all.'

I've been awakened by hearing rooster's crow and that isn't bad. I've been aroused by playful fraternity brothers and that can be endured. Nobody likes an alarm clock but no alarm clock, no matter how grating and raucous, hasn't never heard no swearing that will begin to compare with the forever unprintable barrage of invectives that now assails the insensitive Tannoy.

'It's inhuman! That's what it is!'

'I just got to sleep!'

'Who ever invented that damn Tannoy?'

'Say, what the hell time is it, anyway?'

A long, puffy-eyed stare at my watch finally reveals something resembling numbers and hands and I reply, '0230.'

A spasmodic cursing is my only reward, so I begin the mechanical act of dressing, which eventually drives the urge for sleep into the background.

Bedraggled lines of shadowy forms begin to feel their way to breakfast under a cloudless sky, black as V-mail ink except for a number of feeble stars.

Fresh eggs and a cup of coffee just about complete the waking up process, then, breakfast over, a procession of GI trucks convoy us to the flight line. Cigarettes glow and describe arcs in the blackness as the truck occupants banter with each other.

In the smoke-filled briefing room speculations are still riding high. Howie and I exchange grins as various possibilities are brought to light by the yet uninformed men.

'The target for today will be the Fleugzeug Motorenwerks at—

'Pilots and navigators will brief at 0430, stations 0500, start engines 0510, taxi 0520, take off 0530, forming over Splasher 97 at 11,000 feet, leaving Splasher 97 at 0710 and proceeding on course. The 93rd is leading the wing, 422nd flying high right, 866th low left. Carrying twelve 500-pounders, 2,700 gallons, time at altitude 5 hours, estimated time of return 1330. Time Tick?'

'In 55 seconds it will be coming up on 0337. Coming up on 0337 in 45 seconds. In 30 seconds the time will be 0337. 15 seconds…10 seconds… 5…4…3…2…1…Tick!'

Pop Hamilton takes over and goes over the route in detail, warning us of certain large cities covered by the various-sized red spots on the map. 'Now this town isn't so bad. They have 27 guns and over here there are 32. At the target, you will have about 300 guns but only 187 will be able to bear on you if you stay on course.'

There follows a few more words on fighters, both friendly and enemy, some projected close ups of the target area, a little on our bomb and gas load and weather takes over.

'Stormy' gives us the 'synoptic situation' and declares emphatically that we won't be able to see a damn thing because of the high sitting over Sweden. He predicts nil to one-tenth clouds over the base area and ten-tenths coverage in the target vicinity, so we are pretty confident that it will be just the other way around and that we will have a visual target.

We split up for separate briefing. Pilots get additional taxiing and forming instructions; the navigators begin a hasty struggle with plotters, maps and computers and the bombardiers are warned not to toggle too soon or too late.

By this time the gunners, who have been briefed separately, are dressed and theoretically, at least, pre-flighting the airplane. We take only a very few articles on a mission: heated clothes, Mae Wests, parachute and harness, headset, throat mike, helmet, boots, gloves, oxygen mask and escape kits to mention most of them. A man dressed for combat looks as though he has put on a lot of weight recently and, truthfully, he has.

On our way to the dispersal area we note the approach of dawn and also note a heavy concentration of clouds above. Pre-flighting is a mechanical procedure and is accomplished in a few minutes. This done, we spend our spare time in beneficial ways, such as talking over our missions, laying bets of flak and fighter attacks and discussing the last party, or the previous night's pass to town. All too soon it is time for stations. Chute harnesses are buckled and we clamber aboard.

Men in different positions have set times when they are most nervous. I find that my 'thinking time' falls in the two-hour period involving cranking up, taxiing, take-off and forming, as it is during this period that I have absolutely nothing to do but pull the cotter pins from the bomb fuses before we reach oxygen altitude.

Forming takes quite a while, as it is necessary for each plane to be in its proper place in the squadron, each squadron in the proper place in the right group, etc.

Finally, all is in order and we start across the channel. At this point, I breathe a little easier because we are finally on our way and I breathe a little harder for we are 11,000 feet above the ground.

Joining Howie in the nose, I plug in headset, throat mike, heated suit and oxygen and strive to arrange myself as comfortably as possible in the cramped confines of a heavy bomber.

The sun reflecting on the solid blanket of clouds below gives them a carnival 'fluff' appearance and it almost seems as though you could jump out and sink into them without hurting yourself. As far as I can see, there are formations of bombers ahead and behind us trailing off into flyspecks in the distance. High overhead four Lightnings streak across the sky leaving telltale contrails to mark their passage.

'12,000 feet. Oxygen check,' brings satisfactory replies from all positions from tail turret to nose turret.

The formation is fairly good and we take a little evasive action as we cross the enemy coast. A few bursts of flak break near the group as though in recognition of our arrival. The assault is rather lackadaisical though and we roar on with no damage. Up ahead, clouds are thinning out and we can see patches of enemy territory. Picking up a map, I try to spot our outstanding points to aid Howie who has been doing dead reckoning.

All but a few lingering clouds have disappeared and as I look down, I can't help thinking that the landscape looks about the same as at home or in England. I just about convince myself that combat flying isn't so bad when Mitch's voice rings over the interphone. 'Pilot to crew. Flak at 12 o'clock level.' Looking down, we can see the flashes of the guns, though we can't see the guns themselves. It seems to be coming from one of the larger cities over which we have to pass.

'Boy, these guys are the original squirrel hunters,' offers one of the gunners, as black puffs appear just off our wing in spite of our evasive action.

'Tail gunner to navigator. There's a plane going down at five o'clock. B-24. The left wing is on fire.'

'OK, Palumbo. Keep an eye on it and watch for chutes,' is Howie's terse reply as he makes a notation in his log recording time and position.

'Ten minutes until the IP. Watch for fighters.'

'Roger, Howie. Bombardier to radio. Bombardier to radio.'

'Go ahead.'

'Sergeant Lefty, go down in the bomb bay and stand by.'

'Roger.'

A pause ensues while Fullerton attaches the bomb bay outlet and switches to interphone. Almost immediately the bomb doors of the lead ship creep back to allow a glimpse of its heavy load.

'Open the bomb doors, Lefty.'

'Roger, bomb doors coming open,' is heard over interphone and the ship begins to vibrate heavily under the influence of the slipstream rushing through the bomb bays.

Silence follows. The gunners scan the skyline for fighters. Howie is working industriously at his table, glancing frequently at the compass and other instruments, while my own glances are divided between the lead plane and the ground. I can see check points that have been imprinted in my mind by our previous study and in a moment I can pick out the target off in the distance.

Flak begins to come up in earnest as the uncovering of planes is completed. Uncovering consists of arranging the formation to allow a regular spacing between formations and to get the most effective bomb pattern. I see bombs falling from groups ahead and glance at our lead plane. Flak is bursting above, below and all around us now and the only measures we can take are those the lead bombardier uses as he corrects for course. We no longer have to worry about taking over the responsibility for leading as our leader has come through unscathed.

Tenseness prevails in everyone as we drive on. All my attention is now riveted on the lead ship but I can see plenty of flak out of the corner of my eye. These planes are big and right now they look bigger. How can they miss us? We pass through the after effects of a flak burst. They are breaking closer now. One bursts above us. Wsssst Whooomp! A chilling sound! Whooomp! Now I hear a noise like gravel or stones rattling on a tin root and I know we have been hit, probably just collected a few holes.

I check things in my mind. Switches on...Intervolometer...bomb doors open...Yes, everything is ready. Seems as though this run will never end. Why doesn't he drop? We're practically on top of the target. Whooomp! Whooomph! Then suddenly, even though I have been watching, it surprises me when the bombs begin to tumble from the lead airplane. I hit the bomb toggle switch. At once the sky is filled with bombs and smoke streamers plummeting to earth.

'Bombs away! Bombs away! Let's get the hell out of here!'

'Bomb doors closed.'

'Roger, pilot to left waist, over.'

'Come in, Sir.'

'County, take a look at our rudders, will you? I think we've been hit. They don't feel right.'

'There are a couple of holes in the left rudder but they don't look bad.'

'Roger, thank you.'

All this while the smoke bombs are still tracing their way to the target. They fall short and immediately afterward bombs straggle in increasing volume across our objective. One...two...three...four bursts appear between our formation leader and us and at our exact altitude. On the ground, volcanic splashes of dirt and debris rise up shortly before fires break out and finally the entire area is enveloped in a thick cloud of smoke through which flames lick erratically.

The cameras have recorded forever the bombing results. Radio messages are flying back to our home base. For the first time in what seem ages, we are entitled to turn off the target. In actual time, the run was probably two or three minutes in length but minutes really can drag by on leaden feet at times.

Flak is still a great menace and looking as we make a 90° turn, the sky over the area is a grey-black with the more recent bursts offering little contrast to the whole dark picture. It is hard to believe that it was possible to come through that mess in one piece. There are vacancies in the formation, which serve as mute reminders that we have lost planes. There will be some empty beds tonight.

The pilot's work to get the outfit compact again as a bulwark against fighter attacks and we are on our way home.

A new group of friendly fighters pick us up now and our erstwhile escort dashes for home and the sack. Possibly they will encounter some of the *Luftwaffe* or beat up an airdrome on the way home. 'So long, fellows! Thanks a lot. See you tomorrow!'

Now we become consciously aware of the extreme cold and the wet uncomfortable oxygen masks clinging to our faces. Cords and wires hamper our every movement and we long to get back.

'Hey, Tom! Watch those flaps when I drop below 150mph.' Then half apologetically, 'I'm sorry. I can't help it. This iggerant bastahd in the high right is messin' up the whole formation.'

The return trip takes less time than the penetration and the release of tension is evident in the remarks of the crew. Tom, who has been listening on another channel, switches to interphone, 'Co-pilot to crew. Did someone call me?'

From a waist window, a voice replies, 'G'wan back to sleep! Who in hell would want to talk to you?'

'Quiet back there, or I'll bat you in the mouth with this guy's right wing!'

In a few small towns below, gunners set their stems down long enough to send up a few drunkenly aimed shells.

The clouds thicken under us again and we lose contact with the ground. When next we see ack ack appearing from nowhere, we reason that we are leaving the Dutch coast. We weave a little to play it safe.

'18,000 feet. Oxygen check.' Everyone answers but the top turret.

'Fullerton, take a look at the engineer will you?' After a pause, 'Top turret OK.'

'How about trying to stay awake up there, Balate?' 'MMmmm.'

Like old hens, four ship bunches of Mustangs are still sweeping, scurrying here and there to see that all is well,

Over the Channel we are slowly letting down and Howie who has been working steadily, finally throws his pencil down and leans against an ammunition box. At 15,000 feet, Howie and I rip off our masks and light a cigarette.

The group leader spies a large break in the clouds and successfully lowers the formation through them intact. We reassemble on the flight deck and shout at each other above the roar of the engines.

Another hour and the familiar features of our home base slide into view. Pedestrians, cyclists, housewives and other citizens of the nearby towns are clearly discernible from 2,000 feet as they turn out to stare up at us on our return.

The landing of a formation is a complicated but beautiful thing in itself. The sky is filled with planes peeling oft circling the field and landing.

Properly executed, it is a masterpiece of timing and coordination. But to us at this time, it means home again.

Disembarking, we are surrounded by crew chiefs, armament, ordinance, radio and bombsight men full of a million questions about the mission and the equipment.

We inspect the big holes we have accumulated and decide that we have been pretty lucky again.

Once more the GI trucks roll, take us to the locker room and from there to interrogation where heated arguments are in full sway, each person having his own idea on some particular phase of the mission. S-2 makes detailed reports on the observations of each crew, which are both sent to higher echelon and kept in files to serve as guides on later missions.

Tired but still victorious, we adjourn once more to the mess hall. We've been up a long time already but for lead crews, the mission is not yet complete. Wing critique follows chow. Here the mission is gone over from start to finish, mistakes are analyzed, criticism is given and suggestions for future missions are discussed.

Before we get back to the barracks it is 20:00 hours and we just have time for a drink and a final comment or two at the club before turning in dog tired.

Yes, a mission day is a long, hard, really full day but it doesn't bother me... bother me... bother me...

Charles E. Clague Jnr, 93rd 'Travelling Circus' Bomb Group

CHAPTER 1

Where the Girls are Prettier

I had the front bedroom, along Liliha Street and I was awakened by explosions and bombs going off. 'Jesus Christ' I yelled, 'what the hell's happening?' Maneuvers on a Sunday? What's the matter with those papayas?

My mother turned on the radio. We had one of those big Atwater-Kent radios. 'All military personnel, report to your bases at once' the announcer was saying. Then we heard what was happening. Pearl Harbor was under attack. We tuned to both stations – KGMB and KGU – and we heard the same type of message.

27-year old Rodney L. Rodriggs of 1909 Liliha Street, Honolulu[1]

Every Sunday Augustine Dolim would go fishing in his thirty-foot boat off Pearl Harbor on the Hawaiian Island of Oahu where he worked in the naval dockyards. He rose very early at his two-storey house on the high side of 7th Avenue in Kaimuki, then went to the 6 o'clock mass at the cathedral on Fort Street and usually left Kewalo Basin by 7:30am to fish outside the three-mile limit where it was quite deep. There was always a destroyer patrolling the area and if caught inside the three-mile limit, he could expect a citation. Mr Dolim was born in Kapakalua, Maui, where he had worked for the sugar plantation there, helping his father to cut and haul firewood from kiawe trees. He married Mary Mendonca, who came to the islands from Portugal when she was two years old. In Honolulu the first of their two sons, Abel, was born in 1922 and Henry was born there a year later. Abe worked at the Hawaiian Pineapple Company as a machinist. He went fishing with his father often in the cruiser that they called a 'hapahaole' sampan. Built at the Matsumoto Boat Works down on Kapiolani, near Pier 2, it was launched in 1940. They would fish out at Barber's Point, trolling all the way down there and back and they would deep-fish too, as far down as 2,000 feet. They caught fish that nobody could identify – black devils with sharp teeth – like prehistoric monsters. Mr Dolim was a 'cracker-jack' fisherman and Abe really enjoyed going fishing with him. On Sunday 7 December 1941 however, he did not go out with his father for some reason. That morning the nineteen-year-old teenager, who lived at the family home, got up early, dressed and went to the 7 o'clock mass at St Patrick's. It was about 8 o'clock when he got back. The Dolim house had a front porch that looked down toward Pearl Harbor. Going up the steps, for some reason the young Hawaiian turned around and looked out. He saw white puffs over Pearl Harbor and thought, 'What the heck's the Navy doing having gun practice on Sunday?' He was really surprised at that so he went in and turned on the radio. Then he was really puzzled because KGMB was not on the air at that time.

Sunday 7 December 1941 in North Henderson on the north-western Illinois prairie turned out beautifully, the sun nicely taking the temperature into the windless forties and fifties. Nineteen-year-old Bob Shaver and his buddy seventeen-year-old Tommy 'Sock' Devlin had been invited to go duck hunting on the Mississippi River backwaters with Dick Willett, a one-legged World War I veteran. People in North Henderson did not much like Dick because he was quiet and surly, speaking more in begrudging, short, clipped answers to others' attempts to be pleasant than in civil conversational tones. Possibly he was carrying a 'poor-me' grudge against society the rest of his life for the loss of the whole of his right leg, or so some thought. He never had himself fitted for an artificial limb but always swung himself along on two wooden crutches. His right trouser leg was folded and tucked neatly into his belt line in the rear. His mannerisms and the stark one-leg reminder were thought to be his deliberate chip on his shoulder. He was comparatively well off among most townspeople during the depression years. He had complete disability payments from the Veterans Administration, which meant he could drive late model cars, be the best dressed man in town and afford an Oquauka hunting cabin on the Mississippi River. In his summer light-coloured suits, Panama hat, his swinging brisk gait and dour countenance, he appeared a little intimidating. Even so, the Marine Corps veteran had extended the invitation to the two teenagers to go duck shooting at his cabin that stood on stilts on the great river and they drove there early on Sunday morning in his specially fitted car.

Arriving at the cabin still in darkness, they went by boat to Willett's backwater blind and set out decoys before full sunup. They sat in the blind awhile, getting a little cold. It was a bright, clear and subfreezing morning; very pleasant, nevertheless, for 7 December. Willett pulled out a fifth of whiskey. After swigging deeply he passed the bottle on to Bob and

Tommy. Devlin, the diplomat, took a token swig but Shaver refused politely, which probably meant that he would never be invited to go duck hunting again

Dick was good with his duck call, which he used whenever a flight of ducks could be seen. The flight wheeled, circled and began to drop into the clearing of water in front of the blind; the duck bodies tilting upward, their wings doing full flaps and their landing gears down and extended slightly forward. But something was wrong; maybe they saw paint chips on the decoys; whatever, they quickly changed flight plans and were off safely. Two more flights did the same thing as the morning dragged toward noon. Shaver and Devlin ate their sandwiches and Willett worked on his bourbon. They decided to try their luck by prowling through the backwaters in their rowboat. When Shaver was commanded to shoot he pulled his Uncle Tuffy's double-barrelled 12-gauge shotgun to his shoulder but it was a hen, a no-no at that particular time and season. No shot and no more scare-ups.

As the sun hung low in the afternoon sky, they called it quits and headed for the cabin. They climbed the stairs to the cabin, kindled a fire in the small space heater and Willett made coffee on a small electric range. Devlin and Shaver made toast and Willett removed a cold cooked duck from the refrigerator. He turned on the radio as they began to eat. Willett listened to the radio and insisted that Shaver and Devlin listen as well. The startling news went on and on and was repeated. The Japanese had devastated Pearl Harbor with the tragic loss of thousands of American lives and with the loss of a fleet that seemed beyond recovery. President Roosevelt and Congress would go into emergency session the next day and declaration of all-out war against both Japan and Germany was expected. Willett became outgoing for the first time that Shaver had heard him in such a mood. He was solemn, however. 'It would be a hard war' he said 'and none of us would escape its far-reaching effects.'[2]

As Robert M. Cline and Teresa Pritchard, his high school sweetheart, listened to the news on the radio of the surprise attack by the Japanese on Pearl Harbor, they realized that their lives were in for a dramatic change. Cline was visiting Teresa, a student nurse at Bethesda Hospital in Cincinnati, Ohio. She had graduated from Bath High School in Osborn in 1940 and was valedictorian of her class. Robert was very much in love with her and very proud of her. Shortly thereafter, Bob asked Teresa to marry him and they became engaged. Later they decided that as soon as Teresa passed her state-board for nursing they would get married. Bob Cline also decided that he would enlist, not out of a great desire for heroics but simply to avoid being drafted by the Army. He did not like the idea of fighting in the jungles of the Pacific, or from one hedgerow to the next in Europe.

In Honolulu Abe Dolim had purposefully left the radio on. A few minutes later a very excited KGMB announcer came on and he said, 'We are under sporadic attack by unknown airplanes.' Abe would never forget that he said 'sporadic'. Then the announcer really got excited and he realized that something important had happened – that something was very wrong. Anyhow, his dad was on his boat, out of Kewalo Basin, before the attack and heading for open sea when he came upon the destroyer USS *Ward* patrolling out there. Augustine Dolim watched in amazement as he saw an aircraft drop a bomb near the *Ward*. When he saw the explosion it produced, he turned right around and headed back to shore. He returned home and that was about the time that they were calling all Pearl Harbor workers to report to their shops, so he immediately got in his car and took off.

Abe Dolim watched the whole attack from the front porch. He saw formations of aircraft. He was quite an aviation buff and he had built a lot of models when he was a kid. In fact, that was all he could think of – flying! He saw these high-level bombers – torpedo-type Nakajimas – about a dozen of them flying right over the house, heading north at about 8,000 feet. Martial law imposed a 10pm curfew and anyone caught outdoors in the blackout after that time risked being shot on sight – no questions asked. Fishing was banned and the beaches were barricaded with barbed wire. Martial law allowed the US Coast Guard to confiscate his father's fishing boat. This entitled Mr Dolim to membership in the Coast Guard temporary service, which he declined and sent Abe in his place.

All he ever wanted was to fly but the Air Corps could be a lottery. When his brother Henry joined the Air Force and was assigned to the 11th Bomb Group in the Pacific he was a bookkeeper for the Honolulu Iron Works, so 'naturally' they made him a baker in his squadron!

Robert H. Tays was butchering with his family at the Satter farm in rural New Braunfels in Texas.

> This was a big event for my family and the news of Pearl Harbor was received by crystal set radio. Communications of the time was limited to newspapers and the new medium, radio. Rural areas without electricity used crystal sets for radio and slow mail for newspapers so the lag time between a happening and receipt of knowledge thereof was large and significant and affected the

understanding of vital current world affairs. World War I had made the world 'Safe for Democracy' so a flavour of security transcended on the people who were primarily involved in solving domestic or personal situations. It was tough enough here so why worry about people's problems thousands of miles away.

Most of us never heard the call to war in the late thirties. The nation was coming out of the worst depression it had ever experienced. Life was devoted to making a living and most people focused on (parochial) interests and friends. Teenage thoughts included Model Ts, Model As, girls, school, drive-ins, getting a job and surviving in a dollar-a-day economy. The Comal River and all the beautiful activities at Camp Warnecke were always on our mind. The rapids provided a continuing challenge to good swimmers and entertained the steady stream of tourists to that vacation mecca. In a world where there was little or no money, we constantly sought new ways to entertain ourselves that might be cost free. The river did this exceedingly well. Reports of events throughout the world were dismissed as being far away and of no real concern to the average citizen of the USA.

The older men talked endlessly and conjectured a great many scenarios of things to come. I continued my college programme but registered for the draft, which was instituted immediately. The local National Guard had been mobilized about a year earlier and included many of my friends. With the declaration of war we young folk knew it was just a matter of time and we would be called with that famous letter sending 'Greetings from the President.' [*'Greetings: Having submitted yourself to a local board composed of your neighbors for the purpose of determining your availability for training and service in the land or naval forces of the United States, you are hereby notified that you have now been selected for training and service therein. Your friends and neighbors ask you to serve your country. Report for induction…'*] Having completed two years of college work at Southwest Texas State, working for Servtex during the summer and having Dad check with the draft board to see how close I was to being drafted, I gave much thought to volunteering. The thought was that volunteers may at some time receive special breaks.

Upon graduation from high school, I went to work for Mr Paul Bielstein's service station and stayed with him for a little more than a year. The salary was $5.00 per week with every other Sunday off. Every other day the hours were 8am to 10pm and 6am to 6pm. Mr

> and Mrs Bielstein introduced me to meeting the buying public and provided endless meaningful and worthy experiences never taught in school. I will always be indebted to them for their patience and wonderful guidance. Mr Bielstein was a veteran of World War I and would from time to time comment on world conditions and try to make me aware of what the consequences might be.[3]

Robert Rosenthal, a twenty-four-year-old lawyer who was born in Brooklyn on 11 June 1917, had graduated from Brooklyn College with high honours and a degree in law and worked in a very distinguished law firm in New York City. He came from a close family; his father, a Health Department worker in New York had died in 1940. 'Rosie', as he was to become known, was very frustrated when the war began. He could see what the Germans were doing in Europe, wiping out democracies and killing people. He imagined he was like a lot of other people in those days. It was a period he felt very deeply about and he wanted to be 'in it'. When 7 December happened 'it sort of lifted the load'. On 8 December, instead of going to the office he went down to the Federal Building on Church Street in Manhattan and enlisted in the Air Corps.

Ten minutes after the announcement of the attack on Pearl Harbor Eric Neuhaus of Flushing, New York, tried to enlist but he was not a citizen and was refused. Slim and small, with blue eyes and curly hair he was formerly Eric Neuhaus of Vienna, Austria, where he and his family had once operated a little Viennese chocolate shop. On 15 March 1938 Vienna was overrun by the new war lords. In their black uniforms they strutted about the city. To show their strength they attacked the Jews. They hounded them off the streets and into their homes. Watching from a window Eric Neuhaus saw them on the streets and listened to their broadcasts on the radio: 'All Jews must go or die'. Then he heard that several members of his family; hunted and with their backs to the wall, had killed themselves. He made up his mind. He would escape to America. His family planned to do the same and he hoped to meet them there.

To start out on his own on such a journey was a big decision for a boy of fifteen to make. Hiding in the countryside with a band of boys his age he helped attack sentries and disrupt communications before escaping to the Sudetenland. Finding the Nazis in power there the group split up and Eric was off on his own. He found food and shelter by working here and there for a few days at a time. In time the police would catch up with him and he would have to move on and move fast. From the Sudetenland he went to Yugoslavia, from there to Greece to Haifa on the border of Syria.

Here he met up with the British Army, told them he was nineteen and was accepted as a temporary soldier, joining the Kent Regiment. Transferring to the Hampshire Regiment at Nazareth, he saw action against the Arabs. To get to America he had to have a passport. So he went to Jaffa and by slipping £3 to someone in the German consulate he obtained a German passport. Back to Jerusalem he went to get his American visa. After a long wait, the ticket to America was finally his. All he had to do now was get there. The first leg of the journey was by boat, to Haifa, Beirut, Athens, Naples and Genoa. Being young, he got the urge to do some sightseeing in Genoa. With his German passport and a series of snappy *Heil* Hitler's he had a good time. On the way to Marseilles he talked a fellow passenger, a Danish official, into taking him ashore as his secretary. Then he caught a ship to Gibraltar, where there was a ship sailing for the US but the British would not allow him to sail because his eyes, reddened by the desert sun, were thought to be infected. By now he was desperate. To have come so far only to meet what seemed utter failure was a tragedy. But he settled down to wait and finally his eyes cleared up and he boarded a ship bound for Boston.

On arrival in Boston a nurse on the boat gave him a dime to see the town with. Hopping on a streetcar he rode all over the town, from one end to the other, thoroughly enjoying himself. The New World was all that he expected, even more so. He left the boat in New Jersey, where he started looking for a job. He knew only a very few words of English, but he just started out and went from one store to the next asking for work. His first pay was earned by performing the great American task of dishwashing. Before long he had word of his parents, joined them and went to Wausau, Wisconsin, where he learned to be a machinist and soon found a good job back in New York. On 7 December and for 120 days consecutively, Eric returned to the recruiting office until he was finally accepted into the Air Corps.[4]

On Pearl Harbor day Larry 'Goldie' Goldstein was lying on his bed at home in Brooklyn listening to a radio broadcast of a football game when the broadcast was interrupted by a news flash that the Japanese had bombed Pearl Harbor. Larry was nineteen years old. A trainee draughtsman with the US Coast and Geodetic Survey, he had graduated from Erasmus Hall High School in 1940. He was not a great student; studies got in his way, and sports were important to him. 'Goldie' was a fierce competitor and hated to lose and he was devastated when he did not make the high school football team. He thought he was a great player and was known on the sandlots of Brooklyn as 'Snake Hips' because of the way he was able to run on the football field. While waiting for his draft number to be drawn he was caught up in this patriotic fervour that swept the country following Pearl Harbor. 'Goldie' went to the Marine recruiting office and was told by the sergeant in charge to go home and wait for his number to be called and this after he had passed the physical. He was right. Within two weeks his draft number was called and he waited for his actual reporting day. Just before entering the Army he met Rose Mandel, his first real serious romance and the girl that he wanted to be waiting for him when his service was over. They only had about six months of dating before he entered the Air Corps.

George H. Lymburn had an all-consuming interest in aviation as a boy, making model aircraft out of balsa wood. Then there were the great films – *Test Pilot*, *Dawn Patrol* and *Ceiling Zero*; and reading – *G-8 and His Battle Aces*. 'Whatever you were doing on December 6' he recalled, 'there was a good chance you knew your future would be taking a different path by December 8. I was working in Plymouth, Massachusetts in a department store and I gave in my notice and headed home to Weymouth to enlist in the Army Air Corps.'

On 21 June 1941 the Army Air Corps was renamed Army Air Forces and Major General Henry Harley 'Hap' Arnold was named Chief of Army Air Forces. Arnold was born on 25 June 1886 at Gladwyne, Pennsylvania. His parents wanted him to become a minister. When his oldest brother, Tom, decided to forego his West Point appointment for an electrical engineering career, young Henry entered West Point – motto *Duty, Honour, Country*. One of Arnold's cavalry instructors saw him chewing tobacco and ordered him to spit it out. 'I thought all good cavalrymen chewed tobacco,' replied Arnold. Angered at this impertinence, the instructor disqualified Arnold from the cavalry and Arnold graduated from West Point in 1907 as an infantry second lieutenant. Embittered, Arnold was assigned to the Army Corps of Engineers in the Philippines where he made maps with another lieutenant, George Marshall. Arnold's career would span over forty years from the Signal Corps' three aircraft to the aerial might of World War II.

Although the Japanese bombing of Pearl Harbor brought the United States into the war, her first enemy was Germany and far-reaching decisions had been made in the event that America should become involved in the conflict with the Axis powers. Between 27 January and 27 March 1941, agreements between the United States and Great Britain were made for the provision of naval, ground and air support for the campaign against Germany. On 28 January 1942 the 8th Air Force had been formed at Savannah, Georgia. Brigadier General Ira C. Eaker, the forty-five-year-old Commanding General of VIII Bomber Command, intended to build a heavy daylight bomber force as quickly and as efficiently as possible. Born on 13 April 1896 in Field Creek, Texas, and raised in south-eastern Oklahoma near Durant, Eaker received a commission as a second lieutenant in the Army Infantry Reserve in 1917 and became a pilot two years later. During the 1920s and 1930s Eaker developed and tested procedures for aerial refuelling and in 1936 made history by piloting the first 'blind' transcontinental flight, flying on instruments only from New York to Los Angeles. Funds for new military aircraft were very limited and the only four-engined bomber of note was the Boeing Y1B-17A, which went into service during January to August 1937. This aircraft was conceived for a purely defensive mission – the protection of the US coastline from foreign surface fleets. It was this designation and not the later, formidable, defensive machine-gun armament, which suggested the famous name 'Flying Fortress', which was coined by a watching news reporter. Early in 1939 the USAAC drew up a requirement for a new heavy bomber of vastly superior performance to the 'Flying Fortress', then in production. The Consolidated Company of San Diego, California, submitted the LB-30, a landplane version of one of their Model 29 flying-boat. On 26 October 1939 David R. Davis' high-aspect ratio wing was married to the fuselage for the first time and the XB-24 prototype flew for the first time on 29 December.

In 1940 the 2nd and 7th Groups, equipped with B-17B high-altitude bombers, practised precision bombing using the top secret Norden bombsight until experienced bombardiers could place their practice bombs within yards of the target from as high as 20,000 feet – which led to claims that bombs could be placed 'in a pickle barrel' from some such heights. Precision bombing called for attacks in daylight but the ideal conditions prevailing on the ranges at Muroc Dry Lake in California's Mojave Desert were not to be found in Europe, where first the *Luftwaffe* and then RAF Bomber Command found to their cost that day bombing was unsustainable. Despite this, the accepted theory in America was that a formation of unescorted bombers could get through to their target in daylight if they were properly arranged and armed sufficiently.

Men who a few months before Pearl Harbor had been working in the wheat fields, the factories and in the cities had to adapt to a whole new way of life and quickly. They had no way of knowing what their chances were of survival – no one told them. That they faced long odds only began to dawn on them gradually. Ben Smith Jr found himself volunteering – the last thing he wanted to do.

Why was I there? I had less than my share of physical courage. In my teen years I thought of myself as something of a coward. I cared not at all for bodily contact sports; I did not like to be hurt. At the same time I envied my own more robust companions and I thought there was something wrong with me because I was not like them. This spectre haunted me until I came finally to believe that I was going to have to overdo it or be destroyed in the process. I became a radio operator-aerial gunner on a B-17 crew at Salt Lake City. The combat crews were assembled there and then sent to the overseas training bases. 'Chick' and 'Fish', pilot and co-pilot, were talking together as I went up to them and introduced myself as the radio operator on their crew. 'Chick' Cecchini was a big red-haired Italian from Poughkeepsie, New York. His face fell as he sized me up. He could see I was no bargain, but he was cordial enough. I shook hands with them but I wasn't exactly happy – an Italian and a Jew and I was going to trust my life to these two. After meeting the others I felt better.

Flying, especially military flying, did not appeal to me at first. In training we flew worn-out aircraft and had many hairy experiences in these old B-17s. I used to lie awake in bed dreading the time when I would have to lay it on the line or forever be lost in the infamy of disgrace (I learned later that I was not the only one) this was so real to me. Outwardly, I was light-hearted and jovial, well-liked by my friends. They thought I was a pretty cool customer but inside I was sick, sick, sick! My bravado was sort of a rallying pint though phoney as a three-dollar bill. I wore a 'hot pilots' cap', smoked big black cigars and drank boiler-makers. The only one who wasn't fooled was me.

Finally when overseas training was finished I went home on furlough. My family was very proud of their eldest son and I was carried about town; to be shown off to old friends and relatives. I had been away for some time and it was good to see everyone again. I wore my leather A-2 jacket and showed my aerial gunner wings and staff sergeant stripes to all my admiring aunts, uncles and cousins. I had just gotten a Good Conduct Medal, which tells something about the behaviour standards of the Air Corps. All of the family were very pleased about this ribbon. It did no good to explain that everyone got it; in fact, there was no way not to get it. By some process of reasoning my people assumed that it was as important for a soldier to have good conduct as it was for a Boy Scout. If our soldiers fought fair, were decent and good and never cruel as were the Germans and Japs, then ours would be the victory. God would not permit it to be otherwise. So mother, beaming with pride, would say, 'See his Good Conduct Medal!' She would not have traded it for the Congressional Medal of Honor. I am sure the folks all felt better knowing that I would now be manning the ramparts against Corporal Hitler and his conquering hordes. I managed to create an aura of uncomplaining heroism which I wore like a halo. To anyone who inquired, I and my buddies were ready for anything the Germans could throw at us. We were eager to get at them and get the war over. This was light years from the truth. I was about as eager as someone being prepared for radical surgery to his gonads.

In desolation I spent my last day at home revisiting the familiar scenes of my youth. I borrowed my dad's car and drove out to Senior High and visited all of my former teachers, Mr Walton, the principal, Coach Rushton, Coach O'Rear, Miss Mary Lane, Miss Julia Carnes and all the others. They seemed glad to see me and wished me luck. I drove by the tennis courts where I had spent most of my time in the summer playing tennis with Billy Cromer and Red Henderson. The corner at Elliston's Drug Store, where the old gang had hung out, was now deserted. There was the Standpipe, long a Waycross landmark and a visual atrocity if there ever was one, but it looked like the Taj Mahal to me. My next stop was the old courthouse, which had always resembled a medieval castle complete with turrets, spires and a bell tower. As a little boy I had followed my dad to court and had seen many spectacular trials there. The town clock struck every hour in those days and it was a sound I dearly loved. I drove out the Savannah Highway and stopped for a beer at Riverside, the nightspot which all the teenagers had frequented. I put a nickel in the jukebox and played *Cherry* by Erskine Hawkins and then *Summit Ridge Drive* by Artie Shaw, but there was no one to dance with. Leaving there, I drove to the Memorial Bridge and got out of the car. This was my favourite place, the beautiful Satilla River. As a child I had roamed its length and breadth, fishing and swimming, hunting and camping. Gazing out over the languid, wine-coloured stream, I sat there on the sand bar a long time. I viewed all these scenes as one who was seeing them for the last time. These things were all I had. I was not leaving a wife or a girlfriend behind; I knew nothing of the manifold

> mysteries of adulthood; and I felt at that moment that I was very likely going to be cheated of all those things. Self-pity consumed me, in this case perhaps justified. I had no choice in the matter either; it was a man's place to go. I was only twenty years old. I did not wish to lay down my life for anyone or any cause; yet the idea that I could refuse to do so was beyond my comprehension. It has been said that it was probably wrong of my generation *not* to question; that patriotism of a higher order weighs every action of the State and refuses those actions which seem wrong to it. Perhaps so. I can only compare that misguided patriotism with what has taken its place, a Republic that has lost its nerve and lost its way.[5]

On 22 February 1942, three months after the US entry into World War II, General Eaker was assigned as commander of the first American air headquarters in Europe It was from RAF Bomber Command Headquarters at High Wycombe in Buckinghamshire that he would initially direct operations but Flying Fortresses and B-24 Liberator bombers were slow to arrive in England. When the first raid involving American crews in England took place on Independence Day, 4 July 1942, it was six Douglas Boston twin-engined medium bombers manned by RAF crews and six others manned by American crews of the 15th Bombardment Group (Light) that took off in daylight from RAF Swanton Morley in Norfolk for a strike on four German airfields in Holland. The Independence Day raid was important historically, but it was not an unqualified success. Two of the aircraft manned by Americans were shot down by what the RAF flight leader described as '...the worst flak barrage in my experience'. Despite the disappointing outcome of the raid, the press hailed it as the start of a 'new and gigantic air offensive'.

One of the Bostons carried Lieutenant Boyd S. Grant of the 97th Bomb Group, which provided some of the personnel. This Group, with its four squadrons of Boeing B-17E Flying Fortresses, had arrived in England in July 1942 after flying the northern Atlantic ferry route via Goose Bay, Labrador, Greenland and Reykjavik, Iceland, and was based at Podington and at Grafton Underwood in Northamptonshire.[6] The no-nonsense Eaker soon replaced Colonel Cornelius Cousland, the Group's original commander, with Colonel Frank A. Armstrong Jr, one of his original staff officers who had worked closely with RAF counterparts during the early, formulative days at High Wycombe, to re-impose discipline and get results – quickly. Cousland was sacked for running a 'lackadaisical, loose-jointed, fun-loving, badly trained outfit', which was 'in no sense ready for combat'. Armstrong was a cool, tough, no-nonsense North Carolinian who had served in the 3rd Attack Group. His West Point training, his erect bearing and wind-tanned face – for the last fourteen of his thirty-nine years he had spent most of his time in the cockpits of military aircraft – commanded the respect of those who served with him.

In America meanwhile, more heavy bombardment groups were activated for deployment to Britain.[7] The first of the Consolidated B-24 Liberator groups activated had been the 44th on 15 January 1941 at MacDill Field, Florida, and the 93rd was created using personnel from the 44th. This Group also provided personnel for the 98th commanded by Colonel John Riley 'Killer' Kane, the son of a Baptist preacher, from McGregor, Texas, which was dispatched to North Africa; and the 90th, which went to the South West Pacific. The 93rd would soon be commanded by Colonel Ted Timberlake, who war reporter 'Tex' McCrary once described as a 'broad-backed man who looked like a cross between Spencer Tracy and Bobby Jones'. Born at Ford Hood, Virginia, one of four sons of a career Army artillery officer, who all graduated from West Point (three becoming general officers), Colonel Ted would take his group to the ETO (European Theatre of Operations) and the group soon became known as 'Ted's Travelling Circus'. But this was all in the future. A nucleus of the original personnel in the 44th, which was broken up and pocketed around the world like a gigantic game of pool, called themselves the 'Eightballs'. In June–July the 44th and 93rd were engaged in operations against U-boats, the latter from Page Field, Fort Myers, Florida. One June evening, *Jerk's Natural* was en route from Chicago to Fort Myers when a submarine was sighted. There were two depth charges aboard the B-24 and Lieutenant Darrel L. Sims made a run. Two weeks later Lieutenant William J. Williams' Liberator was over the Gulf of Mexico south-west of Fort Myers when his navigator sighted a U-boat. They made a run and dropped two 300lb depth charges, while passing over the bow-to-stern. Oil rushed to the surface.

At 0930 hours on 10 July a 44th B-24 flown by Lieutenant Robert A. Norsen departed from Barksdale Field, Louisiana, as ordered to patrol a specified area of the Gulf of Mexico. While flying at an altitude of 1,500 feet the bombardier released a 300lb demolition bomb over an area of water, which appeared dark. However, the peculiarity was formed by a school of fish in the area, as was confirmed by some crewmembers. As the aircraft was flying on the last leg of the search, the photographer observed a suspicious boat on the horizon toward the south. This area was located approximately 120 miles south of Mobile, Alabama. The aircraft was approximately twenty miles south of its course. The pilot remained in this general vicinity for approximately fifteen minutes and the co-pilot observed a submarine surfaced at the starboard side. The pilot made an approach against the sun in order to observe the reflection made by the submarine more dearly. Then he made a left turn for half a minute and prepared to make a bombing run. By this time only the periscope of the sub was visible. The bombardier had only fifteen seconds for his bombing run and made an approach at an altitude of 1,500 feet about 30° from the bow of the submarine using PDI instruments. The bombing run was made at 2010 hours. Both the engineer and radio operator observed the bombing results from the bomb-bay section. The bombardier released four bombs, in the following order: one depth charge, one 300lb demolition bomb, one depth charge and another 300lb demolition bomb. All charges were set to go off in train, 50 feet apart. 'Excellent' hits were observed. The first charge hit behind and short of the periscope wake; one demolition bomb hit directly in the centre and the other depth charge hit the bow.

In claiming the successful sinking of the submarine a greater explosion was seen from the dropping of the 300lb demolition-bomb on the submarine than had previously been made with a similar bomb that was dropped earlier in the day on a school of fish. The marker beacon light was on just prior to bombing and also on the actual bombing run. It remained on while two more runs were being made. A great deal of debris was observed in this area as well as an extremely large oil patch. Two large black shadows that were also observed remained on the water for five minutes and then seemed to drift apart and disappear. These observations were made from an altitude of 200 feet. Darkness was approaching rapidly and prevented better visibility. Sergeant D.H. Ingram, the radio operator, radioed two positions of the sinking and the aircraft patrolled the area for about thirty minutes. The pilot was obliged to return to base because of fuel shortage. The pilot commended the bombardier on such an excellent performance; for his bombing run was the most accurate he had ever witnessed. He also wanted to commend the entire crew for such excellent vigilance as they maintained, for they had remained at their stations for nine hours, making continuous observations.[8] The Liberator men never dreamed that within twenty-eight days they would be bombing U-boat pens on the Atlantic coast of France, 4,000 miles away.

While aircrews flew the Atlantic ferry routes to Great Britain, the ground personnel arrived by sea, often on converted ocean-going liners such as the *Queen Mary* and the *Queen Elizabeth*.[9] Trucks took the men from Camp Kilmer, New Brunswick, New Jersey, to the Hudson River separating New York and New Jersey, which were completely blacked out, and they boarded a dayliner, which took them down river to the ship that would take them overseas. As the peacetime excursion boat moved down the Hudson and edged toward Pier 90 on the Manhattan side of the River they saw the *Queen Mary*, now in battleship grey and with her name painted out. Alongside the French liner *Normandie* was lying on her side after a disastrous fire.[10] Loaded with troops, crew, fuel and provisions, the *Queen Mary* moved slowly down the Hudson River, passing the Statue of Liberty, into the Bay and out into the Atlantic Ocean. During the war the *Queen Mary* alone made around twenty-eight voyages across the Atlantic, sometimes calling at Halifax, Nova Scotia, to pick up Canadian troops. Often there were more than 14,000 men on board. She sometimes carried as many as 16,000. In open sea the *Queens* changed direction every three minutes to help prevent U-boat attack. The main rule the Admiralty laid down for the *Queens* was 'no stopping – for anything'. This was because it was feared that the Germans may try to use a decoy to get the great liners to stop and then they would torpedo them.[11] On board *Queen Mary* the men were quartered in the staterooms, lounges, libraries and even swimming pools. There were tiers of bunks made of pipe frames with what appeared to be chicken wire under a thin mattress. Officers were assigned to a stateroom designed for two people. They stacked them, one above the other, with three tiers against three walls. There were no portholes and some of the men were claustrophobic. Some would not bathe. 'Shower parties' were formed and they all bathed with salt water soap. Many of the men were uneasy, three or four decks below, with the possibility of U-boat attacks. Some prayed in groups, occasionally prayers could be heard recited in the shadows. There were far too few lifeboats; certainly not enough to handle all the men and crew. All wore their Mae Wests to reduce casualties in case of an attack. There were two lifeboat and abandon ship drills each day.

There were lectures on what life would be like in Britain. There were movies. Smoking was not permitted. Chewing gum was forbidden because it was difficult to remove it from the decks when it was discarded. Each troop load received a special talk explaining the value of the murals, fine woods and art works on the ship. The men were asked not to deface the art work and were offered an alternative. They could use the 750-foot long teakwood railing on the promenade deck as a 'tree to carve your initials.' The one third mile railing was carved with initials, names, nicknames, girl friends' names, dates and even one expertly carved nude.[12] MPs enforced the ban on gambling. However, poker, blackjack and crap games started when the men were settled. Some spent the whole crossing gambling. There was one-way traffic to move the men efficiently. Moving forward they took the starboard passageways and returned by the port side. They ate and slept in shifts. Two meals were served in six staggered sittings, with breakfast starting at 0630. Each sitting was allowed only forty-five minutes to enter, eat and leave to make room for the next sitting. Approximately 2,000 men were fed at a sitting. For six days they queued up for meals and sleeping time. With her speed *Queen Mary* sailed along without convoy, taking a zigzag course. Her speed of over 30 knots could be maintained for thousands of miles. She could outmanoeuvre a U-boat, even a torpedo. Hitler offered $250,000 and an Iron Cross to the U-boat captain or *Luftwaffe* pilot who would sink the *Queen*.

Having arrived in the United Kingdom via the ocean liner *Queen Mary* one diarist wrote:

> We are on our way by troop train from the Firth of Clyde to East Anglia. The train stops at a station and the inevitable question is asked, 'Where are we?'
>
> 'We are in Bovril', comes the reply from one of our group. Standing at the far edge of the platform is a plain, rectangular sign containing only the name 'BOVRIL' in bold, black letters. Much later, another station and an identical sign also reads 'BOVRIL.' 'What a popular name for towns over here!' Eventually, we learn that these one-word signs advertise a bouillon beverage product in competition with its rival Oxo. Well, we did 'just get off the boat'.
>
> Because of the war, the regular longer-distance trains in England do not carry restaurant cars. However, all railroad depots of at least a moderate size have a tea room. At these stops passengers en route pour off the train, swarm into the tea room and rush back to their carriages, each carrying tea in a china cup and saucer and a biscuit (cookie). At the next station stop no one carries a teacup back into the depot! No, the trains are continually hauling used teacups back and forth across the country. It must be a logistical nightmare to redistribute this chinaware equitably each day.

Conditions on the bases provided further shocks.

> The squadrons' living quarters vary from base to base, but many are Nissen and Quonset huts. Heating is from a single, small, iron stove fed with rationed coke, never enough. Nearby in separate buildings are the unheated sanitary facilities. In a failed effort to avoid the dreaded trek from a warm bed into the frigid winter night for relief

from the 'GI's' (diarrhoea), which does occur occasionally, one suffers the misery of holding on as long as possible. The unheated ablutions building; furnished with a row of shower heads is quite distant from our hut. After several days while everyone becomes riper, three or four of us decide to brave the cold room to take a warm shower. On the way back to the hut, congratulating ourselves on our cleanliness, one of our party has the misfortune to slip and tumble into a mud puddle, to no little amusement of the others. The food in the base mess hall keeps starvation away but makes C-rations seem pretty good. The staple items day after day and month after month are powdered eggs, shredded corned beef (referred to as 'sloppy corn willie') from Argentina, all the Brussels sprouts that England can produce, dark bread (really good!) and barrels of that English favourite, orange marmalade. Some of the more imaginative cooks are able to make the powdered eggs palatable. The flight crews are treated to fresh eggs when they are available.

The Armed Forces Radio broadcasts provide diversion from the business at hand. Most of us tune in during off-duty hours. A favorite is the swing band music served up by *The Duffle Bag* program with its theme, *Opus One*, a rousing Tommy Dorsey Band number. Our side does not own a monopoly on the airwaves, though. The Germans have several transmitters set up across the Channel to blanket the UK with its English-language broadcasts. 'Lord Haw Haw' [William Joyce, Irish-born British traitor] and his cohorts spew forth their propaganda in a futile attempt to demoralize us: 'Welcome to England, crew of the *Blonde Venus*. Our *Luftwaffe* fighter boys will be eager to meet with you in the sky when you fly your first mission tomorrow. We will be waiting for you and so will our incredible flak guns manned by your Germanic cousins. We will teach you to side with the Anglo-Saxons in this war against your kin.' But the enemy also plays the popular music of the day. The plaintive ballad, *Lilli Marlene*, becomes well known to us. Even the English latch on to this one, Anne Shelton giving it a slightly faster tempo…

Since arriving in England in July the 97th had been in continual training at Grafton Underwood, three miles east of Kettering. The village, part of the Duke of Buccleuch's estate, dates back several hundred years and the village church dates from the twelfth century. During the period up to 15 August the 97th lost three B-17Es in accidents. On 1 August *King Condor* had a brake failure on landing at Grafton Underwood and overshot the runway, hitting a British lorry and killing the driver. The crew escaped injury but the aircraft was damaged beyond repair. The second Fort lost was on 11 August when it crashed in the Welsh mountains at Llanrhaeadr with the loss of all the crew. On 14 August Lieutenant Francis X. Schwarzenbeck and crew were on a high-altitude training flight in formation at 32,000 when the No. 4 engine ran away. Schwarzenbeck feathered the prop and when it came into full-feather position, saw that one of the blades had broken off.

Schwarzenbeck, who was from New Jersey, recalled:

> I rang the alarm bell as a safety precaution and put the plane into a glide. At 30,000 feet the No. 3 engine blew up and caught fire. I rang the alarm bell again and ordered the men to bail out. I started the plane down in a circle to the left, keeping the two good engines down. By the time I reached 14,000 feet, fire had spread all the way back to the ailerons, over to the No. 4 engine and all along the side of the fuselage. At 12,000 feet the No. 2 engine sputtered, backfired and then quit. This made me sort of mad. Up till then I'd been too scared to do anything. I looked over at the No. 3 engine. It was hanging over the side of the wing, held by a few cables. The oil tank was visible and on fire. I started to get out of my seat to bail out but the wings were still on and I thought I'd try to get it down. Control was nearly impossible, since the bottom of the right wing had been blown off and a piece of cowling had knocked off the vertical fin. I broke through the cloud layer at 9,000 feet and looked for afield. It was a heavily wooded area. [They were over Berner's Heath, Elveden, in Suffolk.] But I spotted a pasture about 800 feet long. I circled the end of it, losing altitude and as the tyres had been destroyed by fire I came in with a wheel-up landing. The entire right side of the airplane was in flames by this time. I started to leave the ship. The place where I had landed was the rifle range of a British Rifle Brigade. About 500 of them were there and as I came out they came running up, about a dozen of them with fire extinguishers. Though the gas tanks were leaking we managed to get the fire out.

Early in August 1942 the 92nd and the 301st Bomb Groups arrived in Britain. The 92nd, commanded by Colonel James S. Sutton, became the first heavy bombardment group to make a successful non-stop flight from Newfoundland to Scotland. Sutton was a 1930 West Point graduate and was with the 2nd Bomb Group when the war began. When he took the 92nd to England he incurred the wrath of Lieutenant General Carl Spaatz and Ira Eaker by insisting that he fly his group directly from the US to the

British Isles without the customary stops along the way. At the start of the war Brigadier General Spaatz was the chief planner for the Air Corps. His friends called him 'Tooey' after a West Point upperclassman he resembled. He was commissioned in the infantry but became a pilot in 1916 and flew with Benny Foulois and the 1st Aero Division in pursuit of Pancho Villa, the Mexican revolutionary, across the border. Spaatz was in combat for the last three weeks of World War I, time enough to shoot down three German aircraft. In 1929 he was commander of the *Question Mark*, a Fokker C-2A, when it set an airborne endurance record of more than 150 hours in the air. To win authorization for the non-stop flight to England, Sutton had gone directly to General Arnold in Washington. Sutton was later transferred to Northern Ireland as base commander at Langford Lodge and only later became a combat commander when he took over the 306th in September 1944.[13]

On 28 August 1942 the last of the four squadrons landed in the United Kingdom and the 92nd set up home at Bovingdon, Hertfordshire. Meanwhile, the 301st decamped to Chelveston and Podington in Northamptonshire. Early in August Colonel Frank Armstrong was able to report that twenty-four crews in the 97th were available for combat missions. On 10 August bombs were loaded into the bays, ammunition was checked, equipment pre-flighted and procedures checked – only to have the weather 'scrub' the mission. Two days later it was responsible for the loss of a 97th Bomb Group Fortress in Wales when all aboard were killed. Tension mounted again with the cancellation and the sceptics spoke louder. The RAF made every conceivable effort to help the 8th get into the war as quickly as possible but remained sceptical about its ability to bomb in broad daylight. On Sunday 16 August the weather reports were good. The first Fortress strike of the war was scheduled for the following morning, Monday 17 August 1942. Major Paul Tibbets of Miami, Florida, the twenty-seven-year old Group Flying Executive Officer in the 97th, recalls:

> Frank Armstrong and I went to Grafton and conducted the mission briefing and elected to take Butcher's aircraft because of its good crew and maintenance status. Frank Armstrong was not qualified in the B-17, so he elected to fly with me in the lead aircraft of the main group departing from Grafton Underwood. Twelve aircraft were designated as the main group, twelve were designated as the main force to strike at the Rouen-Sotteville marshalling yards in north-western France and another six, from Polebrook, were to act as a diversionary force going to St-Omer.

At 1526 Colonel Armstrong and Major Tibbets took off in *Butcher Shop*. General Spaatz had felt confident enough to allow Brigadier General Ira C. Eaker to fly on the mission. Eaker joined the crew of *Yankee Doodle*, lead aircraft of the second flight of six. As the formation crossed the French coast the German radio proved as sceptical as the Allied critics by announcing that '12 Lancasters' were heading inland. At Ypreville fighters began to make their appearance and Sergeant Adam R. Jenkins, the tail gunner aboard *Bat Outa Hell*, flying 'tail-end Charlie', had his hands full. He later reported: 'There were eight of them in "V" formation and the leader waggled his wings and came for us. When they were about 300 yards away I figured it was about time for me to do something. So I pulled the trigger and it looked like the ends of his wings came off. Then the other seven scattered.'

One fighter was chased into the line of fire from Sergeant Kent R. West, the ball turret gunner aboard *Birmingham Blitzkrieg*, and he became the first American crewman to be credited with the destruction of a German aircraft. Ten minutes before the bomb run began, Lieutenant Frank R. Beadle, the lead bombardier, exclaimed in a sing-song voice: 'I can see the target, I can see the target!' Crewmembers twisted and turned, peering in all directions, probing the beautiful bright blue sky for signs of possible enemy fighter attacks; a movement, that would soon become known as the 'Messerschmitt twist'. Crews were relieved that 'here was the target at last' and the tension they had been feeling began to ease. The Initial Point (IP) was reached and the bomb-run started. Beadle again moved to the centre of the spotlight, for as he manipulated the switch to open the bomb bay doors of *Butcher Shop* he could be heard singing over the intercom, 'I don't want to set the world on fire'!

Packed into the bomb bays of the twelve Fortresses was 36,900lb of British bombs in the form of forty-five 600-pounders and nine 1,100-pounders. The heavy bombs (carried by three of the B-17s) were for the locomotive repair shops and the 600lb bombs for the Buddicum rolling stock repair shops. RAF reconnaissance photos had revealed concentrations of more than 2,000 freight cars at Sotteville, so even if the bombs missed, any damage to what was the largest switching facility in northern France would make spectacular front page news the following morning. Bombing was made from 23,000 feet and a few bombs hit a mile short of the target. One burst hit about a mile west in some woods but the majority smashed into the assigned area. Anti-aircraft fire slightly damaged two B-17s. Three Bf 109s that were moving in for the kill were driven off by the Spitfire escort.

At Polebrook shortly before 1900 hours anxious base personnel, fellow airmen, high-ranking American and RAF officers and about thirty Allied pressmen gathered to witness the end of an historic mission. Cheers were heard when it was realized that all of the B-17s had returned safely. Three, in complete disregard for air discipline, peeled out of formation and buzzed the control tower. Under the circumstances no one seemed to mind. Paul Tibbets concludes: 'Once back at base we were debriefed and then there followed a "victory celebration" at the club with the RAF fighter pilots in attendance.'[11] The first of the congratulatory messages to arrive came from Air Marshal Sir Arthur Harris, Chief of RAF Bomber Command. 'Congratulations from all ranks of Bomber Command on the highly successful completion of the first all-American raid by the big fellows on German-occupied territory in Europe. Yankee Doodle certainly went to town and can stick yet another well-deserved feather in his cap.' The *New York Times* communiqué describing the mission was placed on the front page.

Flushed with success, on 19 August the 97th dispatched twenty-four B-17Es in support of the Allied landings at Dieppe. Their target was the airfield at Abbeville-Drucat in northern France, home of the infamous 'Abbeville Kids' whose yellow-nosed Bf 109 pilots were numbered among the *Luftwaffe* elite. Two of the B-17s aborted because of mechanical failures but the rest of the group plastered the airfield, destroying a hangar and severely cratering or 'postholing' the runways. Fortunately, the *Luftwaffe* was heavily engaged over the Dieppe area and did not appear. British High Command reported that sixteen fighters were either destroyed or damaged as a result of the bombing strike and the airfield itself put out of action for a vital two hours. In addition, the controllers of the whole of the fighter area remained out of action until that evening.

The morning of 20 August brought a hurried call from photo-reconnaissance, informing Eaker that 1,600 goods wagons and seventeen locomotives were parked in the Longeau marshalling yards in Amiens. Twelve Fortresses were airborne and all except one bombed through slight flak. Spitfires protected the formation and a Belgian fighter pilot who witnessed the raid reported that the bombers scored at least fifteen direct hits. The bomber crews were jubilant but senior staff officers were more reserved, well aware that so far they had flown only shallow penetration missions in predominantly fine weather. The case for daylight, high-altitude, precision bombing was as yet unproven. The indications were that the B-17s would not be able to flaunt themselves over enemy targets with impunity for very much longer.

In the early morning of 21 August twelve Fortresses were dispatched to bomb the Rotterdam Wilton shipyards, the most modern in Holland. Crews still felt confident, knowing that the faithful RAF Spitfires would again be on hand to protect them but the B-17s were slow to form up after leaving Grafton Underwood. One Fortress was barely airborne when it was forced to abort and a replacement joined the formation. Three other B-17s suffered generator failures, which caused the gun turrets to become inoperative and they returned to base. Arriving sixteen minutes late for the escort, the remaining crews knew that the fighters would not be able to accompany them all the way to the target. The Dutch coast was in sight when the recall message came through and the Spitfires turned for home. They were immediately 'replaced' by upwards of twenty-five German fighters in what became a prelude to a running fight, which lasted for twenty-five minutes. The bombers' mass firepower was a little more than the *Luftwaffe* pilots could handle and two fighters fell to the Fortresses' guns. *Johnny Reb*'s tail-turret gunner, Sergeant Adam R. Jenkins, drew first blood. Sergeant Roy Allen, the top turret gunner, fired one burst and his guns jammed. John N. Hughes, one of the waist gunners, sucked a lump of ice into the mouth of his oxygen tube in the excitement and was forced to hold the mask with one hand and fire his gun with the other, while nearing collapse from lack of oxygen. In the nose compartment Harold Spire, the navigator, had just fired at a crossing fighter when a burst of cannon fire tore through the windshield. Second Lieutenant Donald A. Walters, the co-pilot, was raked from his legs to his chest and died instantly and Plexiglas splinters seriously wounded Richard S. Starks, the pilot. As he struggled for breath, Starks managed to call for help and 1st Lieutenant Ewart T. 'Ed' Sconiers, the bombardier, and Sergeant Allen came to the cockpit. Sconiers, who had washed out of flight training before becoming a bombardier, removed the dead co-pilot and took his place at the controls, hoping that what he had learned about piloting before washing out of flying school would be useful to him now. Holding on to the wheel the pilot began giving instructions to Sconiers while the tail and ball turret gunners continued to blaze away at their five pursuers. *Johnny Reb* lagged behind the rest of the formation, with its No. 3 and 4 engines hit. Despite this Sconiers managed to nurse the ailing bomber back to England and land at Horsham St Faith, near Norwich. The brave bombardier was awarded a DSC and it was rumoured that he was mentioned in one of FDR's 'Fireside Chats'.[15]

The Press enthusiastically credited the nine Fortresses with six fighters destroyed and praised them for beating off twenty-five Focke-Wulfs. It was a welcome change. The British Press liked to 'twit the Yanks': 'Heard the one about the Yanks who went to a war film? One fainted and the other got a medal for carrying him out.' And a verse that made fun: 'Alas they haven't fought the Hun no glorious battles have they won. That pretty ribbon just denotes. They've crossed the sea – brave men in boats!' Some RAF officers, however, remained sceptical and it later transpired that only a handful of fighters had actually fired on the formation.

Eaker took advantage of the *Luftwaffe*'s inexperience in dealing with American bomber formations and on 24 August dispatched a dozen 97th Bomb Group B-17s to the shipyard of the *Ateliers et Chantiers Maritime de la Seine* at Le Trait. Three days earlier Brigadier General Newton Longfellow, one of Eaker's closest friends since they had served in the 3rd Aero Squadron in the Philippines in 1919, had been given command of the 1st Bomb Wing.[16] In July, the newly arrived Colonel Longfellow had been put forward by Eaker for promotion to brigadier general. On 24 August Longfellow flew his theatre indoctrination flight with Paul Tibbets who led the mission. Twelve of the forty-eight bombs fell within 500 yards of the aiming point but no material damage seemed to have been done to the yards. One wayward bomb luckily hit and sank a U-boat moored in the docks but overall it was the poorest bombing to date. Flak caused damage to the Fortresses and two officers and three sergeants received slight wounds. On the way home the formation was jumped from above by yellow-nosed Bf 109s. Fighters from 12 o'clock attacked Major Tibbets. A 20mm cannon shell ripped through the right-hand window and badly injured the co-pilot, Lieutenant Gene Lockhart, in the left hand. Blood sprayed over what instruments were left in the shattered cabin. Tibbets, who suffered slight injuries to the wrist and left leg, struggled with the controls.

Tibbets later wrote:

> Newt panicked. He started grabbing for the throttles and we had a critical situation. I told him to quit. He didn't even hear me. The only thing I could do was hit him with my right elbow. I was able to catch him under the chin, while he was leaning over and I knocked him flat on his fanny. He calmed down then and when he got back on his feet he spent the next half-hour ministering to the injured. Having done what he could for Lockhart's hand, he bandaged the head of the turret gunner who was lying on the floor unconscious. After lifting Lockhart out of his seat and making him as comfortable as possible on the floor, with a parachute pack for a pillow, Longfellow took over the co-pilot's duties to help me fly the plane.

> When you have wounded aboard, you fire a Very pistol on final approach to the runway. Newt did that and as we rolled to a stop, ambulances moved in beside us to speed the injured men to the base hospital. All recovered in good time, although there were some uneasy moments in the case of Lockhart, who had lost a large quantity of blood. Lockhart recovered and an awards ceremony was arranged.

This event was as much for public relations as to honour the wounded and General Eaker dispatched Beirne Lay, the Public Relations Officer, on the staff of General Spaatz, to cover the ceremony. In 1942 when he was a captain, Lay was one of Eaker's original 'seven' senior officers to arrive in England. The red headed Yale-educated pilot and writer had penned the classic *I Wanted Wings*, which, in 1941, had been made into a successful movie by Paramount and will be remembered as the movie that made Veronica Lake famous. It was written originally to tell what happens inside a boy who 'just has to fly.' At first Lay received no co-operation but after a heated argument with Tibbets he finally got his parade. Lay recalled: 'Later we became great friends and collaborated on an MGM feature motion picture about his Hiroshima experience, called *Above and Beyond*.'

With the good weather continuing to hold, bombing missions were becoming almost everyday events at Grafton Underwood and Polebrook. On 27 August nine Fortresses returned to the Wilton shipyards at Rotterdam, which was once again working to full capacity. Although only seven of the B-17s bombed the target, hits were claimed on two ships and the centre of the target was well covered. Next day the 97th dispatched fourteen B-17s to the Avions Potez factory at Meaulte in northern France. Most of the bombs from the eleven Fortresses that bombed the target fell in open fields, although some 'postholed' the runways. The bombers returned intact but one Spitfire was missing, along with its Canadian pilot. It was on this mission that American fighter pilots were also present for the first time. On 29 August, for the third day running, the 97th was airborne and twelve of the thirteen B-17s dispatched bombed the German fighter base at Courtrai-Wevelgem in France. The results appeared good and even the British Press, which had at first been cautious of American claims, now openly praised them. However, Spaatz and Eaker refused to read too much into the Fortresses' success (they were claimed in some circles to have scored better than 70 per cent of hits). It was early days yet and moves were afoot to transfer the 97th and 301st to the 12th Air Force, activated in Washington DC on 20 August. Although Eaker continued to use the two groups at every available opportunity, it meant he would have to reorganize and plan for the future.[17]

On 5 September the 97th dispatched twenty-five of its newly acquired B-17Fs together with twelve Fortresses of the 301st Bomb Group, flying its first combat mission of the war, to the marshalling yards at Rouen. Thirty-one B-17s bombed and six aborted owing to mechanical problems. Only about 20 per cent of the bombs fell within the target area and some hit the city. The next day Eaker mounted his largest bombing mission so far, to the Avions Potez factory at Meaulte. The 92nd scraped together fourteen B-17Es and crews, filling in with ground personnel and joined twenty-two B-17Fs of the 97th in the main strike, while the 301st flew a diversionary raid on St-Omer-Longuenesse airfield. Thirty Fortresses crossed Meaulte but only six in the 92nd attacked the target. Enemy aircraft were encountered continuously from the French coast to the target and the Americans suffered their first combat losses. Lieutenant Clarence C. Lipsky in the 97th was shot down and Lieutenant Leigh E. Stewart's B-17 in the 92nd was also lost.[18] These first losses had a deep effect on the survivors, as Paul Tibbets recalls.

> Up to this time, the war had seemed a little more than a game in the sense that we flew out in the morning and came back a few hours later after dropping our bombs and eluding enemy flak and fighter fire. We knew the flak was for real and the shells from the German attacking 'planes were dangerous but we still had come to consider ourselves supermen whose skill in the sky would always bring us back safely. That was the state of our confidence up until the moment we saw Lipsky's airplane spin out of formation, burst into flames and make that last grim, smoking dive to earth. Now at last the war was a bloody reality for all of us.

The 92nd had flown the 6 September mission only because VIIIth Bomber Command was so desperately short of aircraft and spares and personnel. This constant drain on its resources was a direct result of the need to supply 'Junior', better known as the 12th Air Force, which few were aware were destined for Operation *Torch* and the Mediterranean theatre. The new air force had top priority when it came to spares, personnel, B-17Fs and even training and Eaker was also informed that the 97th and 301st were earmarked for the MTO, although they would continue to fly missions from England until mid-November. On 7 September, twenty-nine B-17s from these two Groups were dispatched to the Wilton shipyards at Rotterdam again. A storm warning was flashed to the outbound Fortresses and most of the crews received it and returned safely. Seven in the 97th formation continued to the target, where the *Luftwaffe* was waiting for them. The lead ship, piloted by Captain Aquilla Hughes was badly damaged but all B-17s returned safely after beating off heavy fighter attacks. No further raids were flown and on 14 September the 97th and 301st were, on paper at least, assigned to the 12th Air Force. The complete break-up of VIII Bomber Command was avoided by the arrival in England of four new B-17 groups, Colonel Stanley T. Wray's 91st 'Ragged Irregulars', the 303rd, 305th and 306th and two Liberator groups, the 'Flying Eightballs' and the 'Travelling Circus'. The 303rd would take its name from *Hell's Angels*, one of the original Forts in the Group, which became the first heavy bomber in the 8th Air Force to reach the twenty-five-mission mark. During the next two months the crews flew training missions and the aircraft were cycled through the Lockheed plant near Belfast, Northern Ireland for combat modification.

On 26 September approximately seventy-five B-17s were dispatched to Cherbourg-Maupertus and Morlaix-Poireau airfields but bad weather over France forced them to return without dropping their bombs. Unable to see the coastline, the bombers flew on dead reckoning and when they were actually over their target their plotting charts showed them still short of it. Eleven Spitfires of 133 Eagle Squadron ran short of fuel and were forced to land in France. The twelfth, nursing his fast-dwindling fuel supply, attempted to glide back to England but crashed on the cliffs of the Lizard. The Fortresses were able to buck the headwind and return to base.

At 0500 on the morning of 2 October Lieutenant Charles Paine Jr, pilot of *Phyllis* in the 301st was woken up in a Nissen hut at Grafton Underwood. It was dark and for a moment he didn't know quite where he was. Paine dressed quickly and gulped down the tea that was brought him. After that he went to the Intelligence office, where they gave him the exact location of the objective. It was the Avions Potez aircraft factory at Meaulte again, in occupied France. On this occasion thirty B-17s of the 97th[19] and 301st were involved. More than 400 fighter escorts provided cover.[20] When the signal for the take-off came, he was so scared that he could hardly talk. Somehow, though, he managed to make it. They were in Vee of Vees all the way into the target. Their ship was 'Tall-end Charlie', the rearmost left-hand ship in the formation and hence the last to bomb.

Paine recalls:

> We hit scattered heavy flak on our way in but it was slight and did no harm. We got well over our targets, in formation and unmolested and the bombing part was easy. But that's when the enemy fighters

started to pour it on. The German strategy was obviously to pick on the last ship and shoot it down. All the gunners in the crew started calling through the interphones: 'Enemy aircraft at 3 o'clock, Lieutenant! ...At 5 o'clock! ...At 9 o'clock!...' They were all around us. The fighters were employing two tactics that were new to me. When they peeled out of their formation to attack, they came in so close together that by the time one ship had shot up and banked away, the next in line had his sights on us. The other dodge they used was to pretend to come in on one of the other ships and then do a 20° turn and shoot hell out of us. Mostly they came from the rear but at least one of them came up under us from in front, stalled and as it fell off, raked us the length of the Fortress' belly. I could feel his hits banging into us. As a matter of fact, I could feel the effect of all their fire. It was rather like sitting in the boiler of a hot-water heater and being rolled down a steep hill. There was an explosion behind me as a 20mm cannon shell banged into us just behind the upper turret and exploded and I kept thinking, 'What if it hit the flares?' If it hit the flares and ignited them, I knew we'd go up like a rocket. Then I looked out at the right wing and saw it was shot to hell. There were holes everywhere. A lot of them were 20mm cannon holes and they tear a hole in the skin you could shove a sheep through. The entire wing was just a goddam bunch of holes.

About that time, several other unpleasant things happened all at once. First, one of the waist gunners yelled through the interphone: 'Lieutenant, there's a bunch of control wires slapping me in the face,' which meant that the tail surface controls were being shot up. Second, the right-hand outboard engine 'ran away' and the engine controls were messed up so we couldn't shut it off. Third, the left-hand inboard engine quit. And fourth, the ship went into a steep climb, which I couldn't control.

I forgot to say that the whole left-oxygen system had gone out and that I was trying to get the ship down to 20,000 feet to keep half my crew from passing out. One gunner passed out from lack of oxygen and the radio operator, seeing him lying by his gun, abandoned his own oxygen supply and put the emergency mask of the walk-around bottle over the gunner's face. The gunner revived just in time to see the radio operator pass out. He, in turn, took the emergency mask off his own face and revived the radio operator with it.

To return to the fourth unpleasant thing that happened – when our ship went into a steep climb, I simply couldn't hold her level. There

> was something wrong with the controls. I motioned to the co-pilot to help me and between the two of us, we managed to get it forward and assume normal level flight. Then I started to think. The enemy fighters were still shooting us up, we had a long way to go to reach England and safety, we were minus two engines and it took almost full left aileron to hold that damaged right wing up. It was time, I decided, to bail out of the aircraft. So I yelled into the interphone: 'Prepare to abandon ship.' But just about that time the top gunner slid out of the top turret and fell between the co-pilot and me. His face was a mess. He was coughing blood; I thought he'd been wounded in the chest. It later proved that he wasn't but he was clearly in no condition to bail out of an airplane. I called for the bombardier and navigator to come up and help us with the top turret gunner and they did. Back in the waist one of our gunners was manning two guns despite a bad bullet wound in his leg. I don't know how many fighters we damaged or destroyed; there wasn't time to worry about that. We got out over the Channel, finally and a flight of Spits came racing out to meet us. Brother, they looked mighty good. We nursed the Fort across and made a belly landing at Gatwick, the first airdrome we could find. We nicked a hangar on the way in but somehow we made it. Afterward they counted sixteen cannon holes and 300 bullet holes in *Phyllis*.[21]

The locomotive, carriage and wagon works of the Ateliers d'Hellemmes at Chemin de Fer du Nord at Lille had long been earmarked as a target because of its importance to an enemy that was suffering an acute shortage of rail transport. Eaker also saw it as the ideal target to demonstrate high-attitude precision bombing. He waited until 9 October before he had enough bombers capable of destroying the target in one mission. A few weeks before, VIII Bomber Command could muster only twelve aircraft. But by including Timberlake's Group and the 306th, both of which were flying their maiden missions, Eaker was able to assemble an unprecedented 108 bombers for the raid, which would also involve an attack on the engineering works of the Compagnie de Fives. A strong contingent of RAF and USAAF fighters would also fly cover for the bombers while smaller, diversionary forces attacked Courtrai-Wevelgem and St-Omer airfields and the city of Roubaix. Crews remembered Colonel Ted Timberlake's address at the first briefing at Alconbury. He said, 'I know you Joes can do it'.

The briefing finished, Colonel Timberlake in *Teggie Ann* led twenty-four of the Liberators and formed up behind a larger force of B-17s. As the formation approached the French coast Lieutenant Edmund F. Janic, the bombardier aboard *Shoot Luke*, reported over the intercom that the navigator had been taken ill and that to proceed could prove fatal. The pilot, Lieutenant John H. Murphy, turned back. (*Shoot Luke* was so named because in the USA a favourite pursuit of the men was the rolling of dice, accompanied by the expression, 'Shoot Luke, you're faded'.) *Bathtub Bessie* became the first B-24 lost in combat when it went down over France. *Ball of Fire Junior* made the five-hour flight only to crash-land at another airfield on its return.

Seven Fortresses in the 92nd formation returned early to Bovingdon. Henry A. West, the navigator in Major Dean Byerly's Fortress in the 301st formation, had no such problems.

> We picked up our fighter escort at Felixstowe, about three squadrons of Spitfires and three squadrons of P-38s. As we entered enemy territory we had some inaccurate flak but generally we proceeded to Lille without incident. Colonel Ronald R. Walker our CO, who was leading the entire mission, got fouled up somewhere and we just invited trouble by stooging around France for a while doing 180° turns. Finally we found the target but just as Arthur 'Catman' Carlson, my bombardier, was sighting through his bombsight, a formation of B-17s cut in front of us and we were forced to bomb another target. This turned out to be the railway goods terminus.

Colonel 'Chip' Overacker, 'a trim, moustachioed and dashing figure' led twenty-three B-17s of the 306th on its first mission in *Four of A Kind*. Two of the Group's Fortresses aborted the mission before reaching the enemy coast. In the darkness the ordnance personnel were unsuccessful in fully loading all twenty-three B-17s to capacity and nineteen aircraft dropped 159 500lb GP bombs on the primary, while two aircraft bombed the secondary, the airfield at Courtrai, with twenty bombs. 2nd Lieutenant Al La Chasse, the bombardier in the crew of *Snoozy II*, piloted by Captain John W. Olsen, recalls.

> Some smoke and dust covered the target area. As we continued the run a line of B-24s out of position were coming across the target area from the east, heading towards England. Flak hit our right inboard engine and set it on fire. Norman Gates, the co-pilot, somehow extinguished it. Flak increased. I was surprised it came in so many colours. On the bomb run Captain Olsen trimmed the ship before turning the control over to me. After our flak hit, the Norden bombsight automatically made the corrections necessary to 'right'

> the ship on course. I released the bomb load, not knowing there would be several malfunctions causing bomb rack problems. The 'plane lifted; lightened by the bomb drop. The B-24s were now behind us. It was 0942 – time over the target as per mission plan. For *Snoozy II* the war was about to begin and end. Bandits were everywhere. *Snoozy II* began to lag behind the rest of the formation. 'Honest John' McKee's ship tried lagging back with us. Good old 'Honest John'. He tried but *Snoozy II* was too badly damaged and we were ordered to bale out. Our navigator, Bill Gise, got out after some trouble with the hatch. God must have opened it. The ride down was just like the book on parachutes said it would be: scary but nice. I was alive.[22]

Claims for German fighters shot down reached double figures. Tech Sergeant Arizona Harris, an engineer top turret gunner, saw three FW 190s five minutes after the target and as they peeled off at 900 yards to attack the red-haired ranch hand from the deesert town of Tempe, Arizona, opened fire at 600 yards. His bullets hit the cockpit of the leader, setting the fighter on fire and it went down in a fatal dive. Harris would go down with guns blazing two months later when he perished with the rest of his crew on *Sons of Fury* 400 miles north-west of Brest.[23] 1st Lieutenant James M. Stewart in the 'Clay Pigeons' Squadron got *Man O'War* home after losing one engine and two more that overheated.[24] At mid-Channel it seemed that the crew would have to ditch but Flight Lieutenant A. J. Andrews of 91 Squadron in a Spitfire saw them and escorted them safely to Manston. The first rescue of Americans by their Allies took place after Lieutenant Donald M. Swenson, pilot of the 301st Fortress that fell in the drink about a mile from North Foreland. Swenson told the story:

> The fun began as we started home. We were getting plenty of heavy flak and were under constant attack by enemy fighters. We seemed to be getting away with things very nicely until a Focke Wulf 190 winged us with an explosive cannon shell, slightly wounding the bombardier. Then we started to get other hits. One went into our outboard engine, which started smoking badly. The generators were knocked out and the intercom system went dead. The co-pilot and I found that we couldn't hold our altitude. We were losing about 1,500 feet a minute and the English coast was a long way off. After discovering I couldn't talk to the crew on the interphone I turned the controls over to the co-pilot and went aft. We had only about 5,000

feet at this point and there wasn't any time to waste. I got hold of the top turret gunner and told him to get the rest of the gunners together in the radio compartment. Then I climbed down the nose to call the bombardier and the navigator. Then I went back to the controls and got ready to 'ditch' the ship. We had had ditching practice just the day before, so everyone knew what he had to do. We jettisoned the waist guns and adjusted our parachutes and Mae Wests. The water looked cold and I remember thinking it also looked hard. There were waves and I had heard that when you land on water and hit a wave the effect is very much like flying into a stone wall.

It was. We laid her in a belly landing, as slowly as we could, with the tail well dawn. But even at that we hit so hard that it threw the crew all over the ship. A couple of them were stunned for a moment. The navigator was flung from the radio compartment into the bomb bay and knocked unconscious. The top turret gunner had a Very pistol in his lap. It flew up and cut his head. I think all of us were more or less dazed momentarily. The men tried to launch the rubber rafts; but they had been so damaged that, with the exception of one which could be only partially inflated, they were entirely useless to us. Then came another problem. When the men started dropping into the cold water, they realized that the heavy winter equipment some of them were wearing was too heavy for their Mae Wests to support. Splashing around in the icy water, the ones in lighter clothing managed somehow to hold the others up while they got out of their leather jackets, trousers and flying boots and struggled into their life preservers again. The co-pilot had been hurt in the landing and I saw him float out of a window and drift under the wing of the ship. I swam after him and managed to grab him and drag him over to the partially inflated dinghy. Then the navigator's log floated past, so I retrieved that. About then everything began to seem perfectly logical, it's funny but I was doing some very careful reasoning. The trouble was I didn't always get the right answer. The ship went down in about a minute and a half I imagine. Land-planes always sink fast when you 'ditch' them. I ordered some of the men into the partially inflated boat. The rest held on to the edges of it. One of the gunners was bent, bound and determined that we were going to let him sink. He'd go down and then come up and spit seawater and then go down again; but he kept trying to make us let him go. It took a direct order to make him behave. He thought he was hurting our chances of survival.

Then came the worst part – waiting for help to get there and wondering if any help was going to come. What we didn't know was that we were as good as rescued – already. Some time before our ship hit the water the machinery of HM Air-Sea Service started to roll. The lead plane in our Spitfire escort had told them that we were going down over the Channel and gave them our position. Soon a small boat with a rescue crew already on deck came foaming up to us. Right here a strange thing happened. The men on the boat made no sound and scowled at us with cold and gloomy faces. I didn't get it, until one of my men in the water called out something to them. Then one of the rescue crew yelled, 'Hell, they're Yanks!' and after that everybody grinned at us and started calling, 'Hold on, Maties! We'll have you out of there in half a mo'!' We found out later why they had been scowling at us. They thought we were Germans because of the powder-blue colour of the electrically heated jumpers that a couple of the gunners wore. It seems that they pick up Germans too but somehow they can't develop any wild enthusiasm about the job. Our rescue constituted a special occasion for this crew because, they told us, the crew of various Air-Sea Rescue boats had organized a pool to be won by the first crew to pick up some Americans.[25]

Captain Ramsey D. Potts Jr, the 330th Squadron Operations Officer, an ex-Memphis Junior College economics instructor whose father was a Memphis cotton broker, had led an element of three B-24s in the 93rd formation.

Although a successful mission, we sustained numerous losses. Captain Alexander Simpson, my best friend, who was flying [*Big Eagle*] on my left wing, was shot down.[26] My tail gunner was in shock and wouldn't respond. At the base the plane in front of me had to make an emergency landing and skidded off the runway and broke in two. Afterwards, I went back the Nissen hut I lived in and sat in front of the potbelly stove. I was cold, so I put on extra clothes and eventually went to the officers' club for a shot of whiskey. I wasn't frightened during the mission, but I was shaken afterward. I wondered if I could keep doing this. Just then Tommy Taylor, an officer from another group who was in my graduating class and on the same mission, walked in. I said, 'Tommy; that was one hell of a mission.'

But he laughed and said, 'That was a piece of cake.'

> And I thought, 'If he can do it, then I know damn well I can too.' I was never in that kind of shock again.

Four bombers were lost. Only sixty-nine aircraft, including just ten Liberators, had bombed their primary targets. To make matters worse, many of the bombs had failed to explode. The inexperienced 93rd and 306th Groups had placed many of their bombs outside the target area, killing a number of French civilians. Traffic control was bad and some of the bombardiers never got the target in their bombsights. Liberator crews who had to jettison their bombs in the Channel on the way home were termed 'chandeliers' at one B-17 base. At the subsequent interrogations crews revealed that they had had 242 encounters with *Luftwaffe* fighters and put in claims for forty-eight destroyed, eighteen probably destroyed and four damaged. The Germans admitted the loss of only one fighter. At the time the figures did much to compensate for the largely inaccurate bombing. At Thurleigh, one B-17 landed with a critically wounded gunner who died five days later. Another B-17 lost a propeller on the runway after having had its No. 3 engine shot out by flak over the target and two others came in with feathered propellers. Another landed on one good wheel and with a badly ruptured gas tank and another had its tail wheel shot up and destroyed. Ground crew stopped counting holes in two of the Forts at the 170 mark, though there were more; many more. Captain Thurman Shuller, group medical officer, in his diary for 9 October wrote: 'Man must be nothing but a fool to face a hell of fire like that. But that's what we came here for and we'll have to see it through.'[27]

For three months the 97th and later the 301st, had pioneered American daylight bombing from England. Both these and four fighter groups left for North Africa in November 1942 and earned undying fame with raids from the desert and later from Italy. The remaining groups in England still had to prove that high-altitude missions in daylight, often without escort, could justify further B-17 and B-24 groups being sent to the ETO. Shallow penetration missions, or 'milk-runs', as they began to be called, were not the answer but for the time being VIII Bomber Command could flaunt itself in force over the continent of Europe, so 'tip-and-run' missions to the U-boat pens remained the order of the day. On 21 October VIII Bomber Command flew its first mission against the U-boat bases, when a small force of bombers hit Lorient-Keroman. Fifteen B-17s bombed from as low as 17,500 feet and three were shot down in attacks by thirty-six FW 190s. First to go down was *Francis X*, which was flown by Lieutenant Francis X. Schwarzenbeck who on 14 August had crash-landed his Fortress at Elveden. The crew could have bailed out but they were heading into a flock of German fighters so they kept their guns manned and managed two destroy two fighters on the way down. The Forts flown by Captain John M. Bennett and Lieutenant Milton M. Stenstrom, who was taken prisoner, were the other two victims. FW 190s raked the cockpit of *Johnny Reb*, wounding the pilot, Lieutenant Richard F. Starks and killing the co-pilot, 2nd Lieutenant Donald A. Walter, the first 8th Air Force combat fatality. *Johnny Reb* made it back and Starks put the plane down at Horsham St Faith. Eight other B-17s bombed Cherbourg-Maupertus airfield.

Although they had lowered their bombing altitudes by as much as 10,000 feet the B-17s' small high-explosive bombs barely dented the sub-pens. On 31 October General Spaatz told General Arnold that operations against the U-boat pens were proving too costly for the results achieved. He planned to send in the heavies at altitudes as low as 4,000 feet and accept the heavy casualties.

Notes

1. *We Remember Pearl Harbor* by Lawrence Reginald Rodriggs (Communications Concepts 1991).
2. *To Beyond The North Sea And Back; An Eighth Air Force Saga that James Michener Never Wrote*, Robert H. Shaver, 1991.
3. *Country Boy-Combat Bomber Pilot* by R. H. Tays (privately published, 1990).
4. Going to gunnery school at Tyndall Field, Panama City, Florida, he shortly graduated as an aerial gunner and went overseas in March 1943 with the 306th BG. When he had just completed his first mission, to St Nazaire, and was asked how he liked it, 'It was wonderful,' he said. 'I saw three Germans going down in flames all at once. It was terrific.' He got on well with his fellows and met a refugee girl. They announced their engagement and made their wedding plans. The day before the wedding S/Sgt Eric G. Newhouse went on the mission to Kiel and was KIA. See *Clash of Eagles* by Martin W. Bowman (Pen & Sword 2006).
5. *Chick's Crew: A Tale of the Eighth Air Force* by Ben Smith Jr (privately published 1978, 1983, 2006).
6. The 97th had been activated on 3 February along with the 301st, commanded by Colonel Ronald R. Walker and the 303rd BG.
7. The first B-17 group to be activated had been the 34th at Langley Field, Virginia, also on 15 January 1941, but the group was used to train others and would remain in the USA until late March 1944. On 1 March 1942 the 92nd and 93rd Bomb Groups were activated at Barksdale Field, Louisiana, equipped with B-17Es and B-24Ds respectively.

8. Between 12 October 1942 and 6 May 1945 64 U-boats were sunk by actions involving RAF and RCAF Liberators. In 1943 in actions involving the USAF Anti-Submarine Squadron B-24s, seven U-boats were sunk and in actions involving US Navy PB4Ys, July 1943-April 1945, twelve U-boats, mostly in the Bay of Biscay, were sunk.
9. June 1943 saw the start of the Atlantic run from Gourock to New York. It is said that the two liners helped shorten the war by a complete year. *RMS Queen Mary Transatlantic Masterpiece* by Janette McCutcheon (Tempus 2000).
10. With the start of the war all Atlantic liners raced to the safety of neutral countries. New York was a refuge for many of them. There was fear that German agents might try to sabotage them while they were berthed in the Hudson River. While being converted to a troopship the *Normandie* met its end when it accidentally caught fire at the hand of a careless worker wielding an acetylene torch. She capsized under the weight of the water that was poured into her by fireboats and fire-fighters.
11. On her first trip with American troops aboard, *Queen Mary* was to stop at Trinidad for fuel and provisions. While she was at sea, a U-boat slipped into Trinidad harbor and sank two ships at anchor, leaving unharmed in the confusion. The *Queen* received an urgent coded message ordering her to avoid Trinidad. As long as she kept her speed up there was not much chance a sub could score with a torpedo. The crew felt that stopping or even slowing down would have meant disaster. In early 1942, about 100 miles north of Bermuda, *Queen Mary* passed seven lifeboats adrift in the sea with men aboard. Under strict orders, she did not stop or slow her speed -- sending a blinker signal indicating they would send word of the sighting by wireless. The *Queen*'s purser watched the lifeboats bobbing in the water. He did not know one of the individuals in the lifeboats was his son. After being rescued his son said in a message to his father: 'You didn't have to be so haughty simply because you're aboard the *Mary*. I am blood you know.' *The 446th Revisited* by Ed Castens for the 446th BG (H) Association.
12. Not one wall or mural was scratched. No moustaches were drawn on the art. A fact the Captain called, 'An example of the discipline of the American troops.' He wanted the carved railing left intact as a fitting memorial to the brave American fighting men who sailed on her to war. Cunard did not agree and had the railing planed and sanded to remove the carvings – all except a six-foot piece, which was removed and sent to the US Army archives as a war time memento. *The 446th Revisited* by Ed Castens for the 446th BG (H) Association.
13. *First Over Germany: A History of the 306th Bombardment Group* by Russell A. Strong. (Hunter Publishing Co, 1982).
14. Tibbets was to fly an even more historic mission three years later when he piloted the B-29 *Enola Gay*, named after his mother, to Hiroshima, when the first atomic bomb was dropped on Japan.

15. Sconiers was shot down on the raid on Lorient on 21 October 1942 and he was taken prisoner and sent to *Stalag Luft* III. About fourteen months after capture Sconiers slipped on ice in the South Compound and he ruptured an ear drum. His condition worsened without adequate drugs to treat the injury and he died from complications on 27 January 1944.
16. Colonel Charles T. Phillips, with whom Eaker and Longfellow had gone to the Philippines in July 1919, was given command of the 4th Bomb Wing. Phillips was KIA in North Africa on 15 December 1942.
17. Eaker needed a Combat Crew Replacement and Training Center (CCRC) but personnel and equipment were in such short supply that the 92nd BG, with its base at Bovingdon, was selected for the task. Bovingdon became the 11th CCRC and for a few, vital months provided the 8th with badly needed crews. Unhappily for the 92nd, their B-17Fs were transferred to the 97th in exchange for battered B-17Es. However, the time would come when the 92nd would fly combat missions and become known as 'Fame's Favored Few'. The B-17F was supposed to be an improvement on the B-17E. However, it was equipped with only two .30 calibre machine gun mountings in the nose, although it had additional .5 sockets fitted later as a field modification. Externally, the B-17F differed little from the B-17E, its most noticeable distinguishing feature being a frame-less Plexiglas nose but inwardly it incorporated over 400 major design modifications which, although making it 1,000lb heavier than the B-17E, made it better suited for combat.
18. The Red Cross reported later that Lipsky and five of the crew were PoWs.
19. Now commanded by Colonel Joseph H. Atkinson, Colonel Armstrong having moved up to Bomber Command.
20. The 92nd flew a diversionary feint along the French coast and six B-17s of the 97th attacked the airfield at St-Omer.
21. *Target Germany*: The US Army Air Forces official story of the VIII Bomber Command's first year over Europe (1944).
22. Olsen and 2nd Lt Joseph N. Gates were killed. Al La Chasse, Bill Gise and T/Sgt Erwin D. Wissenback, the top-turret gunner, were the only three to bail out. La Chasse was thrown into various jails, including the infamous Napoleonic prison of Saint Giles near Brussels. At *Dulag Luft* he discovered he was only the 18th American PoW. La Chasse finished the war at *Stalag Luft* III, Sagan in Silesia. Wissenback and Giles evaded capture, made contact with the Belgian Resistance and finally reached England via Spain and Gibraltar. One of John R. McKee's gunners was S/Sgt Darwin H. Wissenback, the twin brother of Erwin. Darwin Wissenback was on John McKee's crew when they were one of three Forts in the 306th BG shot down on 19 December 1942. Both men survived and McKee made it home in January 1943. *First Over Germany* by Russell A. Strong.

23. He was posthumously awarded the Distinguished Service Cross, the second highest award for 'extraordinary heroism'. In part his citation said that '...A large force of enemy planes concentrated their attacks on this lone airplane, finally driving it to a crash landing in the sea. Throughout the descent and as the airplane disappeared beneath the waves, Sgt Harris was seen to be still firing his guns at the enemy airplanes...'
24. The 369th Squadron's name derived from the Fightin' 69th Regiment of WWI out of New York. With some literary licence, Lt Kermit Cavedo, a navigator in the 306th BG, gave his name to his Fortress and a special emblem showing two insects sparring, which lasted four months and five days in combat before going down over Kiel. The 369th adopted the nickname and insignia. The 368th was nicknamed the 'Eager Beavers' and the 367th, the 'Clay Pigeons'. The 423rd was known as the 'Grim Reapers'.
25. *Target Germany*: The US Army Air Forces official story of the VIII Bomber Command's first year over Europe (1944).
26. *Big Eagle* was the 93rd's first loss in combat. It took direct hits in the No. 4 engine, which was blazing and in the bomb bay. An explosion sent Simpson and Lt Nicholas H. Cox into a free-fall. In a German PoW camp neither knew how they got out of the disintegrating B-24 or how their parachutes opened. Two other crew survived and were also taken into captivity. Sgt Arthur B. Cox evaded for seven months and crossed into Spain. The rest of the crew were killed. *Ted's Travelling Circus 93rd Bombardment Group (H) USAAF 1942-45* by Carroll (Cal) Stewart (Sun/World Communications Inc 1996).
27. *First Over Germany* by Russell A. Strong.

CHAPTER 2

I Wanted Wings

Most people would have guessed that I would want to be a fighter pilot from the way I drove a car. I was a maniac for speed. So, people would think I was crazy enough to be a fighter pilot. But I liked company. I didn't like the idea of being up there in the air by myself. If I went up in a B-17 I would have nine other guys up there with me and I liked that fine. That was the reason I picked bombers.'

Captain Bob Morgan, pilot of the **Memphis Belle**

From the very beginning Robert Knight Morgan, born on 31 July 1918 in Asheville, North Carolina, the third child of David Bradley Morgan and Mabel K. Morgan, had many things going for him. He grew up in a kind of protective society with nurses to take care of him. His sister Peggy was to break off her engagement to Simon Baring, a member of the London banking family, to marry Alexander Abel-Smith, also of London. Their brother, David Junior, was destined to marry Princess Dolly Obolinsky, a White Russian émigré and socialite from New York. Bob's upbringing did not stop him from hunting and fishing. One of the Vanderbilt estates were located at Asheville and through the Morgan family Bob got to know one of the wardens on the estate. He took him fishing and hunting and taught him how to shoot. Like all boys, Bob was prone to playing pranks – like the time his mother was having a cocktail party on the lawn and he took the water hose, breaking up the party by squirting water on the maids. His dad got out his razor strap and whipped him pretty good. Bob got away with a lot but his father was no 'softie'. He knew how to use that strap. Bob was wild as a kid. He had the world's speed record from Asheville, North Carolina, to Greenville, South Carolina. He used to see a girl there and went almost every day. It was sixty miles and a mountain road but he drove it in fifty-five minutes in his father's Buick. Everybody in town knew about and talked about it.

It appears that young Morgan got the taste of marrying early. Journalist Ruth Reynolds alleged in the *Sunday News* on 22 August 1943 that before he was fifteen he had eloped and married thirteen-year old Doris Newman, a fellow pupil at Asheville Public School. They were wed on 6 June 1931 – and divorced nine days later: their parents took care of that! Things changed with the coming of the Great Depression. Bob's father was president of the Dimension Manufacturing Company, a successful furniture-making concern. When the Depression hit he became the watchman who guarded the locked-up plant for $50 a month. He even had to sell their house. It was an experience Morgan never forgot. The former Cornelia Vanderbilt, a close friend of Morgan's mother, who had inherited *Biltmore House* in 1914 following the death of her father George Washington Vanderbilt, came to the Morgan's rescue. She let them live in a house on her estate rent free and when the Depression eased a little, Morgan's father borrowed some money from one of his friends, bought his factory back and before the Depression was over, owned three furniture factories. In 1936 Morgan's mother contracted thyroid cancer. There was no hope of a cure, no hope of recovery. She took a shotgun, pointed the gun at herself and committed suicide. Bob Morgan continued with his education and in the summer of 1938 he met and married Alice Rutherford Lane whose folks had a summer residence in Asheville. The marriage lasted longer than the first – just – for that fall her parents whisked her away to Florida and divorce followed. Morgan enlisted as an Aviation Cadet at Richmond, Virginia, and in February 1941 he received his orders to report for basic training. Though he was a maniac for speed Morgan became a bomber pilot and by May 1942 he was part of the 29th Bombardment Group. The previous September he had met and married Martha Lillian Stone, an old flame from his University of Pennsylvania days but marriage to Martha ended in divorce in 1942.

Morgan became known as 'Floorboard Freddie' because he wore out more brakes than any pilot in his group. He landed his Fortress hot and always said that he'd rather run out of runway at the other end than not make the runway on the touchdown. During crew training at Walla Walla, Washington Morgan, not yet a 1st Lieutenant, began romancing Margaret Polk, of Memphis, Tennessee, who was visiting her sister in Walla Walla. Legend has it that Margaret inspired the name *Memphis Belle*, which Morgan had painted on both sides of the fuselage of his B-17 at Bangor, Maine, in September 1942 before leaving for Bassingbourn, an ex-RAF bomber station just north of Royston in Cambridgeshire. However, Morgan's co-pilot, Jim Verinis, recalled that he and Morgan went to see the movie *Lady For A Night* starring Joan Blondell and John Wayne. In the movie there is a Mississippi River gambling boat and Verinis remembered that either Miss Blondell or the boat was called the *Memphis Belle*. The romance between Morgan and the Memphis girl would flourish for a time and in England Morgan flew over the French sub pens and German dockyards in a sweater knitted by Margaret. A Hollywood scriptwriter would have had them married and flying off into the sunset but war was no respecter of tradition and Morgan and Margaret later married other partners. The legendary artwork, though, remained indelibly painted on the nose of the B-17 through thick and thin.

The *Memphis Belle* and thirteen other 91st Bomb Group B-17s, led by the CO, Colonel Stanley T. Wray, took part in the Group's first mission on 7 November when the target for thirty-four B-17s was U-boat pens at Brest. Six returned early because of gun and other mechanical problems.[1] Bob Morgan recalled:

> We didn't know what we would run into or what was going to happen. There wasn't anyone to give us any tactical lessons on high-altitude precision bombing. We had to learn for ourselves. We learned the hard way. We made a lot of mistakes and will admit it. Naturally when you go out to do something and no one can tell you what to do, you are bound to make some mistakes. There were only a few B-17s. We had only four groups and all during the winter we got few replacements. We got some planes and a few crews but not enough to make it noticeable. Losses were not replaced. Not until spring 1943 were we back up to the strength we had when we landed in England. That couldn't be helped. We were on the spot to prove that this daylight precision bombing could be done with a minimum loss. We proved it. Fortunately the Germans were unschooled in attacking the B-17s, so it was as new to them as to us. They had to learn just as we did. And happily, they weren't quite as smart as we were. We managed to outguess them and keep ahead of them most of the time. We did run into a lot of trouble. Our first raid was Brest. It was very successful, even though the weather wasn't at its best. We encountered quite a bit of flak; Brest at that time was one of the hottest flak areas. We were at 20,000 feet, flying a formation we thought up ourselves – a pretty loose formation. There were some enemy fighters in the sky but the Groups just saw them. They made one or two feeble attacks at the end of the last Group. We even came home with the idea that this was a snap.

The next day fifthy-three Fortresses with thirty-six RAF Spitfires flying top cover to the enemy coast were dispatched and forty-one B-17s bombed the Abbeville-Drucat airfield and the Atelier d'Hellemmes locomotive works at Lille. Weather conditions over England and above the Channel were clear, with a few cumulus floating over the French coast and the target. The 301st sent eighteen aircraft on this, its last mission with the 8th Air Force. The 306th dispatched twenty aircraft and seven aborted for a variety of reasons. A second run on the target by the 369th Squadron proved disastrous to Captain Richard D. Adams and his crew. During the thirty minutes the squadron was alone, thirty FW 190s made at least 200 attacks on the five-plane formation. Adams' B-17 finally went down to a flak-hit in the wing between the No. 1 and No. 2 engines. Six of the crew including Adams, who evaded, got out of the plane but the radio operator died the next day. The twelve B-17s of the 91st formation went to Abbeville alone. When the lead aircraft, *Man-O-War*, had to abort the mission Captain H. W. Aycock, the 401st Squadron CO, flying the *Sain*t took over as Group lead. The 91st started receiving flak bursts about ten miles east of Ault. Flak was encountered all the way to the target and on the way out, all the way to the coast. Although heavy in places, most bursts were below and to the rear of the aircraft. Only small hits were registered on the bombers.

Short Snorter[2] flown by Lieutenant William D. Bloodgood of Scarsdale, New York, dropped on the target at 1159 hours from 21,000 feet. Bloodgood banked the B-17 a little too soon, resulting in an inaccurate release. Two of the ten 500lb bombs also hung up in the bomb bay and were returned to base. Fourteen fighters attacked the 91st formation as it left the French coast on the way home. The enemy attacked from 5 to 7 o'clock low, closing to within 800 yards. Captain Aycock was hit in the left leg by a .30 calibre bullet at the beginning of the attack. *Short Snorter* received considerable damage from flak and the fighter attacks. Shrapnel from an exploding 88mm shell broke the window in front of Bloodgood. Shrapnel also punctured the No. l gas tank. Three fighters pressed their attack to within 500 yards of *Short Snorter*. All four propellers were penetrated by bullets, while both wings had numerous .30 calibre bullets in them. A 20mm cannon shell went through the No. 4 engine cowling. Another exploded in the rear of the fuselage. Explosions tore away the elevator control cables and the auxiliary cables, leaving a gaping hole in the fuselage. The radio receiver was knocked out and the oxygen line to the radio compartment cut. In spite of the severity of the damage, Bloodgood brought *Short Snorter* safely back to base. The only injuries to the crew were steel splinters in the face of the bombardier, Lieutenant William St Chubb and the radio operator, T/Sgt William Steele. Neither was serious. Chubb was the regular bombardier but was manning a waist gun in place of Sgt Sams who was unable to fly on this mission. Because of the extent of the damage, *Short Snorter* would not be in the air again until 12 December. The *Bad Egg* in the 91st landed at Hunsdon on return. *Panhandle Dogie* was shot up so badly that it became a 'hangar queen' and was cannibalized for parts.

Bob Morgan's next mission, on 9 November, was entirely different to the last.

> It was St Nazaire at 8,500 feet – a mission I am sure none of my crew will ever forget.[3] We formed over England, four Groups. At that time we were not flying close Group formations. The Groups weren't in sight of each other when we left England. We came down to France outside the water area, down low. We were almost on the deck. We came straight into St-Nazaire and then began to climb to 8,500 feet, made a run to the northwest and dropped back to the water.[4] The main idea was to fool the Germans. It did surprise the pursuits, which never got up but it didn't surprise the flak guns. Our plane had 62 holes in it and we got off better than anyone else. We learned a lot about flying and we learned that you had to stick together for protection.[5] We went back to St-Nazaire four times but always at high altitude. Twice we went in over land, over the southern part, trying to fool the Germans and make them wonder whether we were going to St-Nazaire or Brest or Lorient. We would head for Lorient, then change and go to St-Nazaire. The Germans didn't have too many fighters in that area. The controllers apparently couldn't figure out where we were going. Many times we would get almost to the target before we would see a pursuit ship, because they didn't want to take a chance on outguessing us and sending ships one place, only to find we had gone another. When they did hit us – and they did many times before we got to our IP – flak didn't seem to follow us, even though this was the hottest flak area in this stretch of France. The pursuits would attack us right through the flak, right on the bombing run. My gunners said they have seen them shot down by their own flak. We didn't try to bomb the submarine pens themselves, because a 2,000lb bomb bounces off them. We knocked out repair installations and the locks. And when they got them repaired, we knocked them out again. The theory was that this made the pens useless.[6]

There was a brief respite and then missions to St-Nazaire resumed on 14

November when twenty-one B-17s and thirteen B-24s were dispatched and returned without suffering loss. Three days later thirty-eight B-17s, including sixteen Fortresses in the 'Hell's Angels' at Molesworth, making their maiden mission, flew to the U-boat pens at St-Nazaire. Cloud obscured the target and they returned to base without dropping their bombs. Fifteen B-24s went to Abbeville-Drucat airfield. *Shoot Luke* in the 93rd formation shrugged off three flak shells, which exploded under the port wing, almost turning the aircraft upside down. On the homeward flight Ju 88s attacked the formation for forty-five minutes. *Shoot Luke*'s gunners dispatched one of the fighter-bombers, which burst into flames and crashed into the sea.

On 18 November Eaker sent his small force of B-17s and B-24s to the U-boat bases at La Pallice and Lorient-Keroman. Nineteen bombers hit La Pallice and thirteen bombed Lorient but the 303rd formation, dispatched to their briefed target at La Pallice, veered 100 miles off course and bombed St-Nazaire in error. One B-17, *Floozy*, in the 306th was lost.

On 22 November seventy-six bombers attempted to hit the submarine pens at Lorient again. Eleven B-17s in the 'Hell's Angels', which was still smarting from a navigational error four days before, were the only Forts to bomb the target. Over Lorient a bullet from a Ju 88 entered the cockpit of *Ball of Fire* in the 'Travelling Circus', smashing pilot Lieutenant Howard M. Young's arm and ricocheting off the control column into the leg of Lieutenant Cleveland D. Hickman, the co-pilot. At the same time Sergeant Warren U. Sherwood, the tunnel gunner, was twice hit in the stomach. One bullet that had passed entirely through his body was found protruding from his hip by the navigator, who administered first aid. Sherwood took the bloodstained piece of metal that was handed to him and put it into his pocket, remarking that it would make a good souvenir. Young, clinging to the controls with one hand despite the pain of his shattered arm, was lifted out of the cockpit and placed on the flight deck. 'Kelly' Yenalavage, the bombardier who was from Kingston, Pennsylvania – real name Anthony Cristopolus Yenalavage – had some flight training but he had never been at the controls of a four-engined ship, took his place. He and Hickman took it in turns flying the ship. Near the English coast visibility began to grow bad. The navigator took an Aldis lamp and flashed word to the other ships that they intended to land their wounded at the first available airfield. Shortly afterward they left the formation, climbed above the overcast and started hunting for a break in the clouds. Yenalavage's flat, unemotional report told the rest of the story.

> At about 6,000 feet we came into the clear over the overcast. I asked the engineer how much gasoline we had. He checked and said we had about an hour's supply. We decided to fly along for about forty-five minutes and look for an opening. We flew on a 65° heading that the navigator gave us. Just about the time this period was up we found an opening, came through and sighted the runways of an airdrome. We had discussed the matter of landing while flying along. The co-pilot could not use the rudders and on the landing we were both on the wheel. I was using the rudders and working the brakes. We made a fast landing. I turned off the runway to the right as we came to the end of it. After landing we immediately called for an ambulance and rushed the three wounded to the hospital. The plane was not damaged on landing.

The 'Hell's Angels' had been blooded and now it was the turn of the 305th. In April 1942 1st Lieutenant Clifton Pyle was one of the original pilots in the Group who served under Curtis LeMay at Salt Lake City and Muroc Dry Lake, California. He had been designated one of the flight commanders in the 422nd Squadron, which was commanded by Major Thomas McGehee. The immediate mission of the Group had been to train three cadres of primary flight crews, a pilot and engineer in each, for new groups that were being organized. Then they had accepted and trained a new cadre of personnel, this time the whole crew, and proceeded overseas. Pyle recalled that LeMay demanded the best from each man. If the man did not 'produce' he was fired. Several examples were made in this regard and it took little time for the entire group to start stepping in line. LeMay began his Army career in 1929 as a fighter pilot and transferred to bombers eight years later when he was put in charge of the navigation school at Langley Field in the 2nd Bomb Group, the first AAC unit equipped with the B-17. He was only thirty-five when he took over the 305th. LeMay was a believer in exactness in flying, abiding by the book as far as possible but wanted the job done. He would not tolerate laziness of any type and he did not want any 'unlucky' person on his team. He would fire a person for being 'unlucky' as quickly as incompetent. All during the training period Colonel LeMay was a strict disciplinarian. He explained that it was for their benefit and the best chance of survival. Most of the crews thought that he was a little too rough. LeMay was soon known as 'Ole Iron Ass' and was referred to in public as 'Ole Iron Tail' or 'Ole Iron Pants'. Regardless of his persistent firmness, he soon gained the Group's respect, admiration and full support. He was one who believed in flying with his crews and did so on numerous occasions.[7]

When on 19 October the air echelon departed for Gander, Cliff Pyle was among those who made the trip. It was one day after his wife had given birth to a baby girl and it would be nearly a year later before he had a chance to see her for the first time. When LeMay's Group had been scheduled to fly a practice mission on 15 November they had been at Grafton Underwood only a short time and they had had little time to flight test their aircraft before they were scheduled for combat missions. Ball turret problems were evident and they would result in nine aborts when the first few missions were flown. Pyle's aircraft had a peculiar problem of losing power as they gained altitude and the cause was difficult to locate. Consequently, the crew named their plane 'SNAFU' ('Situation Normal, All Fucked Up'). Pyle and the crew were not too fond of this name and after a couple of missions they would change the name to *We The People*, a name recommended to them by the Gulf Oil Company, whose popular radio programme had the same name.

Colonel LeMay gathered all his pilots and crews in one of the huts and told them that they were on their own now. He further stated that he had done his best in training and he believed they would benefit from it. He said that they would be 'face to face with the best of the German Air Force.' On 17 November LeMay led ten B-17s on a diversion mission but four Forts were forced to return early with defective ball turrets and an engine problem. Next day he set out with twenty B-17s and this time five more Forts returned with ball turret problems. On the 22nd LeMay led twenty-two B-17s to Lorient. On 23 November LeMay's Group came face to face with the *Luftwaffe*, when Eaker sent his bombers to St Nazaire for the fifth time in two weeks. On almost every mission bombers were hitting the target but not in large enough concentrations to damage them seriously. Experience was proving that a single bomb or even a few bombs did not have enough destructive power. LeMay, who again led his Group, was determined to alter this and decided to try and achieve greater bombing accuracy by flying a straight course on the bomb-run instead of zigzagging every ten seconds, a tactic that had been designed to spoil the aim of the German flak batteries. His plan was to cross the target faster and therefore reduce the amount of time the German flak had in which to fire on the formation. It was a big step for a group commander to take on a group's maiden bombing mission and one that caused his crews great concern.

Fifty-eight Forts flew to Davidstowe Moor, Cornwall, to refuel before setting out for the Bay of Biscay and St Nazaire. Bad weather and mechanical problems forced thirteen B-17s to abort and one Fortress in the 306th was shot down just before the target. Colonel LeMay led his B-

17s over the target in the longest and straightest bomb run yet seen over Europe. Strike photos later revealed that his fourteen B-17s that had got their bombs away had placed twice as many bombs on the target as any other outfit. Despite their fears, no crews were lost to flak. On previous missions the B-17s had been intercepted from behind, where enough guns could be brought to bear on enemy fighters. However, *Luftwaffe* experiments had now proved that the frontal areas of the B-17 and B-24 offered very little in defensive firepower and despite the dangers of very high closing speeds, a frontal attack was considered the best method of shooting them down. The B-24 normally carried two .5 guns in the nose and the B-17E was equipped with four .30 calibre moveable machine gun mountings but they had to be operated by the over-committed bombardier. Whichever mounting he used, it only offered a very poor field of fire. Fortress navigators could also operate a moveable mounted .5 Browning machine gun from enlarged windows on either side of the nose (often called cheek guns) but these suffered from the same problems as the bombardier's position. In each case a blind spot was left in front which neither the ball turret nor upper turret could cover. *Oberstleutnant* Egon Mayer, commander of III *Gruppe*, JG 2, who led the attacking fighters this day, is credited with developing the head-on attack. The new tactic worked well. The 91st lost only two bombers to head-on attacks but two squadron commanders, the group navigator, bombardier and gunnery officers were among the casualties. Two other B-17s were badly hit. One crashed near Leavesden, Hertfordshire, while trying to make it home to Bassingbourn and three of the crew were killed. *Quitchurbitchin'* was the only 91st B-17 to return. *Lady Fairweather* in the 'Hell's Angels' was shot down in flames near the target.

On 27 November the 329th Squadron in 'Ted's Travelling Circus' transferred to Hardwick to evaluate the British *Gee* navigational device. A special force, consisting of selected crews from all four squadrons, was to test the device on behalf of the USAAF because in October 1942 the 8th Air Force had agreed to spare eight valuable Liberators to help in the work.[8] While the 329th was engaged in 'moling' missions Colonel Timberlake received orders on 5 December 1942 to lead the 328th and 409th Squadrons to North Africa to participate in ten days of disruptive raids against Axis ports and shipping. One Liberator crashed into a mountain south of Tafaraoui and all aboard were killed. In the desert base facilities were almost non-existent. At Tafaraoui bouts of heavy rain turned the short runways into a sea of mud and at Gambut Main dry and dusty conditions played havoc with the B-24Ds. The 'Circus' flew more than a score of missions from North Africa. On 22 February 1943 the 'Circus' flew their twenty-third and final mission of the African campaign. In the three-month stint in the desert seven B-24s had been lost on missions.

During their absence, the heavy bomb groups in England had continued to suffer in raids on the U-boat pens. Some, like the 'Flying Eightballs' at Shipdham and the 305th, which early in December moved from Grafton 'Undermud' to the mud at Chelveston, were still trying to come to terms with the English climate.

On Sunday 6 December the 67th Squadron in the 'Flying Eightballs' at last received its full quota of Liberators and they flew their first full group mission – a diversionary raid to the airfield at Abbeville-Drucat in Picardy. By now, crews had flown so many diversionary missions that they had painted ducks on their B-24 fuselages, each representing a decoy mission. Nineteen B-24Ds, including *Little Beaver* piloted by 1st Lieutenant Chester Lucius 'George' Phillips, a moustachioed Texan from Greenville and his co-pilot, 2nd Lieutenant Bill Cameron, were dispatched. Cameron, a twenty-one-year old from California, had joined the USAAC two days before Pearl Harbor. On 9 October he and Phillips had struggled out into the darkened sky through clouds and pouring rain at Gander, Newfoundland, heading for Britain on the Northern Ferry Route. Cameron had wondered then if 'this flying business' was really for him. In short, he had serious doubts concerning the probability of a long life. Christopher Columbus and his crew could not have been more excited – or relieved – when they had reached England. Phillips had decided to name their B-24 previously known only as '807' after the comic strip character. Since even artists from Walt Disney's studios were on base, they had no trouble in finding an artist to paint Little Beaver in the act of throwing a bomb on the nose of the ship. Cameron recalled that from then on it was not just an aircraft; it had personality and character and it was part of the crew and they were proud of it. Every one of the Group's B-24s had a 'Flying Eightball' emblem on the nose but *Little Beaver* differed in having a 'Flying Eightball' with a shark's mouth.

Shortly after take-off at Shipdham things began to go wrong. *Little Beaver* lost an engine when the supercharger controls were over-advanced during their climb to altitude. When the throttle was pulled back to slow down in formation the superchargers rammed in too much air and the engines were starved of fuel. The other B-24s continued to the target as *Little Beaver* returned to base. As they neared the French coast an abort signal was radioed to the group after British radar tracked approaching enemy aircraft. Two squadrons only received the signal, leaving six B-24Ds in the 68th Squadron to continue to the target alone. The small force bombed the airfield and was then bounced by thirty yellow-nosed FW 190s. The 'Abbeville Kids' shot down the Liberator flown by Lieutenant James D. Dubard Jr and it went down in flames in the Channel. It entered the water with guns still blazing. The pilot from Marked Tree, Arkansas and his crew perished. A FW 190 fired at *Victory Ship* piloted by 1st Lieutenant Walter 'Tommie' Holmes and a shell burst about a foot above the pilot's head, knocking him and Lieutenant Ager, his co-pilot, out cold. A second burst knocked out the No. 3 engine and a third exploded into oxygen bottles just aft of the main cabin. *Victory Ship* barrel rolled to the left and was diving steeply. Centrifugal force kept the crew from baling out and despite the roll, they kept flying. Minutes later when Holmes recovered consciousness, he looked through a hole on the top of the Liberator, he was staring at water; *Victory Ship* was upside down! Lieutenant Howard Klekar, the bombardier, gave his pilot oxygen and he recovered sufficiently to bring the B-24 back to Shipdham, his head aching all the way. For this raid Holmes was awarded the DFC, Purple Heart, a British DFC and French *Croix de Guerre*.[9] Five other Liberators received hits. The Germans did not press home their attacks and further losses were denied them.

Sixteen squadrons of Spitfires escorted thirty-six B-17s to the Atelier d'Hellemmes locomotive factory, railroads and repair shops at Lille. Cliff Pyle recalls:

> The 305th was No. 3 in the formation, stacked up. Major McGehee led the squadron but he had to turn back with aircraft problems and I took over the lead. Twelve FW 190s attacked our squadron and my tail gunner claimed two shot down and the waist gunner one. Ten minutes from the target Lieutenant William A. Prentice left the formation in flames and five parachutes were seen to open.[10] We encountered very little flak in our position and there were no casualties among my crew.

Following the Lille mission, plans were formulated for an attack on the Romilly-sur-Seine air park, 150 miles southeast of Paris on 20 December.[11] Bob Morgan recalled:

> We went after the main air depot between Germany and Africa. We went in all the way without fighter escort. We came in south of Paris and went on southward. German fighters picked us up. First one squadron hit us and stayed with us a way then another and another.

> That kept up all the way to the target. We were shot at, at the target, on the bombing run and off the run. By that time the first enemy planes had been down and refuelled and picked up more ammunition. For one hour and fifty-eight minutes they followed us. I never saw so many attacks in my life. We learned a particular lesson that day. That was to keep your eyes open for fighters. That was the only mission that German fighters slipped in without us seeing them. Two German fighters came in at 2 o'clock high and I still don't know where they came from. The first indication I had of them was that our top turret gunner was firing his guns: he didn't have time to call them out before he started firing. We were caught asleep and if they had been able to shoot straight we would have been shot down. That was a successful mission. We hit the hangars and the depot. We wrecked 100 airplanes on the ground and we hit the Officers' Club at lunchtime. We heard later there was a cellar full of cognac, which we blew up.

Short Snorter was flown by Captain William Harris in the No. 2 position of the Lead Element of the Low Squadron. Flak was light and only minor hits were recorded on the aircraft. Between fifty and seventy-five Bf 109s and FW 190s began harassing the bomber stream about thirty-five miles inland from the French coast. The attacks kept up to the target and on the return, about fifteen miles out over the Channel, the fighters split into pairs and attacked head-on. A 20mm shell exploded in the cockpit, shooting away the engine and mixture control for the No. 4 engine and setting off two of the flares stored in the cockpit. The oil line to No. 4 was cut. A number of small holes appeared in the aircraft, two in the ball turret; one in the left horizontal stabilizer, four in the tail section and one the tail assembly. Large holes were blown in the nose and left wing, just at the back of No. 2 engine nacelle as well as three in the left wing. In spite of extensive damage from the attacks, none of the crew was injured and Captain Harris brought *Short Snorter* safely back to base.

Nine B-24s were forced to abort with oxygen and machine gun failures. *Little Beaver* again experienced supercharger failure and was forced to abort. Major Donald MacDonald, the quiet, soft-spoken CO of the 67th Squadron who was from Tampa, Florida, refused to credit the crew with the mission because of their abort. MacDonald, whose brother Henry was also a major and a squadron commander (in the 305th), was held in high regard by his crews and despite his quiet demeanour, was a strict disciplinarian. Bill Cameron began to realize that the 'price of a ticket back to the ZOI' [Zone of the Interior] might be 'pretty high'. Twelve Liberators continued to the target with the Fortresses. A dozen squadrons of Spitfires flew cover but they were soon low on fuel and had to return to England just before the heavies reached Rouen. Yellow- and black-nosed FW 190s met the bombers at the coastline. For fifteen minutes the bomber crews came under fire from head-on attacks.

Captain Howard F. Adams a twenty-five-year old, 1941 graduate of West Point, from Rutland, Vermont, the pilot of *Maisie*, probably a reference to a series of B-movies starring Ann Sothern, recorded in his diary:

> I was leading the second element of four planes while 'Wild Bill' McCoy led the first element of the 66th Squadron. It was bitter cold – way below zero – but in a few minutes, we all forgot about that as we were attacked by some FW 190s. I closed in behind the first element until we almost touched wing tips but all of a sudden a FW 190 came down in a screaming dive shooting at Major Key's ship just ahead of me and passing between him and my ship. This was my first sight of a German plane despite having been in England almost three months now! He was so close that I could easily see the pilot and the beautiful yellow and silver markings of the plane. I watched him until he disappeared some five or six thousand feet below us but it didn't take long as he was going close to 600mph. I was too busy to be scared but managed to call the crew on the interphone and told them to keep their eyes peeled for more fighters. My navigator had fired a quick burst on his .50 calibre nose gun at the first FW 190 to no avail. It took all my time and energy to keep in tight formation and so I did not see Paris as we passed almost over it. The Germans kept buzzing around us but I didn't see them. One of them dived on Major Key's ship just to my front and fired his 20mm, which hit one of the gunner's square in the head and that was the end of him. Now and again I would hear a short burst from one of our guns and would look over at my tiny co-pilot, 2nd Lieutenant Stanley M. McLeod, huddled underneath his steel helmet. I returned his weak smile and went back to flying, which was real work now as my fingers were like ice and my oxygen mask was full of water and ice.
>
> Every once in a while my plane would rock viciously and I knew that the flak was getting uncomfortably close. Being faster than the B-17s we flew back and forth over the top of them, finally working our way up so we were in the middle of the formation, which was lucky as the FW 190s were concentrating on the front and rear. We continued our running dogfight and after a wee bit, I saw Paris

> spread out beneath us. The Eiffel Tower stood out like a sore thumb even from our altitude. It was not long before I saw several squadrons of RAF Spitfires cutting capers high above us. The white vapour trails against the blue sky were beautiful and a comfortable sight. *Maisie* roared along as faithful as ever but I thought I never would reach the English Channel. We soon passed up the B-17s and headed for home feeling very happy and gay about our good luck. We chattered over the interphone like silly schoolboys though when our radio operator told us that there was a wounded man on Major Key's ship we sobered up some. I peeled off and landed very cold and tired. Food and sleep were all we could think about after our five-hour ordeal. So ended our first real raid!

Two B-17s in the 91st were shot down. Lieutenant Robert S. English piloted one of these. Ralph J. Tomek, one of his waist gunners, on only his fourth mission, recalled:

> Sixty fighters ripped through our formation and made decisive hits on one Fortress [*Danellen* flown by Lieutenant Dan W. Carson] flying in the rear element. The tail broke off and there was only one survivor. Salvador Dalteris, the tail gunner, was fortunate enough to be in the part that broke off and managed to bail out. Later, he told me that Carson had told everyone to wear their parachutes on the mission. If he hadn't he would never have made it. Our ship was the next to be picked off. The fighters made head-on attacks and put two engines out of action and killed my pilot. Our B-17 nose-dived about 1,000 feet but by some miracle Sergeant Mandell, the top turret gunner, scrambled out of his turret and managed to get the aircraft straightened out. The two engines were on fire and we were losing altitude rapidly. Near Paris Mandell sounded the alarm to bail out.[12]

The slower Forts flying below the Liberators soaked up most of the punishment. As the initial FW 190s broke off to refuel, another fifty joined the running fight and continued making attacks until shortly before 'bombs away'. Cliff Pyle, pilot of *We The People*, saw his squadron's bombs drop short of the target. 'We were using the tactics of squadron aircraft dropping on the lead squadron aircraft,' he said. 'However, the target was hit by the mass with good results.' The *Luftwaffe* fighters, which had broken off to refuel reappeared on the homeward trip and made repeated attacks on the B-17 formations until the Spitfire escort showed up to cover the bomber's exit across the Channel. Apart from the two 91st ships, four B-17s in the 306th were also lost and twenty-nine Forts were damaged.

On return Lieutenant Bruce Barton in the 91st crash-landed the badly damaged *Chief Sly* at Parsonage Farm, Fletching. All the crew, including the tail gunner who was hit in the face as a 20mm shell burst in front him, were safe. *The 8 Ball* in the 'Hell's Angels' was belly-landed at Bovingdon after eight of the crew had bailed out. Only seventy-two aircraft had bombed the target and they had caused only minor damage to the German airfield. Despite this, Romilly had proved a turning point in the daylight aerial war in Europe. For the first time VIII Bomber Command had penetrated 100 miles into enemy territory and had successfully beaten off incessant fighter attacks without the aid of escorting fighters.[13]

As the year drew to a close, officers and men were still working on improving the methods of bombing and aerial gunnery. At Chelveston Colonel Curtis E. LeMay tried 'stacked up' formations of eighteen aircraft before finally deciding upon staggered three-aeroplane elements within a squadron and staggered squadrons within a group. To avoid complicated individual bombing procedures in which each aircraft would have to manoeuvre for accurate bombing, LeMay discarded individual bombing and introduced lead crews comprising highly trained pilots, bombardiers and navigators. The formation bombed on the lead bombardier's signal.

On 30 December the technique was tried again over the U-boat pens at Lorient when each bomber carried two 2,000lb bombs in the hope that they would penetrate the thick concrete over the pens. One abort after another forced the 306th leader to abandon the mission when fewer than nine planes remained, as they were about to penetrate enemy territory. Moderate, but generally inaccurate flak was encountered from flak ships in the Channel and along the route to the IP at Pos Dorden. Heavy flak hit the bombers, the bomb run was made into the sun and its glare gave the experienced *Luftwaffe* pilots a blind spot from which to attack the Fortresses. Approximately thirty FW 190s made skilful head-on attacks and they succeeded in shooting down three B-17s, including *Short Snorter* in the 91st with Lieutenant Bill Bloodgood at the controls. The No. 3 engine was set on fire just as Bloodgood cleared the target. The plane immediately started going down. About five minutes later, as *Short Snorter* went out over the Atlantic, two chutes were observed to come from the aircraft just before it exploded, the debris falling in the water. None of the ten crewmen survived. *Short Snorter* was credited with just three missions.

On the return flight over the Bay of Biscay Lieutenant Floyd E. Love pulled out of the 305th formation to assist a loner in the 306th. It was the Fortress flown by Captain John B. Brady, who had taken off from

Thurleigh a few minutes after the Group and did not find the formation in the murk over England. Brady found the 305th instead and he had proceeded with the group to the target. During flying training at Westover Field, Springfield, Massachusetts, Brady and crew had flown under the bridge at New London, Connecticut. Although the bridge looked wide enough when they reconnoitred it, there was actually a clearance of only six inches on either wing tip as they flew through. Another crew had buzzed the *Queen Elizabeth* at sea. On the St-Nazaire mission on 17 November Brady and another pilot had fallen into position on the wings of another B-17 in difficulty to provide protective firepower against the German fighters. Higher HQ disapproved of such heroics and action could be taken. On this occasion the heroics proved futile as both Love's and Brady's ships were shot down. There were no survivors from Love's ship and though Brady and his crew bailed out they were fired on while descending in their chutes over the sea. All were killed either by their attackers or by exposure once they hit the cold waters of the Atlantic.[14]

Owing to a terrific headwind the 305th formation thought it was over England when they sighted land but it was France. The formation became lax and the aircraft were spread out more than usual. Fighters badly damaged Captain Everett E. Tribett's Fortress and P.E. Galloway, the radio operator, and C. Kicklighter, the tail gunner, were hit by cannon fire. The latter had his right leg amputated. J. Morris, the top turret gunner, suffered back and head wounds. *Cherry*, piloted by Captain Clyde B. Walker, was also badly shot up and G.C. Bentinck, the bombardier, was killed. Walker managed to make it to Portreath with three wounded aboard.[15]

For the Americans' sixth raid on St-Nazaire on 3 January 1943 Eaker for the first time completely abandoned individual bombing in favour of group bombing. A total of 107 bombers were dispatched but mechanical failures accounted for many aircraft returning to base early, leaving only eight B-24s and sixty-eight Fortresses to continue to the target. The Liberators started out behind the Fortresses but caught up with them by the time they had reached the target and were ready to bomb at a higher altitude. B-17s and B-24s were stacked upwards of 20,000 to 22,000 feet. Visibility was unlimited so an unusually long bomb run was ordered but airspeed was reduced to more than half by a 115mph gale during the run-in and the bomb run took twice as long as briefed. For ten minutes the bombers flew almost straight and level, taking all the flak the anti-aircraft gunners could throw at them. Colonel Frank Robinson, who was leading the 'Eightballs', abandoned the bomb run and the eight B-24s headed out to sea, jettisoning their bombs as they went. They made for home at a height of 200 feet above sea level. The return over the sea was made in thick fog and crews could see only a few feet in front of them.

Captain Vincent B. Evans, a genial twenty-three-year-old Texan and the bombardier on *Memphis Belle* in the 91st formation, recalls:

> It was a small target but very important and we were glad of the opportunity to lead the VIII Bomber Command. As we turned to make a run on the target, which I knew by its relation to other buildings, we ran into a strong wind, which we hadn't anticipated. That caused the plane to go wide on the IP and we almost went over Nantes. It also caused our ground speed to drop to 85 or 90mph. There we were sitting up there like clay pigeons. I told Captain Morgan and Major C. E. Putnam, who was riding as co-pilot and wing leader, that it was going to be a long run. They said let's settle down on it. We were anxious to get it right. We had a 2½-minute run. The usual one was about 55 seconds. We were really sweating out the last few seconds of that run. The flak was terrific. I could see the flashes of the anti-aircraft fire through my bombsight and occasionally a fighter crossing underneath. I could hear flak slapping the side of the ship like kicking the door of a Model-T Ford. Later we discovered that we had a lot of holes in the ship and a tyre was blown to hell. Captain Morgan asked me when the hell I was going to drop the bombs. I told him to take it easy. I put my cross hairs where I knew the target to be, although I couldn't make it out at that distance. The second I released the bombs; I knew they were going to be good. The bombardier can usually tell. They were squarely on the target.

When the Liberators neared the Brest Peninsula the fog began to clear, but after passing the area the Isles of Scilly were mistaken for Brest and the small formation flew further and further up the Irish Sea. It was only when the very real threat of internment loomed before them that Colonel Robinson led the 'Eightballs' into a turn towards the Bristol Channel. Fuel was getting low and in any case they had only allowed for landfall at Lizard Point. Realizing they had missed Land's End, the crews searched for airfields in Wales but there were few to be found in this part of Britain. Lieutenant John B. Long, from May, Oklahoma, flying *Texan*, discovered Talbenny airfield in Pembrokeshire, only to have his last engine fail through fuel starvation just as he made his approach. Fortunately, all of the crew managed to escape from the Liberator, which was destroyed in the ensuing crash. Others were not as fortunate, including two B-24s that crashed into stone walls obscured by hedges. Three crewmen were killed and three were injured. The survivors flew into nearby airfields. *Little Beaver* eventually landed at Talbenny airfield and remained there for five days, buffeted by snowstorms.

The 306th, which had lost two B-17s in combat, put down at St Eval in Wales where bad weather kept the Group grounded until the 6th when with the promise of clear conditions at Thurleigh they departed only to return when conditions were not as forecast. At Chelveston Colonel LeMay and his senior officers eagerly sought confirmation that the new bombing tactics had paid off. Intelligence revealed that most of the 342,000lb of bombs had fallen smack on the pens. The 305th suffered no combat losses but two B-17s were so badly shot up by flak that they were left at Talbenny. Four B-17s in the 'Hells Angels' failed to return. One of these was *Snap! crackle! pop!* (the original pilot, Captain Jacob Fredericks, had worked for the Kellogg cereal company before the war) flown by Lieutenant Arthur Adams. The B-17 was hit by flak just after turning off the target. The nose glass shattered from an almost direct hit, which killed the bombardier and badly wounded Lieutenant Glen Herrington, the navigator. S/Sgt Alan Magee, the ball turret gunner, was hit in the face, but he managed to get back up into the aircraft. As the B-17 dropped out of formation, it was attacked by two FW 190s. They made only one head-on pass at the crippled bomber. Immediately, almost the whole of one wing sheared off completely and the rest of the Fortress fell into a flat spin. *Snap! crackle! pop!* crashed on a sand dune behind a school house, breaking apart and burning. The wing section landed in the town square of La Baule, ten miles west of St-Nazaire. Only three of the crew of ten were able to get out of the doomed bomber. The navigator and tail gunner, S/Sgt James Gordon, landed in the sea about 100 yards off the French coast and were picked up by German soldiers in a row boat. S/Sgt Alan Magee was thrown from the burning B-17 without his parachute. He blacked out and fell around 20,000 feet, crashing through the roof of the St-Nazaire railway station, where he was found, severely injured, but alive.[16]

In all, seven Forts had been lost over enemy territory and forty-seven B-17s plus three B-24s were badly damaged by enemy fighters and ground fire.[17] These were the heaviest losses VIII Bomber Command had incurred so far in the war.

The following day Colonel Frank Armstrong Jr took command of the battle-weary 306th at Thurleigh, Vice Colonel Overacker, although his stay would be short, lasting just over a month. The 92nd minus key personnel and all of the 326th Squadron left Bovingdon for Alconbury airfield and bomber crews were sent to the 91st and the 'Hell's Angels' Group as 'temporary replacements'. Very few returned to the 92nd. Crews in the 'Flying Eightballs' arrived back at Shipdham on 8 January to find that the well liked and respected Colonel Robinson had been replaced by twenty-nine-year old Colonel Leon Johnson. Johnson, born in Columbia, Missouri, graduated from the US Military Academy at West Point in 1926, at which time he was commissioned a second lieutenant in the infantry. In 1929 he 'decided that things looked more interesting from the air' and transferred into the then Army Air Corps and learned to fly at Brooks and Kelly Fields, Texas, followed by assignment to the 5th Observation Squadron at Mitchell Field, New York. In 1936 he decided he would have to know something about weather if he intended to be a leader in the Air Force so he took a special course for Army men at the California Institute of Technology and got his master's degree in meteorology. 'I thought I'd be able to look out the window and decide whether we'd be flying that day or not' Johnson said. He had reached the rank of major by August 1940 and early in the war he joined the 8th Air Force as Assistant Chief of Staff for operations and went with it to England in June 1942, as a lieutenant colonel and one of the first flying officers in the organization.

On 13 January seventy-two B-17s set out to bomb the locomotive works at Fives-Lille once more but only sixty-four got their bombs on target. Captain Oscar O'Neill's crew in the 91st were assigned *Short Snorter II* for the B-17's first mission since it arrived at Bassingbourn in early January. While still over England a series of technical failures occurred. The No. 1 engine started running rough as she climbed above 20,000 feet. There was a leak in the right oxygen system, which was almost empty by the time they formed up. Oil temperature was too high on No. 4 and the ball turret was leaking oil and the guns wouldn't fire when tested. The intercom was in poor working condition and the left waist and tail guns were not adjusted correctly. O'Neill had no choice but to abort the mission. Most of the problems could have been avoided had *Short Snorter II* been test flown before being sent on a mission.

The 44th flew a diversionary raid over to the Dutch coast in an attempt to draw the enemy fighters away from the real raid. Howard Adams brought up the rear of the seventeen-ship formation. He wrote:

> As the sun streamed into the cockpit a feeling of peace and serenity settled over me as I lazily shifted back and forth behind our leader, 'Wild Bill' McCoy. The German fighters and the bark of their guns

were remote from my thoughts though the ever-present sense of danger kept us all on our toes.

In the Fortress formation the 305th again flew lead, with Brigadier General Hayward 'Possum' Hansell, Commander of the 1st Bomb Wing, flying in the lead ship. Captain Cliff Pyle was flying his seventh mission with the 305th this day.

Everything went well until we reached the target area, then everything seemed to happen at once. Six Focke Wulfs attacked us simultaneously, head-on, concentrating their fire on the third and fourth squadrons, while others attacked the second squadron. During this burst, the No. 2 ship in the second element in the third squadron was shot down. Our ship received four cannon holes, two in the left wing, one in the right wing and the fourth went through the floor of the bomb compartment into the pilots' compartment, bursting the hydraulic lines. Hydraulic fluid spewed throughout the pilots' compartment blinding Lieutenant Fred Gilbert my co-pilot and myself. Only moments later the windshield shattered inwardly. I believe this was caused by a hit on the side of the aircraft and was aggravated further by the top turret guns firing forward. Gunfire from two other fighters entered the lower turret, wounding Sergeant L.G. McCoy, the turret gunner. There were about 150 .30 calibre holes in the wings, along with the two cannon shots. There was a hole in the leading edge about the size of a bushel basket. A tracer bullet entered the radio compartment, setting fire to the upholstery.

Luckily I managed to stay in formation. The No. 1 engine was misfiring and spewing black smoke and we feathered the props immediately. The No. 4 engine was also smoking. We feathered it for a few moments at a time until we reached the coast. Then we began to lag behind but we arrived over Chelveston in time to land with other damaged aircraft first. We had to extend the landing gear by hand. On the final approach it required both of us to hold the 'plane steady. The crippled engine was unfeathered and used on the final approach. Both tyres were flat and we landed far too short. This was lucky, because we had no braking action. We had to abandon the runway for other aircraft landing behind us, so we blasted the engines with full power and managed to swing off and clear the runway. We ended up in the ditch alongside. The aircraft landing immediately in front of us was *Dry Martini & The Cocktail Kids*.

Major Thomas H. Taylor, the 364th Squadron CO, had volunteered to take the place of Captain Allen V. Martini who had been hospitalized. After passing the French coast on the way to the IP, moderate to heavy flak was seen over St-Omer. On the bomb run at 21,700 feet, FW 190s began weaving and circling in front of the formation and began to attack one at a time. At the same time moderate to heavy flak was seen to burst close to the formation. In spite of the attack *Dry Martini & The Cocktail Kids'* bombardier, Gardner, was able to get his bombs away accurately and on target. Soon after the bomb run was completed a FW 190 came in weaving at 11 o'clock level. All guns that could be brought to bear on the fighter and others were firing. As the fighter kept boring in it kept up a steady fire and many shots found their mark. One of the cannon shells came in through the windshield and exploded, killing Taylor instantly and wounding 2nd Lieutenant Joseph B. Boyle, co-pilot, who came from Teaneck in New Jersey. The aircraft dived almost 2,000 feet. Brigadier General Hansell, watching the episode from his station in the leading Fort, thought the *Dry Martini* was done for. Boyle thought at first that the engines were gone but after pulling the dead pilot away from the controls, he managed to pull back the stick and level off. The aircraft was then out of formation and was being subjected to continued attack from enemy fighters. More hits pierced the nose, top turret and ball turret. The top turret gunner, Staff Sergeant Bill Beach, a cowboy who used to bust broncos at the 'Flying A's' ranch in New Mexico and the radio man, Staff Sergeant O. E. Ballew, carried Taylor's body into the nose. In the meantime ball turret gunner Staff Sergeant J. F. Hill had been shot through the thigh and, although in great pain, continued to fire until he was pulled out of the turret by Technical Sergeant H.L. Marby, the right waist gunner. Beach returned to his turret while Ballew administered first aid to Hill.

While all this was going on the plane was receiving hits in the nose, fuselage, cockpit and tail. The radio was completely out except for interphone communication between co-pilot, tail gunner and navigator. Cannon shells exploding in the nose blew the oxygen masks off the navigator and bombardier, who maintained continuous fire while they found new masks and put them on. Meanwhile Boyle had managed to get the ship back into formation. Shrapnel hit Bill Beach in the leg a minute or two later and he had his oxygen mask blown off also. Beach continued firing without his mask until Ballew, finishing the task of putting a splint on his leg and assisted by Marby, helped him down and tendered first aid. In both cases aid was so efficiently rendered by Ballew that neither Hill nor Beach were permanently injured. Marby then got into the pilot's seat and assisted Boyle in flying the aircraft. Sergeant Hise, the waist gunner, was firing his gun and Marby's alternately. The tail gunner, Sergeant Willis, kept up his fire as each fighter dived away. He had the shoulder of his flying suit blown away by bullets and the parachute on his back was riddled with shrapnel. Boyle, although in pain from a wound in his leg and shrapnel wounds on his face, skilfully continued to pilot back to base and landed with Marby's assistance. Beach later recovered and in November he married his childhood sweetheart, Helen Croom, at Lordsburg, New Mexico. While she had been waiting for Bill Helen had become a singer on Tucson local radio station KVOA with the country and western band Larry's Sunset Riders. She also sang at War Bond rallies and Army bases in the area.

General Hansell had some words of praise to offer.

> I was profoundly impressed with Lieutenant Boyle's skill and courage in flying a B-17 in good defensive formation at high altitude when he had been painfully wounded around the face and shot through the leg. Flying a B-17 in formation requires a great deal of physical effort at any time. I am still amazed that Lieutenant Boyle, despite the difficult conditions, could exert enough stamina to land his plane safely at its base. He and his crew deserve the highest credit.[18]

The bombers were stood down on 22 January. The next day sixty-seven Fortresses and six 'Flying Eightballs' Liberators mounted raids on the U-boat pens at Lorient and Brest. Eighteen of the bombers hit the target at Brest and thirty-six attacked the sub pens and supply shed at Lorient-Keroman. At Lorient German fighters employed new tactics of co-ordinated attacks in groups of six aircraft and five B-17s in the 303rd were shot down.[19] One of the Fortresses that aborted was *Short Snorter II*, this time with Lieutenant Earl F. Riley at the controls. As he climbed through 15,000 feet the oil temperature on No. 4 engine again became too high, 110 degrees; 22 degrees above the upper limit. The No. 2 engine began to vibrate and the Vickers unit (that drove the ball turret) and the oxygen system in the ball turret went out. Once more *Short Snorter II* aborted and returned to Bassingbourn.

The Groups were stood down for three days to lick their wounds but something big was in the offing. On 24 January Ira C. Eaker returned to Britain aboard *Boomerang* flown by Captain Cliff Pyle in the 305th after attending the Casablanca Conference in North Africa. *Boomerang*, a borrowed B-17F, which Pyle and the crew of *We The People* used to fly the General to North Africa nine days earlier,[20] was escorted into Eglinton,

Northern Ireland, by Spitfires of 501 Squadron; leaving later for Langford Lodge. Eaker had decided that his forces were now ready to attack Germany.[21]

In the south-western part of Friesland Province in Holland on the morning of 27 January the weather was glorious – a little cold, but there was bright sunshine and the sky was of a spring-like blue. It was the sort of weather that made Frisian housewives' fingers itch to start spring-cleaning. Sixteen-year-old Jan van der Veer was doing his school homework, mostly mathematics – which he hated. For the rest, all was quiet outside. If there was any air activity, it would be German; chiefly Messerschmitt Bf 110 night fighters just to the northwest of Leeuwarden, or maybe some FW 190 single-engine fighters. Usually they were greeted by 'Drop dead, you bastard!' or something, like that. Allied air activity was at night when RAF armadas flew over for their raids on Germany. Up until now the sound of the Lancasters, Stirlings and Halifaxes had kept up Dutch morale, which was just as well since the German terror regime was getting worse. Jan van der Veer thought it had reached the summit, but its fury would increase to a degree to which the Dutch would want only one thing: 'to wring their necks with their bare hands'.

The target selected for 27 January was the U-boat construction yards at Vegesack on the Weser. Throughout 1942 the RAF had heavily bombed the port and it had long been earmarked as a possible target for the Americans. The RAF night bombers had caused severe damage to the town and had destroyed a large naval ammunition dump but some of the U-boat slipways, dry docks and shipyards had escaped damage. It was an ideal opportunity for Eaker to demonstrate that daylight precision bombing could be more effective than RAF night bombing. Colonel Frank Armstrong, CO of the 306th who, six months before had led the equally momentous first American heavy bomber raid on France, led sixty-four B-17s out over the North Sea, flying a dog-leg route to confuse the enemy. Twenty Liberators took off from Shipdham and seven more in the 329th Squadron at Hardwick joined the 'Eightballs' on a diversionary raid aimed at Wilhelmshaven. Four of the B-24s aborted and haze over the North Sea made it very difficult for the rest to keep formation, which was being led by Colonel Leon Johnson in *Captain and His Kids Ride Again* flown by Captain Thomas R. 'Fritz' Cramer of Washington. A navigation error caused the Liberators to fly too far south and the haze worsened until they found themselves over 10/10th clouds. By the time the enemy coast came into view only fifty-five Fortresses remained. All but two dropped their bombs blindly from 25,000 through a German smoke screen, which drifted lazily over the shipyards, while the other two bombed Emden. The Forts lost one of their number. Of the Liberators there was no sign. Jan van der Veer recalls:

> At exactly 11:45 there was some strange, high-pitched sound in the distance and some dull explosions, which sounded far away – a sort of distant rumble, coming from the south. We had heard that rumbling before: exploding bombs. We had seen more than enough of the air war and being used to that faraway noise it did not register with us very much. But that other sound, which could best be described as a tenor-like, metallic singing – must be aero engines, but we had not heard that sound before and wondered what it might be. It was unlike the sound of any British or German aircraft. The rumbling died away and we could not see any smoke in the distance, but the singing noise increase in volume and we all looked upward, trying to spot the planes, which were making that strange sound. It was very difficult, since one had to look almost right into the sun – but finally someone said, 'I can see them – there are twenty of them!' We strained our eyes and yes, indeed there they were, at least 25,000 feet high and flying very close together. No contrails. It was very hard to count them, but we managed to do it. There were twenty-three, flying very closely together and they were overhead. Their sound now reached a crescendo and at that moment some sharp-eyed fellow yelled, 'A fighter!' And then things happened very quickly. I realized that those twenty-three aircraft must be Allied – the only RAF fighters we had seen had been Mustangs of Army Co-Operation Command shooting up trains. We were out of range for Spitfires and Hurricanes and why should RAF Mustangs come here to shoot at a German formation? The attacking fighter must be German so we should be in for something sensational. As indeed we were and we did not have long to wait!

As the B-24s flew over the Zuider Zee and started a wide left-hand turn the clouds suddenly disappeared and crews were bathed in brilliant sunshine. Now they could see land and navigators pinpointed their position accurately: after having gone south as far as Amsterdam they were approaching the small town of Lemmer on the south coast of Friesland. Colonel Johnson decided to make a wide sweep over Friesland and the Waddenzee and to bomb Lemmer harbour to draw German fighters away from B-17s attacking their German targets. He gave the order while the formation was approaching Lemmer from the south. At

1155 hours the twenty-three Liberators were over Harlingen, the port on the Waddenzee, twenty miles west of Leeuwarden and from there they flew on across the Waddenzee.

Jan van der Veer continues:

> A fisherman, having just left Lemmer harbour, told that he could see the Liberators approaching the Frisian coast, but at the same time he heard the snarling sound of other aero engines. Four FW 190s of JG 1 came flashing in from the southwest, practically at zero feet. They passed his fishing smack and next they were climbing almost vertically towards the bomber formation. Next there was a sound as if a piece of sail cloth was being ripped in two and a fighter started falling. The bombers must have fired at the Hun simultaneously and the burst of fire did not last longer than a second and probably not even that long. Next we saw white silk fluttering and realized that the fighter pilot had got out. The parachute filled up and was carried away gently by the breeze, which was coming from the south. The fighter was falling faster and faster and broke up over Lake Fluessen, 1½ miles away. Must have been a part of a wing or something like that. We saw it splash into the water. The rest of the fighter crashed beyond the lake.

JG 1 started attacking the formation in earnest from 1 o'clock high. Twenty-five-year old *Feldwebel* Fritz Koch of Osternburg was flying FW 190A-4 'Yellow Three' of 3/JG 1 and he dived on *Captain and His Kids Ride Again*. Captain Cramer's gunners let fly, causing Koch to break off his attack and taking position just behind the B-24's starboard wing tip. Sergeant Charles L. McMackin, the right waist gunner, did not hesitate and he opened up on 'Yellow Three'.[22] Koch was either killed outright or wounded to such a degree that he could not retain control of his fighter. 'Yellow 3' slammed into the B-24D flown by Lieutenant Nolan B. Cargile of Tulsa, Oklahoma, on the right of the lead ship and slightly lower. The larger part of Cargile's port wing was torn off and the whole tail unit practically disappeared. With part of his wing gone the B-24 dropped away like a fluttering leaf, finally going into a tight spin, its fate sealed. It crashed into the Slenk, a gully ground out by the tides in the rather shallow Waddenzee about halfway between Harlingen and the Island of Terschelling. None of the crew was seen to jump. Koch's fighter also went down and was soon lost to view in the slight haze that was now forming over the Waddenzee. Immediately after, the lifeboat *Brandaris*, named after the famous Terschelling light-house, left harbour in search of survivors. Despite a large-scale search, only the body of one American airman was recovered. Also, the German fighter pilot could not be found.

At about 1205 hours a 20mm shell hit *Spirit of '76*[23] flown by 1st Lieutenant Maxwell W. Sullivan of Washington DC and a West Pointer. The B-24 exploded and disintegrated into two pieces, the rear fuselage and tail unit falling into Terschelling harbour and the rest scattered over the Noordsvaarder Shallows and Terschelling beach. The *Brandaris* was able to save only 2nd Lieutenant Albert W. Glass, the bombardier who suffered leg injuries, and he was taken into Terschelling harbour. Dr D. Smit, the only doctor on the island, was sent for immediately but he was attending a woman in childbirth and he arrived too late to save Glass's leg. While he was working on the American, the Germans would not leave them alone for a moment and Dr Smit did not get a chance to talk to him. Glass was later transported to a Friesian hospital where his leg was amputated.

The battle was not over yet. The Liberators were now heading west and the FW 190s continued their attacks. *Black Jack* flown by 1st Lieutenant John H. Diehl Jr of Carlsbad, New Mexico, filled the hole in the formation caused by the destruction of *Spirit of '76* . In so doing *The Rugged Buggy* flown by Captain James E. O'Brien from Monongahela, Pennsylvania, to the left and slightly behind the lead ship, could be better protected. Immediately after this a 190 pounced almost vertically on O'Brien's ship and passed between *The Rugged Buggy* and *Black Jack*. Sergeant Gentry, one of the waist-gunners on Diehl's ship, opened fire immediately and was certain that he had downed the enemy fighter, which turned out not to be the case. *The Rugged Buggy* sustained considerable damage and a shell hit the fuselage and wounded S/Sgt Harold L. Guilford in the leg. Sergeant Manford S. Deal of Williamsburg, Michigan, was hit by a bullet and was killed. The machine guns in the nose were destroyed by a 20mm shell and the tail turret was also inoperative. The radio equipment had been destroyed and smoke was coming from the fuel cell behind the No. 2 engine. *The Rugged Buggy* lost 5,000 feet of altitude and O'Brien was unable to keep the badly damaged B-24D on course and he drifted out to the left of the formation. Diehl could do little to help O'Brien as his navigator told him that the lower machine gun in the nose was useless and the gun on the right side of the nose was almost out of ammunition – only eight rounds remained. In the meantime the Focke Wulfs delivered four concentrated attacks.

Diehl's Liberator was now 300 yards behind the front of the formation and then he left the formation altogether to join O'Brien's ailing B-24.

Using sign language O'Brien told Diehl to fly in front of his ship and when overtaking Diehl noticed the damage in *The Rugged Buggy*'s nose compartment. The bombardier and navigator were not to be seen. A study of the fuselage nose with the aid of binoculars established that something had exploded there and that the two men were either dead or seriously wounded. (The bombardier, 2nd Lieutenant Reginald D. Grant of Thurnston, Georgia, and 1st Lieutenant Leroy Perlowin, the navigator of Philidelphia, Pennsylvania, were hit by 20mm shells, killing Grant and seriously injuring Perlowin). Both bombers descended to 8,000 feet and Lieutenant George J. Kelley, Diehl's navigator, managed to navigate them home to Shipdham by way of The Wash. The other nineteen Liberators also succeeded in getting back safely.

The high-pitched engine noise died away and there was no more shooting. In the meantime, the American formation opened its bomb doors and each B-24 dropped four 1,000lb bombs on Lemmer.

Jan van der Veer had heard the hellish screaming sound of bombs falling before. He dived for cover and had to sweat out the time the bombs took to hit the ground, which seemed a long time.

> If it was just a case of bad aiming I don't know. Maybe the arrival of the first German fighters had something to do with it. Anyway, by the grace of God, the whole load went astray. Had that load come down in the harbour area, the whole town of Lemmer might have been blown off the map. The bombs were scattered far and wide and a number of bombs exploded south of the harbour, in the Noord Oost Polder, which was under construction. Other bombs landed close to the harbour in the vicinity of the old tram station, but caused only glass damage by blowing in a lot of windows. Most of the bombs landed alongside the Lemmer to Sneek road four miles to the North. Only superficial damage had been done and as far as known no civilian casualties. But at dinner time Jan Huitema, a farm labourer of Follega village, did not return home. He had been working in the fields in the area. A party set out to search the meadows. They found Huitema's body. There were no external injuries. He had been killed by the shock wave of one of the bombs. He was the only Frisian casualty.
>
> We kept asking ourselves what aircraft these twenty-three might have been, but we were terrifically excited. The Germans never stopped shouting that their *Luftwaffe* was invincible, but we had just watched the contrary. That night, clandestinely listening to the BBC news, it was announced that US bombers for the first time had raided

> Germany proper and I listened to Colonel Stanley T. Wray giving his account of the raid – the first time I heard the American way of pronouncing English. We had seen American bombers, either B-17s or B-24s.

In England the bombing of Vegesack was described as 'fair' but the Press was ready to fete the B-17 crews. The Fortress was rapidly becoming the favourite of the American public, much to the chagrin of the Liberator crews. They received barely a mention and resented being used as bait while the Boeing boys captured the headlines. It was not until 20 February that a story about the 'Flying Eightballs' by Nat A. A. Barrows at 'A US BOMBER FIELD, SOMEWHERE IN ENGLAND' appeared in the *Chicago Daily News* under the banner headline 'BOMBER PILOT SAVES PALS FORCED OUT OF FORMATION.

> Up there in the sub-stratosphere over Nazi Europe, where American bomber crews are flying their tight formation daylight patterns as part of the intensified attempt to knock out German industry and bases, Johnny Diehl saw his best friend, piloting another huge Liberator bomber, begin to struggle behind. A few minutes later when Johnny Diehl's ship, *Black Jack,* had made its run over the target and salvoed its bombs it was too late for him to go to the rescue – Messerschmitts and Focke-Wulfs had pounced on the wounded Liberator like wolves trailing a cattle herd. Johnny Diehl saw his pal's ship explode into bits...

The Liberators' mission was a fiasco, but as a diversion flight it may have been useful. Still this was a Pyrrhic victory: two B-24s lost against two German fighters, twenty-one dead American airmen and one Frisian farm worker for one German fighter pilot.

Howard Adams, who had to abort the mission at 17,000 feet with a clogged line to the supercharger on No. 3 engine, went down to watch the others return to Shipdham after dinner. He did not know that the 'Eightballs' had failed to locate their target and that crews bombed through cloud somewhere near the Dutch-German border. Also, he was not yet aware that navigation had gone uncorrected and the 44th had continued out over Friesland where it encountered heavy fighter opposition but he did notice that two Liberators were missing. Adams wrote:

> Later I found out that they were my friend and West Point classmate, Maxwell Sullivan and a Lieutenant Cargile, both of the 68th. On talking with the others, I learned what had happened. During one of

> the numerous frontal attacks, the Huns scored a hit on Sully's No. 3 engine, setting it on fire, which soon grew in fury as he dropped out of formation. Soon the fire had burnt a large section of the wing away and in no time the right wing folded back along the fuselage and Sully plummeted down for his last landing. The crews in the other planes watched helplessly as his plane disintegrated in the air and fell into the sea like a burning rag. Two men were seen to jump out and float towards the sea in their parachutes. A third man jumped but his chute trailed out behind him, never seeming to open fully. Their fate is still unknown.
>
> A little while later another FW 190 came in on a head-on attack aiming at Cargile's plane. Either through accident or design, as he went to turn away, his wing clipped the wing and then the right tail fin of Cargile's B-24, knocking both off. The FW 190 seemed to fold up and then go into its last dive. Captain Oscar Wilkenson, a very swell fellow and friend, was the navigator in Sullivan's ship. As the attack continued many of our ships were shot up but no more were knocked down. Captain James O'Brien had a waist gunner and bombardier killed and his navigator wounded. Nearly every ship had a hole in it somewhere; Billings having a shell come through the cabin between him and his co-pilot. This raid sobered everyone up and we're beginning to realize that war is no picnic.

Next day Jan van der Veer learned that the German fighter (FW 190A-4 0629 *Weisse Vier* ('White Four'), of the Fourth Staffel of JG 1 had almost buried itself completely in a field at an area known as '*De Hel*' the Frisian word for 'Hell'. He said:

> Don't ask me why' since there is nothing hellish about this place, somewhere between the village of Gaastmeer and the coastal town of Workum. The only thing visible of the fighter was its tail, marked with the Swastika – so it was a German plane all right! That fighter had found the right spot in which to crash – it had really gone to Hell and that amused us no end. The pilot (*Unteroffizier* Ehrhard Bruhnke, twenty-three, who was from Mackensen in Pomerania) came down just across Lake Fluessen in a sparsely populated area known as the 'Land of the Heathens'! The pilot landed on of all things, an American windmill at Heidenschap; a steel mast with a large vertical bucket-wheel at the top, which could pump out the surplus water of a polder. He was not too sure of a warm welcome by the Frisians of the Heathen Country and drew a pistol. Still, he could not get down

> without help. Now the 'heathens' like all of us, were not overly fond of the Germans, but they helped the pilot down from the windmill.[24] As luck would have it, a week later there was another American formation passing overhead, but this time they were B-17s and left contrails. Again, exactly over our heads, they were attacked by German fighters and promptly sent another one of them to the bottom. We could not help cheering!

Only two members' bodies on Cargile's aircraft were recovered: those of Captain Wilkenson and T/Sgt Saul Suskind the bombardier. All the other crew members' bodies except Sergeant Thomas W. Crook, Jr were recovered. On 17 April, more than two months after the first US raid on Germany, the body of the German fighter pilot, *Feldwebel* Fritz Koch, washed up at the seawall near Roptazijl, just north of Harlingen. His wife, Magda, was informed that her husband 'had given his life for the *Führer* and the *Reich*'.[25]

By the end of the month bomber casualties exceeded replacements, with only twenty-four B-17 and B-24 crews arriving to replace sixty-seven lost on missions during January. There had been talk suggesting that the small American force should be incorporated into the RAF night bombing campaign. Despite the value of daylight bombing, losses had continued to rise and many senior officers in the RAF remained unconvinced as to its ultimate success. General 'Hap' Arnold, Chief of the American Air Staff, was under pressure from various quarters from those who wanted to know why Eaker had been unable to mount more missions and why French, rather than German targets, were being bombed. Once again the future of VIII Bomber Command as a separate bombing force was in question and answers were desperately needed if it was to survive.

Having bombed a German target for the first time, Eaker now decided to crack an even bigger nut. For years RAF crews had referred to the industrial German heartland of the Ruhr as 'Happy Valley', feared and respected for its lethal concentrations of heavy flak. Twice bad weather postponed the strike and on 2 February the heavies actually got into the air only for the mission to be aborted because of worsening weather conditions. Finally, on 4 February, eighty-six bombers took off and went all the way, flying a long, deceptive flight over the freezing grey waters of the North Sea before turning for Hamm. Bad weather forced the Fortresses to seek targets of opportunity at Emden and off the coast. The Fortress formation became strung out, offering an open invitation to the *Luftwaffe*, as Captain Cliff Pyle, who was flying *We The People*, explains.

> Everything went well until we were about 100 miles inland. There about fifty enemy fighters met us. They attacked us continuously to the target and until we were thirty miles out to sea. The battle reached fever pitch and five Fortresses were brought down as the *Luftwaffe* single- and twin-engined fighters tore into the depleted ranks of the bomber formation.

Five B-17s were lost. In the 91st *Pennsylvania Polka* was ditched in the North Sea by 1st Lieutenant Alan L. Bobrow with the loss of nine of the crew and Lieutenant Kenneth H. Futch crash-landed *Texas Bronco* on the beach at Terschelling in Holland. Eight men survived to be taken into captivity. In the 305th *El Lobo* and Lieutenant William K. Davidson's B-17s failed to return. Davidson's crew perished and five men died on *El Lobo*. In the 'Hell's Angels' *Memphis To* and four of Captain Lloyd R. Cole's crew were lost when the aircraft crashed at Zwolle.

Bad weather grounded the 8th until 14 February, when the B-17s flew an abortive strike against Hamm. On the afternoon of the 15th twenty-one B-24s of the 'Flying Eightballs' attacked Dunkirk. Their target was the *Tojo*, a German Fighter Control ship. The 67th Squadron was led by Major Donald MacDonald in *Betty Anne-The Gallopin' Ghost* flown by Lieutenant Arthur V. Cullen, who was from Dallas, Texas. *Little Beaver* flew on his left wing in the No. 3 position in the lead element. Just beneath them were three B-24s of the second element and six more to the left. The formation crossed the Channel to Le Havre. Cullen's navigator, Lieutenant 'Ben' Franklin, plotted a course to make the Germans believe that the Liberators were headed inland but they changed direction and flew straight and level up the coast of France to Dunkirk. However, their long straight run had enabled the German gunners to determine their speed and height. From their high altitude the B-24s could release their bombs some distance out over the Channel and let their trajectory carry them in. Lieutenant Paul D. Caldwell, *Betty Anne*'s bombardier, called out 'target in view'. Flak enveloped the formation and just as the bomb-release light came on, at 1540 hours, the B-24 took a direct hit. When Art Cullen recovered from the shock the Liberator was in a dive, with no other ships in sight. There was no cabin roof; just a windshield – and the cowlings were blown off No. 2 and 3 engines, which were smoking. He could not operate the rudder because his leg was broken. MacDonald, in the co-pilot's seat, had a bad stomach gash but signalled to bail out. For a few moments the nose-less bomber flew on, only to fall away to starboard with the port inboard engine aflame and the right inboard ripped from its mounting. Finally, the starboard wing fell off and a huge explosion scattered debris among the formation, hitting another Liberator, whose pilot managed to re-cross the Channel and force-land it at Sandwich. MacDonald bailed out in extreme pain, Cullen helping by pushing him through the hole where the roof had been. He then followed MacDonald, hitting the tailplane and breaking his arm and then breaking his leg a second time. MacDonald died later in a German hospital.[26] *Railway Express,* flown by Lieutenant Rufus A. Oliphant of Chester, South Carolina, was hit by flak. It exploded and was finished off by fighters. All eleven crew were killed. Tom Cramer, the pilot of *Captain And His Kids* and a friend and West Point Classmate of Howard Adams had three engines shot out by fighters but made it back across the Channel to put his B-24 down on a beach at Sandwich. Despite the efforts of the 'Eightballs' *Tojo* remained afloat. Adams was killed eleven days later when his B-24 was shot down by German fighters on a raid on Bremen.

On Monday 16 February Howard Moore assumed command of the 67th Squadron and led them to St-Nazaire. Colonel Leon Johnson flew Group lead. Shortly after leaving the English coast *SNAFU,* flown by Lieutenant Fred M. Billings of San Diego, California, fell away to port, hit the port wing tip of *Miss Marcia Anne* flown by Lieutenant John B. Long and locked there. Seconds later they exploded, scattering debris into the Fortress formation below. One man survived from Billings' crew and was taken prisoner but there were no other survivors.

At the target 'George' Phillips lined up *Little Beaver* for a bomb run but the bomb bay doors refused to open. Lieutenant 'Chubby' Hill, the bombardier, entered the bomb bay and released the bombs manually. The closed doors splintered on impact and Hill realized they had to be tethered quickly before they broke off and damaged other B-24s in the formation. Clinging precariously to the catwalk, 20,000 feet above the earth, Hill went to work. Using pieces of wire, he secured the remnants of the doors in what must have been the highest trapeze act of the war.

The Fortresses climbed to the briefed bombing altitude of 26,000 feet. Passing over the French coastline, heavy flak started penetrating the 305th formation. As *The Hun Hunter* flown by Henry R. 'Hank' Burman, approached the target, they took a hit and several crewmembers were wounded. Captain Lyn H. Mokler, a fellow pilot in the Group, described Burman.

> He was a tall dark handsome Philadelphian, athletic from top to toe and took up a space of six foot three from the ground up and miles around all the shoulders. Always fond of horseplay and although he

could be serious, he usually had nothing more on his mind than a new joke or his next pass day.

Shortly after releasing their bomb loads the formation started receiving head-on attacks from the 1 o'clock high position by gaggles of FW 190s. A second wave of fighters scored hits on the right hand wing root and No. 3 engine of *The Hun Hunter*, causing a rampant fire all over the inboard wing area. Co-pilot Robert Mericle activated the fire extinguisher but it made little impression and on Burman's command he rang the bail-out bell and the crew prepared to abandon ship. At around 16,000 feet the wing snapped off causing the ship to roll and tumble. Navigator Dominick N. Lazzario was preparing to jump out through the nose hatch exit, when the Fort flipped on to its back and he found himself having to climb up to get out. Swinging in his parachute he watched their ship flip-flop crazily earthwards trailing smoke and fire, before hitting the ground and exploding near the town of Redon, France.[27]

'Hank' Burman was vacating his seat and clipping on his parachute, when the wing snapped off. The violent manoeuvre threw him against the windshield pinning him with centrifugal force and he passed out. He regained his senses on the ground amid the fiery wreckage. Somehow he had survived a crash from 16,000 feet! Crawling free of the wreckage he again lost consciousness and was dragged clear by French farm workers. There were no other survivors. *Boomerang*, flown by Captain Charles J. Steenbarger, was hit by enemy fighters who set the No. 2 and No. 4 engines on fire and the Fort, which Cliff Pyle had used to fly General Eaker to North Africa on 15 January, went down in a glide.[28] The 305th formation failed totally because of a bombsight malfunction in the lead aircraft.

Flak enveloped the twenty B-17s in the 306th formation and immediately after 'bombs away' 1st Lieutenant Joseph A. Downing's Fortress in the 367th 'Clay Pigeons' Squadron was hit in two engines. Enemy fighters knocked out a third engine after the target and Downing had no alternative but to dive the aircraft from 10,000 to 4,000 feet and disappear into some clouds. He lost the fighters and ordered the crew to bail out. Harvey J. Ross, one of the waist gunners, was killed but Lieutenant Kelly, the co-pilot and Staff Sergeant Allen H. Robinson, the engineer, evaded capture with the help of the French Underground. Six FW 190s attacked 1st Lieutenant William H. Warner's B-17 in the 423rd 'Grim Reapers' Squadron, head-on, killing Warner and three of his crew. Tech Sergeant Eddie Espitallier was seriously wounded in the left leg and hip by 20mm cannon fire. Lieutenant Arnold Carlson, co-pilot, pulled

Warner's body off the controls and put the B-17 into a rapid descent. He and Sergeant Walter C Morgan, who could not be extricated from his damaged ball turret, went down with the aircraft. Altogether, eight bombers were lost and most of the bombardiers missed their aiming point at the south-western corner of the submarine basin.

The 'Clay Pigeons' were not the only Group to gain publicity in the American press in 1943. On 20 February Nat A.A. Barrows of the *Chicago Daily News* paid tribute to John Diehl in the 'Flying Eightballs' in a story titled: 'BOMBER PILOT SAVES PALS FORCED OUT OF FORMATION.

> Since that day over Abbeville [sic – on 27 January, when he went to the aid of James O'Brien and the crew of *The Rugged Buggy*] Captain John H. Diehl, Jr has made a point of watching out for stragglers limping behind from flak or fighter cannon wounds. Two Liberator crews are still alive and bombing Europe because of Diehl's protecting gunfire. 'We'd go through hell and half of Georgia for him', said Captain Diehl's tail gunner, Sergeant Milford L. Spears of Springfield, Montana. Imagine how the crews of those two planes feel about him then. They wouldn't be alive today but for Captain Diehl...
>
> Last Monday coming back to England after the Liberators' own raid on Dunkirk, the whole group ran into severe fighter opposition over the Channel MEs and FWs flashed at the Liberators like streaks of lightning seeking a weak spot, hoping to find a straggler. Massed gunfire, with enough guns always bearing from the tight formation, drove the Germans away. But two Liberators had been hit badly by flak. They began to lag. Diehl spotted them losing altitude and promptly peeled out of formation to their rescue. The enemy had already hamstrung the weakest Liberator and it exploded and crashed into the sea before Diehl's gunners could get range. The doomed gunners still were firing when their ship disappeared. At the controls of the other Liberator Captain Thomas Cramer was trying desperately to keep his ship from going into a spin. He was losing altitude rapidly and soon Diehl and his team, diving in behind, were able to remove their oxygen masks and take off their heavy gloves. Eight German fighters already were working on Cramer and it was only a matter of a few minutes unless he got help. *Black Jack* came in with all guns blazing while Diehl and his co-pilot Lieutenant Rowland Houston jockeyed *Black Jack* about in incredible positions so as to bring as many guns as possible into bearing.
>
> Cramer's gunners were firing madly all the time despite the crazy

angles of the plane as it continued its steady fall toward the Channel. Two Germans exploded and fell into bits. Another German pilot suddenly slumped forward as his plane went out of control and disappeared in a cloud of black smoke. A fourth German gave up the battle and scurried back to France. But the remaining four climbed just out of range and hung on, tagging along until the English coast was reached. 'We got our breath then and looked around to see how the other ship was doing – and she wasn't doing too well' recounted Sergeant Canton. 'We could see she would fall short of the beach and crash into the sea if she kept on losing altitude. Her No. 2 engine was feathered and completely useless and her No. 3 was wind-milling. The other two were pulling but smoke was coming out. Then we saw three men jump out in parachutes and go into the sea.' Cramer had called for three of his men enabled their team mates to live, for with the decreased weight Captain Cramer was just able to get his ship into a crash-landing in the water, so near the beach that when it bounced it landed on the beach.

They don't talk much about such things out here where the Liberator bomber crews are based. Always they discuss German fighters, German flak, German targets and how finally they were given a raid entirely of their own, (the Dunkirk sortie), how their Command Officer and his flying companion, Colonel Leon W. Johnson since, has praised them for accuracy in that day's pinpoint bombing. How they would like to get it over with and go home. But the way these Liberator youngsters look at Captain Diehl and the way their eyes light up when *Black Jack* is mentioned doesn't need words. It tells its own story....[29]

Notes

1. The 'Flying Eightballs' received its first baptism of fire when eight B-24s flew a diversionary sweep to Cap de la Hague in Holland.
2. Membership in the Grand Order of the Short Snorters was a tradition prevalent among overseas air travellers of all nations from the late 1920s to the early 1940s. To become initiated into the Order, upon completion of a trans-oceanic air crossing, you were required to give $1 each, to all members present. You then produced another dollar bill. You would sign this bill, which when countersigned by a minimum of two members of the Order became your membership card in the Order, your Short Snorter. When Short Snorters subsequently travelled to another country, they would take a currency bill of that country, have it signed by two Short Snorters present and tape it onto the end of the previous bill. After visiting a number of

countries, the Short Snorter could become up to several feet long. Short Snorters had to be in possession at all times and whenever challenged by another member, the possessor had two minutes to produce his Short Snorter. Failure to do so required that he either pay each member present $1 or buy all a drink (a short snort, thus, the origin of the name of the Order) Over time, the Short Snorter bill came to be considered a good luck talisman.

3. The 'Flying Eightballs' flew their first bombing mission, when twelve B-24s drawn from both the 44th and 93rd BGs accompanied thirty-one B-17s to St-Nazaire. Bombing results had been so inconsistent on earlier raids that Eaker decided to experiment with attacks at lower altitudes.
4. The force swept out over the sea towards the mouth of the Loire in Brittany at 500ft to avoid being tracked by enemy radar. As it neared the target the leading 91st BG formation climbed to their briefed bombing altitude of 10,000ft, while the 306th, the last B-17 group, climbed to only 7,500ft to drop their bombs. The Liberators climbed to their briefed altitudes of between 17,500 and 18,300ft and followed the Fortresses.
5. Over fifty heavy anti-aircraft guns were situated at St-Nazaire and the Germans were in the process of installing more. Light flak, 20mm and 37mm, bracketed the low-flying Fortress formations but the Liberators came through without any serious damage, although some crews reported instances of frostbite caused by the lack of protective clothing. The heavier dual-purpose 88mm AA guns caused the most damage and the Fortresses bore the brunt. Every B-17 but one in the leading 91st BG formation was peppered with flak but all managed to return safely to base. By the time the trailing 306th BG element crossed the target, the *Flieger Abwehr Kanonen* (flak) crews had their height and speed. Their aim was so accurate that a shell was seen to make a direct hit and explode against the nose of one B-17. The 306th lost three B-17s and twenty-two B-17s in the total force were damaged. The intense flak succeeded in breaking up the formations and they flew back to England in disarray. Thenceforth St-Nazaire became known, as 'Flak City' and bomber crews would not venture below four miles high. Missions to the U-boat lairs became an almost established routine and the Germans moved in more and more anti-aircraft guns. By November there were seventy-five ringed around the city alone. Gradually the number was increased until it passed 100. Soon flak was so accurate that it was even dangerous well in excess of 20,000ft. The truth of the motto 'The higher, the fewer' was established.
6. Major William Wyler, a Jew from Alsace who was a famous Hollywood director who had produced *Mrs Miniver* in 1941, was sent to England late in 1942 to make a documentary about 8th AF operations, principally for American cinema audiences. Wyler was given a great deal of help by General Eaker, Chief of VIII Bomber Command, and his subordinate staff, not least Lt Colonel Beirne Lay Jr, a Hollywood screen writer with *I Wanted Wings* among his list of credits. Wyler headed for Bassingbourn and was given more

help by Colonel Stanley T. Wray, Commanding Officer of the 91st BG. *Memphis Belle* caught Wyler's lens more than most, probably because of its emotive and eye-catching name. Filming for the morale-boosting documentary began early in 1943 after bad weather had delayed its start. On occasion additional scenes were shot at other bases and ground shots were inter-spliced with real live action over the continent. Dangers were many. Lt Harold Tannenbaum, one of Wyler's original cameramen and four other combat photographers were lost aboard B-17s which failed to return from raids over the continent. In the spring of 1943 several B-17s at Bassingbourn were running neck and neck for the honour of being the first to complete twenty-five missions (a combat tour for the crews). Those lucky to survive the fatigue, flak, fighters and possible mental breakdown were given a certificate and admitted to the 'Lucky Bastard Club'; this at a time when the average survival rate amounted to no more than a handful of missions. More importantly, they could go home.

7. Adapted from Cliff Pyle's account in *Castles In The Air* by Martin W. Bowman (PSL 1984). Colonel LeMay led the first five missions that the 305th BG flew. Two were diversions and the other three were combat missions.
8. The 329th Squadron moved to Flixton airfield, near Bungay, Suffolk, after only a week at Hardwick. Flixton was still in the throes of development when the squadron arrived. Its task, as of an experimental nature, involving 'intruder' or 'moling' flights over Germany in an attempt to disrupt working schedules in German factories by causing air-raid warnings to sound, upsetting civilian morale and impairing industrial output. Seven 'moling' missions were made over Germany, the last taking place on 28 March 1943. Some crews later formed the nucleus of the USAAF Pathfinder units set up perfect blind-bombing techniques.
9. *8 Ball Tails; Journal of the 44th BG Veterans Assoc.* (Spring 2008).
10. Nine were KIA; three were taken prisoner, nineteen B-17s aborted and only three of the twenty-six Fortresses dispatched got their bombs away.
11. Bad weather resulted in the cancellation of the mission on 10 December and two days later ninety bombers had already crossed the French coast before thick cloud resulted in a recall. In the 303rd seventeen dropped their loads on the Rouen Sotteville marshalling yards, two B-17s being lost in the action. Bad weather prevented a return raid until, finally on 20 December; Eaker sent 101 B-17s and B-24s in a third attempt to bomb the air park.
12. Tomek was captured and admitted to hospital in Paris before being sent to PoW camp for the rest of the war. Six others were taken prisoner.
13. Gunners once again submitted high claims and the initial score of fifty-three 'kills' was reduced to twenty-one, plus thirty-one 'probably damaged'. The true figure was three enemy fighters shot down and one damaged.

14. See *First Over Germany: A History of the 306th Bombardment Group* by Russell A. Strong (1982).
15. *Cherry* was lost with 2nd Lt John J. Hall's crew on 22 June 1943. Four crew were KIA and six survived to be taken prisoner.
16. *Pride of Seattle: The Story of the First 300 B-17Fs* by Steve Birdsall (Squadron/Signal 1998).
17. The fighter opposition was provided by III/JG 2, which claimed 15 *Abschusse.* See *The JG 26 War Diary Vol 2* by Donald Caldwell (Grub Street, London 1998).
18. Despite claims by three pilots of JG 27 in the Lille area (two of which were confirmed) just one of the Fortresses in the 305th BG (41-24601 flown by Lt Conrad J. Hilbinger (ten KIA) was lost on the raid. Two B-17s in the 306th, including *Four of A Kind,* which Colonel Overacker had flown on the Group's inaugural mission, were lost in a mid-air collision north of Lille. Gunners claimed six fighters destroyed and thirteen probably destroyed. If anyone needed proof that LeMay's tactics were right, the Lille raid had provided it. The bombing was so effective that VIII Bomber Command never needed to return to Lille.
19. Five aircraft – *Beats Me, Hell Cat, SUSFU, Green Hornet* and *Jerry Jinx* – were MIA with the loss of twenty lives. Twenty-two men survived and were taken prisoner and the others evaded capture. The 303rd had dispatched twenty-one B-17s but only twelve returned. Of these five were damaged, three of them extensively. *Werewolf* limped back on one engine. Lt George J. Oxrider ordered his crew of nine to bail out over the south coast and he then landed *Werewolf* in the grounds of a mental hospital at Dawlish, South Devon. Later, the aircraft was fitted with three new engines and in order to make a runway 2,500ft long so that *Werewolf* could be flown out to Honington Air Depot for major repairs, trees, walls and hedges were cleared away. *Idaho Potato Peeler,* flown by Lt Ross C. Bales, made a safe crash-landing at Chipping Warden airfield with no injuries to the crew. [This B-17 was later re-named *Ramblin Reck* and was lost with Lt Ambrose Grant's crew on 5 November 1943]. *Thumper* flown by 1st Lt John A. Castle and Lt Kent McHenry Fitzimmons belly-landed at Lulsgate Bottom after eight crewmen had bailed out. S/Sgt Billie L. Stainer was killed when his parachute failed to open and five others were injured. Captain Billy B. Southworth Jr put *Bad Check* down at Exeter after the starboard inner engine had failed when badly damaged by flak and cannon shells from FW 190s and Bf 109s damaged the wings. See *Airfield Focus 40: Molesworth* by John N. Smith (GMS 2000). *Leutnant* Otto Stammberger's *9th Staffel,* flying from Vannes with III./JG 2, were credited with two of the 303rd BG B-17s and 7./JG 2 claimed four bombers. See *The JG 26 War Diary Vol 2* by Donald Caldwell (Grub Street, London 1998).
20. On 14 January 1943 Eaker, who since November 1942 had been acting Commanding-General of the 8th AF in the absence of General Carl Spaatz,

had received a cable from General 'Hap' Arnold, asking to meet him at the forthcoming Casablanca Conference. 'Our flight en route to Marrakech was uneventful,' says Pyle, 'flying in broken clouds all the way. General Eaker went by car to the Conference site and we waited at the airfield for further orders.' The Conference of President Roosevelt and Prime Minister Winston Churchill and the combined heads of staff took place at the Anfa Hotel, on a hill just south of the town, overlooking the Atlantic.

21. Arnold warned Eaker that Churchill and Roosevelt had agreed that VIIIth Bomber Command would cease daylight bombing and join the RAF in night bombing. Eaker was shattered but was determined to reverse the decision. He wrote his now famous 'memorandum', less than a page long, which summarized his reasons why the daylight-bombing offensive should continue. Although not fully convinced, Churchill was particularly impressed with Eaker's 'round the clock' bombing strategy. The British Prime Minister agreed to extend the time Eaker needed to prove daylight bombing and the conference approved additional aircraft for VIII BC.
22. McMakin was KIA on the Ploesti raid, 1 August 1943, flying on Captain Rowland B. 'Sam' Houston's crew. It was McMakin's twenty-sixth mission having already completed his tour.
23. Named after the B-24D's serial number, 41-23776.
24. According to German reports Bruhnke had sustained a sprained right thigh and a bullet had grazed his chin. Bruhnke was taken to the German hospital in Leeuwarden. He recovered and was killed in combat on 31 August 1943.
25. Koch was buried at the German War Cemetery in Leeuwarden, but after the war his remains were re-buried in the German War cemetery at Ijsselstein in the Province of Limburg. The German part of the Leeuwarden Cemetery has ceased to exist. Some RAF airmen are still there, surrounded by the graves of Frisian Resistance men and women who did not live to see their country freed. *Meeting the Flying Eightballs for the First Time* (unpublished account by Jan J. van der Veer).
26. Besides MacDonald and Cullen, only two other men made it out of the B-24 in which seven men died. Cullen was repatriated in September 1944. Major Henry G. MacDonald, Donald's brother, who was CO of the 364th BS in the 305th BG, was severely injured on 3 March when he was flying a Douglas Boston on target towing duty for B-17 gunners. One of the B-17s got ahead of the target tug and a gunner mistakenly fired into the cockpit of the Boston hitting Henry MacDonald in the shoulder, shattering his shoulder blade and collarbone. MacDonald managed to put the Boston down on the unoccupied airfield at Polebrook and he was rushed to hospital at Lilford where doctors told him that he would probably never fly combat again. When he heard of his brother's death in combat Henry grew more determined to return to operations and he put himself through a tough regimen that enabled him to

get back 60 per cent use of his shoulder. He resumed operations and took command of the 305th BG on 23 October 1944. See *Mighty 8th War Diary* by Roger A. Freeman (Jane's 1981 and Arms & Armour 1990).

27. With the aid of the French Resistance, Lazzario was able to evade capture for twenty-eight days, before being apprehended by French Gendarmes and eventually handed over to the Germans.
28. One man evaded, one was KIA and eight were taken prisoner.
29. *Black Jack* was lost on 1 October 1943.

CHAPTER 3

The Legion of the Doomed

We could see the coast of Sweden and opted to try for it but it soon became apparent to all of us that it was hopeless. We were flying near 30,000 feet but couldn't go any higher to avoid the prop wash of the B-17s. The navigator was killed instantly in the plane by a 20mm shell which decapitated him. The waist gunner was hit in the knee just as he bailed out. The belly gunner was hit in the shoulder and chest and in several other places, but managed to bail out with the rest of us. He died in a hospital shortly thereafter. After the crew was out (I thought) I started to leave as well but our engineer had passed out from lack of oxygen and was blocking the exit. I must have beaten and abused him very badly when trying to get past him. I finally made it and was about to jump when something stopped me. I thought, 'My God! I can't leave the engineer.' I reached back and grabbed him by the collar of his fur flying jacket and backed towards the bomb bay, falling out and dragging him with me. I saw him later on the ground and it looked like he had been through a meat grinder.

1st Lieutenant Wilbur E. Wockenfuss, co-pilot,* Sad Sack, *66th Squadron in the 'Flying Eightballs' 26 February 1943

On 25 February the number of Liberators was increased, on paper at least, by the return of the 'Travelling Circus' from North Africa, which flew into Hardwick. At Shipdham the 66th Squadron suffered the loss of popular pilot Captain 'Wild Bill' McCoy from Los Angeles, California, and his crew when their Liberator lost its tail assembly at 4,000 feet during a training flight. Immediately after, the Liberator went into a flat spin and dived into the ground, killing everyone on impact. Next day, when the Forts and the 'Eightballs' were assigned Bremen, seven reporters in the 'Writing 69th' or 'The Legion of the Doomed' as they called themselves –

Andy Rooney, aged twenty-four, a graduate of Colgate University, lead correspondent of the *Stars and Stripes*, Walter Cronkite of United Press, Gladwin Hill of Associated Press, Denton Scott of *Yank* magazine, William Wade of the International News Service (INS), Homer Bigart of the *New York Herald Tribune* and Paul Manning of the Columbia Broadcasting System (CBS) – prepared to fly on the B-17s. An eighth reporter, Harvard graduate, Robert Perkins Post, a thirty-two-year old *New York Times* war correspondent, asked to fly with the 'Eightballs' on the mission. His request was granted and he went in *Sad Sack* flown by 1st Lieutenants Robert H. McPhillamey of Sheridan, Wyoming, and Wilbur E. Wockenfuss who was from Watertown, Wisconsin. Cronkite flew in *S-For-Sugar* flown by Captain Glenn Hagenbuch, the new CO of the 427th Squadron, and Bigart, in *Ooold Soljer* piloted by Captain Lewis Lyle of Pine Bluff, Arkansas, both in the 303rd. *Ooold Soljer* had flown General Eaker and his entourage to Casablanca in December 1942. Gladwin Hill went with Major Joseph Preston in the 305th. Rooney went with Lieutenant 'Wild Bill' Casey in *Banshee II* in the 306th at Thurleigh. Scott missed the mission and William Wade's B-17 turned back with engine trouble.

At Bassingbourn the mission started out routinely with the crewmen up at 0230 hours for a quick breakfast and briefing at 0315 hours. Lieutenant Beman E. Smith's crew were assigned *Short Snorter II*, which up to now was experiencing a rather unproductive combat tour. Its first two missions had been aborted while still over England. Another abort occurred as *Short Snorter II* had crossed onto the continent. One mission was recalled before the Strike Force reached the target. On the only mission *Short Snorter II* was able to complete, bombing results were of uncertain effectiveness. But, the Fortress had not been hit by fighters or flak. All aircraft were in the air by 0815 hours. Paul Manning climbed aboard the B-17 to which he was assigned and went forward to the nose gun he was to operate. Manning said:

> After take-off we climbed through the clouds and broke out into brilliant sunshine at 6,000 feet. Over the Channel, at 11,000 feet, all of us went on oxygen and kept a look-out for fighters as the German coast appeared. They did not attack until after we had passed over the Frisian Islands and were headed straight for our target.

At airfields on the Continent, *Luftwaffe* fighter pilots lay in wait for the Liberators and Fortresses. At Leeuwarden thirty-year-old *Hauptmann* Ludwig Becker, *Staffelkapitän*, 12./NJG1 and a great night-fighting tactician with forty-four night victories, waited to fly his very first daylight mission.[1] The 'Night Fighting Professor', as he was known, was instrumental in introducing the *Lichtenstein* AI radar into the night fighter arm in 1941.[2] Shortly before taking off from Leeuwarden at 1135 hours in a formation of twelve Bf 110s led by *Hauptmann* Hans-Joachim Jabs, Becker was informed of the award of the Oak Leaves to his Knight's Cross, which had been bestowed on him on 1 July 1942 after his twenty-fifth night victory.

The weather was clear and from all indications it would be a routine mission but the American strike force was ten minutes' late coming together as some of the Groups had difficulty in moving into their proper places in the formation. On the way across the North Sea, the lead navigator of the 305th did not check his wind velocity. As a result, the entire Strike Force drifted several miles south of the briefed route, taking it over the anti-aircraft positions on the Friesian Islands and a number of aircraft received flak damage. *Short Snorter II* was reported turning back just before reaching the islands, under control and reportedly undamaged. Almost immediately after leaving the formation, the B-17 was attacked by five Ju 88s. There were no further observations. *Short Snorter II,* along with her ten crewmen, went to the bottom of the North Sea. The aircraft was credited with four missions, only one of which resulted on bombs being dropped on the target.

A heavy undercast forced the bombers to abort the primary target at Wilhelmshaven. About thirty miles for the coast they were attacked by fighters so determined in their mission that they sustained their attacks all the way to into the target. IV./JG1 returned to Leeuwarden with claims for two bombers shot down. A dozen pilots in I./JG1 at Jever-Wangerooge returned having shot down five B-17s and B-24s (they claimed thirteen). Of *Hauptmann* Ludwig Becker there was no word. Completely at ease and master in the night battle against the RAF bombing offensive, the 'Night Fighting Professor' had fallen victim to the gunners of B-17s and B-24s of the 1st and 2nd Bomb Wings.

Kickapoo became the second B-17 in the 91st to be shot down when it was ditched in the North Sea by Captain John Swais and the 305th was missing three. About fifteen minutes from Bremen *Sad Sack,* flown by Lieutenant George E. Stallman and the lowest Fort in the entire formation, came under attack from two Bf 109s. They made several passes and the Fortress took hits in the right wing and No. 4 engine, knocking the ship out of formation. A burst of flak hit *Sad Sack* as Stallman tried in vain to catch up with the rest of his formation over Wilhelmshaven and he ordered the crew to bail out. The two other ships that were lost were *Arkie* flown by Captain Everett E. Tribbet and *Devil's Playmate* flown by Lieutenant Isaac D. Benson. In a newspaper article by Captain Lyn H. Mokler, he described the loss thus.

> First Lieutenant Isaac Dortch Benson, lawyer statesman and polished southern gentleman from Austin, Texas, had no business being in an airplane – any airplane. He was slight of build with delicate blonde hair and a moustache. It's true he had no business in an airplane but that doesn't necessarily mean that he didn't do a good job once he was there. Our airplanes are full of such people from all walks of life who don't appear to have anything at all common with flying but who get results. Benny looked as if he'd never seen a Fortress and yet he could fly with the best. He could play poker with the best too! We were having a pretty rough time of it over Wilhelmshaven heavy flak and fighters. One engine was smoking a little and Bennie's flying got a little erratic but he radioed that he was OK. We were all pretty busy, so it wasn't until the last fighter left us that we discovered Benny wasn't along. Back at base, we waited anxiously for reports of him from all over England but he didn't come home that night or any other night.[3]

Paul Manning continues:

> The Me 109s and FW 190s were coming at us from all directions. Our 76 bombers were now flying tight, in a box formation and the guns from each B-17, front and rear, top and bottom, were firing in a continuous stream. Our fire did not keep the *Luftwaffe* away, for their fighter aircraft came in at the front of the formation in an attempt to knock out the lead plane...One Me 109 came directly at me. I was able to shoot it down, causing it to explode in mid-air. My gun then malfunctioned. I fixed it in thirty seconds and started firing as another Me 109 zoomed in then looped and rolled away. All this time, the bombardier was aiming his Norden bombsight at the submarine works below. The German ground defences had lit smoke pots in order to obscure the target, but the winds blew the smoke away and the bombardier sighted it easily, 'Bombs away!' he called over the intercom and we lifted up suddenly as our heavy load fell to the target.
>
> The pilot swung our B-17 around and away and the entire formation of fortresses followed our lead, Far off to the left I could see a formation of B-24 Liberators having rough going; two of them

spiralled down, one with its engine on fire. Later I learned that this had been Bob Post's B-24.[4] The aircraft bearing Walter Cronkite, Bigart, Gladwin Hill and Andy Rooney, all returned to base safely.

Southern Comfort in the 305th was lucky to make it home to Chelveston. Hugh Ashcraft, the pilot, recalled:

We had disposed of six of our bombs when the ship shivered and we knew we had been heavily hit. The bombardier sent away his four remaining bombs on the docks of Wilhelmshaven before turning to see if the explosion of a 20mm shell in the nose had killed the navigator. The navigator was alive and uninjured, although the shell had exploded only 3 inches away from his head and dented the steel helmet he was wearing. The explosion drove his head down on the navigator's table, which broke under the impact of the helmet. The only ill effect he suffered was that he could not calculate the course of the plane for about twenty minutes. During this time the bombardier handled the navigator's gun as well as his own. A moment later the right waist gunner phoned: 'Sir, No. 3 engine has been hit and is throwing quite a bit of oil.' The oil had spread over the wing. A tongue of flame appeared. The co-pilot closed the cowl flaps and pulled the fire extinguishers. The fire went out. The propeller of the crippled engine was now windmilling and chewing away at bits of cowling. Sparks were bouncing off the oil-covered wing. At this point I noticed that the rudder did not respond. Presently we found that four square feet of it had been shot away. When the tail gunner reported the condition of the tail, or rather the lack of it, he also reported that still another shell had burst just in back of him inside the fuselage. There was no time to appraise the damage. *Southern Comfort* had lost airspeed caused by the drag of the windmilling propeller and an attempt to rejoin several of the formations proved futile.

It was then that I realized that if we were to return to England we were going to have to do it alone, crippled and out of formation. The loss of the supporting guns of other aircraft in the formation was serious, but more serious was the choice of course. We flew due north, to put as much sea between the enemy fighters and us as possible. Meanwhile the No. 3 engine was vibrating and the wild prop kept taking bites out of the cowling. We were out over the North Sea when I announced over the intercom: 'Those who want to, please pray!' Not long after that we sighted land. We weren't sure, but we

> thought it was England. As we neared our home base an inquisitive Mosquito spotted us and finally came so close that we could see the pilot shake his head at our battle-scarred condition. He waved his hand and left. Shortly afterward, we picked up our field.[5]

Wayne H. Gotke, the navigator on *Maisie*, wrote a letter to Waldron K. Post, Robert Post's father, on 6 August 1945 after returning from PoW camp.

> Dear Mr Post,
>
> [Regarding the death of your son] the only person I can be positive on during the flight was Bill Hannan, the bombardier, who was riding in the nose of the ship with me. I'm completely at a loss to understand his fate after the ship blew up. He was standing by me, I believe, when the ship blew up. He was not injured at that time. He had passed out twice from lack of oxygen, and I had replaced his mask and brought him back to normal. We were using the old style masks then, bladder types.
>
> Our ship was under constant fighter attack from the time we reached the island of Texel (Holland) until we were shot down. We fought off the planes with very minor damage until we were just short of Oldenburg (south of Wilhelmshaven). Then all hell broke loose. I spent most of my time with navigator's position reports, trying to get short cuts filled into the flight to allow us to gain and catch the rest of the formation. However, I'm reasonably sure no one was injured up to this point, except for William F. Welch, the belly gunner, who had passed out from lack of oxygen. As far as I know, he never regained his senses.
>
> When we were near Oldenburg, fighters hit us from all sides. Robert K. Vogt, the engineer, shot the first fighter down and I shot down the next (after he has sent 20mm shells into the nose and cockpit). James W. Mifflin, shot down a third from his waist gun position.
>
> At this point, my left gun jammed and at least two planes made direct hits on the nose and flight deck. I am sure that someone was hurt on the flight deck. Engines #3 and #4 had been hit and were on fire. I believe the fire spread to the wing tank and caused the ship to explode. I was working with my guns when all at once it seemed someone pushed me from behind – and all went black. I woke up falling through space and I pulled my rip cord with no results. I reached back and tore the back of my chute out. My last look at the

altimeter (before the explosion) showed 26,000 feet. The Germans claim that they saw my chute open at 5,000 feet.

They picked me up after I dangled 20 feet in the air between two trees for about 25 minutes. They took me to a first aid station for treatment of cuts around my head. I also had 20mm wounds. It was here that I saw Mifflin.

The co-pilot of the other ship, Wilbur Wockenfuss (shot down the same time we were), said he saw the leather jacket [belonging to our pilot, Captain Adams] and it appeared that the man had been killed. The ship's loading list was removed from Adams' jacket by the Germans. The Germans asked me about Robert Post, as they could not identify him on the loading list. I gave them no information whatsoever as my orders were to say nothing in hopes, if men were at large, their chances of getting home would be better. The Germans asked questions about Sgt Donald Bowie and 2nd Lieutenant William J. Hannan. From that, I believe those two men could not be identified. They asked questions about Johnson because they could not find any information about a Johnson on the list. My belief is that your son was wearing Johnson's 'Mae West' and perhaps through that lead, you may get some information. I'm under the impression all bodies were not found and if found, they could not identify them all. I regret this is all I can say ... Rest assured, I will forward any additional information I find to you.

We all felt that your son was doing something beyond the call of duty to fly with us and we held the highest respect for him. We knew him as a very fine person, and I regret his loss greatly. I can understand how you feel – as boys on a mission are like brothers. I'm sorry I can't give you more information. I hope this will help.

One of the Liberators claimed shot down by I./JG1 was *Night Raider*, also called *Heavenly Hideaway*, in the 'Travelling Circus' flown by Captain Beattie H. 'Bud' Fleenor. The events that followed caught the attention of Corporal Carroll 'Cal' Stewart, a *Stars and Stripes* staff writer:

At the briefing, the Liberator known as *Night Raider* was tagged for one of the hot spots, an outside position on the next-to-the-last V-formation. That was nothing new: since early the previous October *Night Raider* had been a veteran of flight over enemy territory though never, despite its name, in a night raid. The skipper, Captain Bud Fleenor, 25, of Manhattan, Kansas, was at the wheel as usual. The Kansas State College alumnus tucked his long, gangly legs into the compartment while the engines warmed; beside him sat the co-pilot, 1st Lieutenant James J. Leary, 25, from Omaha, Nebraska. *Night Raider* went thundering down the runway and the take-off was uneventful; a few spurts of lead were fired into the thin air or into a cloud hank as the gunners warmed and tested the guns.

Then things began to go wrong. As the raiders reached the Dutch coast and enemy opposition began to appear, Sergeant Elmer J. Dawley, 19, the youngest of the crew, passed out in the high altitude: his oxygen mask was frozen. Staff Sergeant T. J. Kilmer, also 19, waist gunner went to investigate and found icicles on the kid's eyelashes. The effort to revive Dawley, plus oxygen trouble of his own, soon had Kilmer himself unconscious, clinging desperately to wire cables that control the tail assembly. The skipper and Leary managed to stay in formation.

T/Sgt Louis Szabo, 28, the 150lb waist gunner and engineer, had an almost impossible task in trying to release Kilmer's grip, his own mask being torn from his face in the struggle. A few moments later Kilmer relaxed and lay there blacked out, unconscious. As they approached the target, flak was puffing all around; cannon hits were heard; and shrapnel was spraying the fuselage everywhere. Enemy fighters had already made an estimated thirty passes at the *Raider* and even when the flak was heaviest they continued to attack. Then the *Raider* began its run; its yawning bomb-bay doors wide open. Wilhelmshaven rocked under the bursts: 2nd Lieutenant George A. Pinner, 25, the bombardier, had pinpointed his mark. But trouble mounted last as this B-24 limped back toward England, its big belly empty. The supercharger was knocked out, ack-ack fire was intense and German fighters were still submitting them to deadly attack – even a destroyer lying thousands of feet below in a Dutch harbour sent up a barrage of flak and hot lead.

The *Night Raider* made its way doggedly into the clear, high over the Zuider Zee. The sister ships that had led the attack were now disappearing, far out on the horizon. The skipper knew the *Raider* couldn't possibly catch them up, not with the supercharger out and one engine dead, the result of enemy cannon fire. The radio, too, was dead, so it was impossible to call for help. S/Sgt Robert P. Jungbluth, 24, the fair-headed radio operator, from Arlington, Nebraska, left his position on the flight deck to administer first aid to Kilmer, whose face was now purple. Others who saw him thought that he was dead but 'Jung' fixed an oxygen supply on him and worked hard with artificial respiration and finally Kilmer showed signs of life.

By now the *Raider* was losing altitude as one of the remaining three engines began to vibrate and cough. Jung left the reviving Kilmer and worked on Dawley, the tunnel gunner who had been unconscious since first reaching the Dutch coast. Ellis left the nose to go to the rear and lend a hand. 'Big Jung saved the lives of those two fellows, all right,' The North Carolinian testified later. Then the skipper sent word for Ellis to hurry back to his gun in the nose because more trouble was brewing. Jungbluth took over one of the waist guns and Szabo was on the other.

Suddenly twenty German fighters appeared, FW 190s and Me 109s, Me 110s and Ju 88s; they had been lurking in the sky in the hope of picking up a straggler and this was their chance. Peeling out of the bright sunlight, they came in a vicious running attack that was to last for forty minutes. *Night Raider* had taken care of enemy fighters before – one, two or three at a time – but this was different. Captain Fleenor eyed a large friendly cloud in the distance, perhaps a half-hour away at the speed they were travelling. It was their only hope – and a slim hope at that.

The guns of Sergeant Edward M. Bates, 22, the curly-haired 175lb tail gunner, had long been silent – they had frozen up tight after he had poured only eight volleys into the Huns on the way to the target. He was bluffing now, training the sights on the MEs and FWs as they came in. One Ju 88 sat out there, about 200 yards off our tail, for several minutes. 'I could have shut my eyes and hit him if my guns had been working,' he complained from a hospital bed, where his hands and face, frozen early in the flight, were being treated. One Jerry planted a 20mm shell inside the rear turret, barely missing him and causing the hydraulic fluid to spurt from the turret mechanism in numerous places. 1st Lieutenant Earle E. Ellis, 25, navigator and Pinner were pulling their triggers on everything that came into sight and up in the top turret Staff Sergeant Ronald L. Nelson, 31, was shooting round 360° – he didn't even have time to 'follow through on the shots'. Later he said, 'I was shooting over 2 o'clock for a Me 110 when an Me 109 came in from 11:30, putting a 20mm into one engine. If he'd been any lower he'd have sure hit Captain Fleenor and Lieutenant Leary and if he'd been any higher he'd have hit me!'

Dawley picked off a Me 110. Big Jung hadn't been on Kilmer's waist gun long when he sent one Me 109 plunging in flames into the sea and Szabo bagged another off the starboard side. Besides the three knocked down for certain, there were three 'probables'. 'A FW 190 came toward us,' Szabo recounted later. 'His wings were pure red and I could almost see the lead coming point-blank. I froze onto the trigger. His left wing dropped off and he went hell bent into the water. But he'd fired first and he hit Jung and me. I knew Jung was hurt worse than I was because I looked up and saw part of his arm hanging above the window – then looked around and saw his side intact. The 20mm blast had ripped his arm from his body! The shrapnel had hit us both.' Kilmer began to administer morphine and sulfa to Big Jung, the Staff Sergeant who'd saved his life a few minutes earlier. 'When I got to look around, I realized I was injured pretty bad' said Jung later from his hospital bed. 'We'd been expecting the end for so long that we figured things couldn't be much worse.'

All the while there was no respite for Ellis, Pinner and Nelson and their guns blazed steadily. Nelson, from the circular top turret, was covering the dead spots, where *Night Raider*'s fifties had been silenced – there wasn't even a split-second time for intercom orders or questions. The skipper knew his boys in the back were 'catching hell' but he also knew that the big cloud formation was much nearer now. Ammunition was getting low: Szabo's gun had only three shells left when he was hit. Dawley's parachute was hit and began to blaze. Then suddenly, Fleenor put the *Raider* into a dive and they disappeared into the cloud. There was no gunfire: visibility was almost nil. 'Four Jerries followed us in,' one crewman related, 'but that was the last we saw of them.'

Night Raider was still some distance from England, however and gaping holes as big as a fist were draining precious gasoline. Ellis, the navigator, gave the skipper a course to steer. Nelson went out on the catwalk, checked the remaining gasoline and diverted it to the two good motors. None of the fuel gauges was working and one engine was cut and feathered. Pinner went back and helped adjust Mae West life preservers, because a dunking in the North Sea seemed imminent. As Szabo said afterwards, 'I figured Jung and I wouldn't have a chance if we were forced down at sea.' Big Jung himself said later, 'I guess everyone took time to pray.' Bates climbed out of the tail turret to stand guard with a waist gun. 'How are you doin' Lou?' he asked. 'OK,' was the reply from Szabo. And Jung recalled, 'When Bates shouted, "There's land!" I knew that our prayers had been

> answered!' Both the skipper and Pinner had been in the rear helping Kilmer, who was doing a superb job of administering first aid. Dawley had taken over Szabo's gun. Ellis' uncanny navigation had steered Fleenor and Leary straight for the nearest landing field and England's friendly coastline fields stretched out below. Emerging from the cloud at 1,500 feet, the *Raider*'s two engines struggled and strained to climb to 5,000 feet. 'Just as we reached the coast,' Fleenor explained later, 'our two remaining engines petered out – we were out of gas.'
>
> The wounded didn't know that the undercarriage had been shot out, that the hydraulic system was knocked out, that the tyres were punctured and that a forced crash-landing was inevitable. The skipper sent word round that he'd 'have to crack 'er down'. Ellis and Pinner went back-ship again to arrange the wounded in such fashion as to lighten the shock. Dawley held Szabo in his lap to cushion his side and Kilmer lay down with one arm around Jung's body and used his free arm as a brace. But the shock never came. Skilfully the skipper set the *Raider* down [at Ludham, Norfolk]. Said Ellis, 'It was a smoother landing than when we had wheels!'
>
> The ground crew chiefs handed the skipper his report on *Night Raider*'s wounds.[6] One ground crew man muttered, 'This one shouldn't have come back.' But it had and so had the crew and death had been cheated into taking a holiday.[7]

On landing after the mission Paul Manning travelled immediately back to London and wrote up his account of the raid on Wilhelmshaven. One copy was for Edward R. Murrow, CBS Bureau Chief in London, two copies were for the American and British censors and a fourth went to General Ira Eaker. Then Manning walked to the BBC studio, where he broadcast his account of this raid to CBS in New York for the entire CBS radio network. Both Cronkite and Hill filed their own stories, with UP and AP respectively. After that first mission, Manning went on flying missions with the 8th Air Force for two reasons:

> First the 8th Air Force was 'The Big Story' in 1943 and also because General Ira Eaker, who read the transcripts of my broadcasts, expressed to me his wish that he would go on flying the B-17s and bringing into American living rooms my eye-witness accounts of American courage.

In his letter to Manning he wrote:

> It is important to the morale of these young men who risk their lives

> every time they go on a mission that they know people at home are aware of the dangerous job they are doing in the skies over Germany... I read the transcript of your last mission and it is remarkable reporting and exactly the sort of message I want the people at home to hear.[8]

In London Margot Post waited for news of her husband.

Wilhelmshaven was the last mission of the month for the 'Eightballs'. February had been a bad month for the 66th Squadron, which had lost three ships and their crews. Combat losses were to be expected and although not liked, were accepted as part of the game of war.

The next day sixty-five bombers hit U-boat pens and naval facilities at Brest. Altogether, the February missions had cost twenty-two aircraft. On 4 March four B-17s were shot down and thirty-four casualties suffered during strikes by twenty-eight and sixteen B-17s respectively on Rotterdam and Hamm; the first time the bombers had attacked the Ruhr. Losses might have been higher but for the introduction of new, armoured flak vests, developed by Colonel Malcolm C. Grow, Chief Surgeon of the 8th Air Force, in association with the Wilkinson Sword Company of Great Britain and worn by ten crews in the 91st this day.

Twenty-two-year-old night fighter pilot *Leutnant* Dieter Schmidt-Barbo had joined 8./NJG1 in September 1941 at Twente airfield near Enschede on the Dutch–German border. As with many young and enthusiastic but inexperienced night fighter crews, he only got a few opportunities to prove himself in the *Himmelbett* night fighting system – the most experienced and successful crews were usually assigned to the 'best' *Himmelbett* zones where they kept accumulating their *Abschüsse*. Keen but green men like Schmidt-Barbo had to wait or patrol in those zones that were seldom flown through by the RAF bombers. In the spring of 1943 the round-the-clock bombing of western Germany presented an opportunity to pilots such as Schmidt-Barbo to score his first victory, albeit in daylight, against American bomber formations. Schmidt-Barbo recalls:

> Because the German Fighter Arm at this time was engaged mainly in operations over the Eastern Front, and had only a few units at its disposal in the west, we were at this time called in to repel these American attacks. This meant that we had to be at readiness both day and night, and our aircraft constantly had to be modified. Well, we usually were much too late to take off and intercept the Americans. However, on 4 March, it was a different story.

10.30 am. I am still in bed when I receive a call from Werner Rapp (who on this day is our unit's officer in charge of day fighting). 'The whole Squadron on *Sitzbereitschaft* [cockpit readiness]!' I inform Gustel Geiger of this message. He tells me, 'What nonsense! We won't catch them anyway and we'll be too late as usual!'

'Well, we'll get out of bed anyway!'

The Chief, *Hauptmann* Lütje, has not arrived yet and I phone Werner and ask him if he has arrived with him. Werner is very excited. 'Yes, yes, I've just spoken to him. Aren't you out yet? The Americans will arrive shortly over the airfield. Twenty bombers! End of message!'

Well then, I'll be off. Perhaps I will see them after all. I drive off on my motorcycle, meet *Hauptmann* Lütje on my way; he is fetching the aircrews, having slept at the Station HQ. Our aircraft are prepared for the mission. The ground crew technicians have been at work already. I phone Wemer once again from the Operations shed and ask him if we should proceed with getting strapped into our machines.

'Yes, where are you for God's sake? How much longer will it take you to get ready; how many crews are at their aircraft?'

'Four.'

'Good, over and out!'

I am now as eager as can be! When all the crews have arrived, I phone once more.

'At last! Yes, of course, everybody get strapped in! Over and out!' Today I will fly the *Kurfürst-Siegfried*, a Bf 110G-4. I call in a ground crew member who explains to me the counter of the MG-151 machine-guns and get strapped in as I've done so many times before. Suddenly, I hear on my left side, where the Chief is standing, the roar of his engines, but from the Operations shed no orders have come to take off yet. To be on the safe side, I switch on everything, and there from the left they sign to 'start engines'. When I switch on the engines the thought flashes through my head: 'Keep your fingers crossed and hope no gremlins are in the engines.' The Chief already taxies in front of me. I queue behind his tail. Becker is still in the hangar and I can't see other aircraft. Out on the airfield it's a bit chaotic – in front of us a plane of the 9th takes off. Behind him cross two from the 7th, then one more from the 9th, clouds of dust billowing and the feeling that at last something is going to happen! There, the Chief is accelerating. Should I take off together with him? I hesitate a bit too long and now have my work cut out to get out of his slipstream and the cloud of dust which his plane throws up, but I manage it. I tuck in with him and we fly in the direction of 4-*Berta* – of the other two only one, Heinzelmann, has managed to take off, as we find out later.

We climb steadily. Over the radio we hear wild chattering but soon this is solved too and we clearly receive the orders from ground control; we have set course for *Caesar*. The Chief sets course and there we hear Leo's calm and steady voice: 'Mailcoach [course of the enemy aircraft] 300 or 330.'

I don't listen very carefully to what he says. It is only important to the Chief anyway. Suddenly, he waggles his wings and is speeding up. Something must be going on! I look ahead, but in vain. Our speed is increasing all the time, course north-west. We can already see the Zuider Zee in the distance. Then, all of a sudden I hear over the R/T: 'From *Karin 1*, message understood. We can still see them.' I ask Schönfeld: 'Karin, that is us three, isn't it?'

'Yes.'

'But I can see zero!'

'Me too.'

Then all at once I see them, in front of us and a little to the right. They are almost over us already. They are cruising along 2,000 metres higher than us, quite a lot of them, four-engined, in close formation. A flight of three on the right outer side of the box, which are not as closely tucked in as the rest, formed vapour trails, which in turn formed black streaks against the blue sky – a very powerful sight. Slowly, we get closer and now we can see them well. They are Boeings, painted brown on top, which look like dorsal fins. One of them is trailing a bit.

The lone formation that was intercepted in the Texel area comprised sixteen B-17s of the 91st led by Major Paul Fishburne in *Chief Sly II* in the 322nd Squadron. They had taken off from Bassingbourn and should have formed part of a large force of seventy-one B-17s, which were bound for Hamm, but due to very bad visibility over East Anglia and the North Sea, the Groups did not find each other. Fishburne had then taken the decision that the 91st would continue to Hamm alone.[9]

Fishburne's formation, having bombed Hamm whilst under fighter attack all the time, was returning over Friesland Province in northern Holland when they were attacked by *Leutnant* Schmidt-Barbo and his fellow night fighter pilots. As he approached the 91st he saw a single Me 110 already approaching the formation from the rear. Schmidt-Barbo continues:

Our fighters have arrived at last – one or two carry out head-on attacks and streak straight through the formation and the bombers tuck in even more closely together. Heinzelmann is still flying behind me and now we're at the same height as the formation, sixteen in all. Occasionally, the fighters press home their attacks, but they don't attack in close formation. From behind, another one or two Me 110s have arrived at the scene and one of the *Amys* that trailed a bit has regained his position in his box. The three of us slowly but steadily fly over the formation and overtake the bombers.

'We will go in for a head-on attack.'

'Understood. Understood. We are ready.' Every now and then I squint at the Boeings. They are now to the right, behind and underneath us. The leading bombers are taking pot shots at us. One can see the threads of the tracer bullets. The weather is fine, a bit hazy but the sky is cloudless. A little while ago the haze in front of us looked like clouds and the *Amys* descended to get shelter in the clouds, but it was nothing. In the meantime we have arrived over the mouth of the Zuider Zee just to the west of Texel; time 11.30 am. The Chief is curving towards the formation. I turn with him and there I already have the *Amys* in front of my nose. We go in a bit from the right to the left. The automatic gunsight is on. Full throttle, and there we go in. I immediately have one in my sights. Aim is in front of him. Press the tit! The guns roar and dust flies around. The tracer curves away over him. Aim a little lower. Press the tit again and I race past him already. There is the next one. Aim precisely. Cracking and banging. Dirt flies around in the cockpit, into my eyes. This time the tracers disappear in his fuselage and wing roots and I flash past. I see no one in front of me any more. What next? One instant I don't know where to head to. There I see in front of me a Me 110 breaking off and curving down. I follow him. The fat one [Schönfeld] gave them a burst with his twin pop guns when we curved away; twenty-eight bullets!

'Are you still alive?'

'Yes.'

'No damage?'

'No.'

With me everything is OK. Both engines still running smoothly. Can't see any hits. Great. I look over my shoulder. I'm now underneath and to the right of the formation. As we flew through the

> formation, I saw one of the leading bombers peeling off and plunging towards the earth, as if to crash-land on Texel. In front of me I see a pair of Me 110s, without flame dampers as far as I can see, so they are from Leeuwarden.[10] Where the Chief is, I can't tell. A short distance off Texel, one bomber plunged into the sea. A column of black and white smoke still hangs over the ripples in the water. Another one has sheered off from the formation. I see him to the left and underneath me. Just when I decide to finish him off, I watch how a Me 110 in front of me raced up to the aircraft and at the same time several FW 190s also went into the attack, so there is no need for me to share in this! There is no one left near the formation. The Me 110s have also disappeared. We get in touch with the Chief. He will touch down at Bergen. His engines were damaged, but this was not caused by hits during the engagement; the driving unit of the fuel pump had crammed into the engine, so he has to have an engine change.

The B-17 gunners put up stiff resistance in the face of overwhelming odds but three B-17s were shot down.[11] Lieutenants Alan Brill and his co-pilot, Allan W. Lowry, both drowned after ditching *Excalibur*. They were posthumously awarded the DFC. Major Fishburne and Captain James Bullock, his navigator, were both awarded the DFC for successfully leading and completing the mission. The Germans did not escape unscathed. American gunners claimed thirteen destroyed, three probables and four damaged.[12]

Schmidt-Barbo sums up:

> This was the only daytime mission of the IIIrd *Gruppe* in this period which resulted in an encounter with the enemy. Losses: *Unteroffizier* crew Heintszch-Hendel; possibly they were one of the Me 110s that had approached the formation from behind on their own. As the proceedings had clearly shown, our Me 110, which was specially equipped for night fighting duties, was much too slow and cumbersome for daytime missions. And especially our crews, apart from the double burden of daytime and night-time missions, were completely inexperienced in daylight air combat. Thus, it was practically suicidal to attack such a formation of Boeings from behind as we were used to do at night. Still, only the death of *Hauptmann* Ludwig Becker during such a daylight attack on 26 February, slowly led to the insight by the 'powers that be' that the losses amongst the highly skilled night fighter crews were much too high in comparison to the possible, meagre results. So, after this day, we were not called

> upon to combat these formations of bombers penetrating our airspace at daytime.[13]

On 6 March sixty-three B-17s bombed the power plant, bridge and port area at Lorient while fifteen Liberators made a diversionary raid on a bridge and U-boat facilities at Brest. Denton Scott, who had missed the mission on 26 February while suffering from pneumonia, went along. In *Yank* magazine on 14 March he wrote:

> You are moving at several hundred miles an hour and things are coming at you at several hundred miles an hour and you dearly love life and your wife back in the States and the sooner you get the hell out of there the better it will suit you.

Two days later sixteen Liberators bombed the marshalling yards at Rouen in a diversionary raid to aid fifty-four B-17s attacking the marshalling yard at Rennes. Brigadier General Hayward Hansell flew in the 305th formation, which lost *Carter and His Little Pills* flown by Captain Joseph W. Carter when it was shot down about ten miles south of Selsey Bill. All ten crew perished. *Sam's Little Helper* flown by Lieutenant A.R. Kuehl landed at Manston with one engine out and a wounded crewman aboard. Fifty B-17s plastered the marshalling yards from end to end and effectively stopped any supplies reaching German bases in Brittany for up to four days. Several squadrons of RAF Spitfires and for the first time, the 4th Fighter Group's P-47 Thunderbolts, flew interdiction strikes against airfields ahead of the bombers. The fighters encountered heavy opposition and the 'Flying Eightballs' were left to fend for themselves. FW 190s of JG 26 led by Major (later *Oberst*) Josef 'Pips' Priller attacked head-on and *Miss Dianne* flown by Captain Clyde E. Price went down in flames with bombs still in their racks. The victory was awarded to *Hauptmann* Wilhelm-Ferdinand 'Wutz' Galland, brother of *Generalmajor* Adolf Galland, who was leading II/JG 26. *Emma Lou* flown by Lieutenant Robert W. Blaine quickly followed. *Oberfeldwebel* Willi Roth finished off *Emma Lou* after *Unteroffizier* Peter Crump shot it out of formation. Only 2nd Lieutenant Morton P. Gross, the bombardier, who was mortally wounded and three gunners, bailed out of Price's ship and 2nd Lieutenant Leo C. Frazier the navigator was the sole survivor in Bob Blaine's crew. Both B-24s were from the ill-fated 67th Squadron, now reduced to only three original crews and aircraft. The Spitfire escort finally appeared and prevented further losses. Even so, two B-24s barely made it back to Shipdham. Fifteen kilometres southeast of Hastings *Oberleutnant* Johannes

Naumann of II./JG 26 attacked *Peg* in the 'Travelling Circus' and claimed it as a victory but the B-24 crashed at Bredhurst in Kent.

On 12 and 13 March the bombers hit marshalling yards in France and the good fighter cover helped prevent any loss to the bombers. Some 'Travelling Circus' Liberators joined the 'Flying Eightballs' in flying effective diversion raids for the Fortresses. Bob Morgan, pilot of the *Memphis Belle*, recalls.

> We had a raid on Abbeville airdrome, which was not scheduled. We were going to Amiens. The lead Group was supposed to turn northeast of Dieppe but instead went over Dieppe. We got a little flak. I figured he had missed it and we turned back and found Amiens. There was just one little hole and it was closing over at that time. The crew made so many zigzags to find the target, because they couldn't find a check that we never got on the bombing run. So we had to quit our run because we were afraid we would drop some bombs on one of the planes. We had fighter protection up in the vapour trail. We could see them occasionally and knew they were up there. We had to make a decision – either to make another run on the target or to pick out another target. We knew we wouldn't be able to see it if we turned around. We knew the fighters were about out of gas and would go home any minute. And we knew there were a lot of enemy fighters in the area. While doing this concentrating we were making a left turn and saw Abbeville airdrome. We made a bombing run on the dispersal area and hit a great deal of it. We found out later that we were lucky, because we had just got to the French coast on the way home when 120 German fighters were screened just behind us. If we had made another run we would have had every one of those planes on us. When we checked with the other crews the next morning we found almost everyone had bombed a different target. They had bombed up and down this section on the way home. We were the only ones that hit Abbeville.
>
> We learned a lesson about not turning to go back on a target unless everyone goes back on the same target. We learned that eighteen ships were not enough of a formation to fight German pursuits. The Germans got pretty hot on the B-17s. They started coming in from the nose of the ships and at that time we had only two .50-calibre guns, which wouldn't go straightforward. We were working on the problem but hadn't solved it and hadn't put any more guns in. We had found that by flying all four Groups very close together we could get good fighter protection. That worked fine for a while. We would

> set one Group at 22,000, one at 23,000, one at 24,000 and one at 25,000, always about 1,000 feet difference, on the same line with each other or behind each other. If the enemy attacked the middle Group, the firepower of all the other groups could be concentrated on the fighters. Trouble was, the Germans thought about things too. They worked out the best method of attacking our planes. They picked on the low front Group while all the back three Groups couldn't help out. We solved that by moving the second Group up in front, the first Group behind them. In other words, the lead Group was higher than the second. It has worked fine ever since.[14]

With morale high, plans were laid to bomb the Vulcan shipbuilding yards at Vegesack on the Weser, a few miles north of Bremen and ranked fourth largest producer of U-boats in Germany. On 18 March Eaker ordered a maximum effort and seventy-three Fortresses and twenty-four Liberators – the highest number of heavies yet – were assembled for the raid. Near Heligoland the bombers came under attack from the *Luftwaffe* and the leading 'Hell's Angels' formation of twenty-two aircraft bore the brunt of most of the enemy fighters' aggression. During the bomb run the group encountered some concentrated and accurate flak. 1st Lieutenant Jack Mathis, twenty-two-year old lead bombardier on *The Duchess* piloted by Captain Harold L. Stouse, was posthumously awarded the Medal of Honor, America's highest military award, for completing his bomb run despite being mortally wounded. As lead bombardier, Mathis, who was one of two brothers from San Angelo, Texas, was doing the aiming for all the other aircraft in the 359th Squadron, using Automatic Flight Control Equipment (AFCE) for the first time. This equipment gave him lateral control of the aircraft through the Norden bombsight's connection to the autopilot.

Mathis was just starting his bomb run when the Fort was hit by flak, light at first. The navigator described the sound like 'hail on the roof'. He glanced over at Mathis, who was crouched over the bombsight, lining up the target. He knew him as an 'easygoing guy' and the flak didn't bother him. But a whole barrage of flak hit the squadron and one of the shells burst out to the right and a little below the nose. 1st Lieutenant Jesse H. Elliott, the navigator, thought that it could not have been over 30 feet away when it burst.

> If it had been much closer it would have knocked the whole plane over. A hunk of flak came tearing through the side of the nose. It shattered the glass on the right side and broke through with a loud

> crash. I saw Jack falling back toward me and threw up my arm to ward off the fall. By that time both of us were way back in the rear of the nose – blown back there, I guess, by the flak burst. I was sort of half standing, half lying against the back wall and Jack was leaning up against me. I didn't know he was injured at the time.

But Mathis' right arm had been shattered above the elbow; a large wound was torn in his side and abdomen. The navigator continued:

> ...without any assistance from me he pulled himself back to his bombsight. His little seat had been knocked out from under him by the flak...he didn't let anything stop him. I heard him call on the intercom, 'Bombs.......' He usually called it out in a sort of singsong. But he never finished the phrase this time. The words just sort of trickled off and I thought that his throat mike had slipped out of place, so I finished out the phrase, 'Bombs away!' for him. I looked up and saw Jack reaching over to grab the bomb bay door handle to close the doors. Just as he pushed the handle he slumped over backwards. I caught him. 'I guess they got you that time, old boy' I remember saying but then is head slumped over and I saw that the injuries were more serious than just some flak in the arm. I knew then that he was dead. I closed the bomb bay and returned to my post.

Back at base Staff Sergeant Dick McAllister, from Patterson, Missouri, took Jack Mathis' body out of the nose of *The Duchess*. 'It was just one little piece of flak that went through his left arm and then through his chest. Gee, he was a good guy. Another couple of inches off for that flak and he would'a been okay.' Only the day before at a bombardiers' party on the base Jack Mathis had told his brother Mark, who was a bombardier on Marauders, 'Listen, why don't you get a transfer into our outfit?' Jack Mathis had asked Lieutenant Robert Yonkman, another bombardier, to substitute him on the Vegesack mission, his 15th, so that he could spend more time with Mark. Jack Mathis awakened Yonkman a little later; stating the 'Old Man' would give him 2–3 more days with Mark if he would make the Vegesack run. Mark Mathis hated the Germans and was determined to avenge his brother and complete his 25 missions for him. He moved to the 'Hell's Angels' and went into *The Duchess*, flying in the nose where his brother had been and used his old bombsight.

Meanwhile, the Liberator crews found the trip uneventful until flying 2,000 feet below the Fortresses they reached their bombing altitude fifty miles from the German coast. It was a running fight throughout but while the 44th encountered heavy opposition, the only B-24 shot down belonged

Podington being handed over to the USAAF by the RAF. (USAF)

Airfield under construction for the 8th Air Force. (USAF)

B-17E 41-9023 *Yankee Doodle* was first assigned to the 92nd Bomb Group at MacDill Field on 13 March 1942. On 1 May the aircraft was transferred to the 414th Bomb Squadron. 97th Bomb Group and once in England it was one of 12 E-models that took part in the Eighth Air Force's first B-17 mission of the war, flown on 17 August 1942. Piloted by John Dowswell, it carried Brigadier General Ira C. Eaker to Rouen. Seven days later, 41-9023 returned to the 92nd Bomb Group where it served until 31 March 1943, when it joined the Blind Approach Training Flight (BAT Flight) at Bassingbourn. (Note the RAF-style camouflage). In August 41 -9023 was transferred again, this time to the 322nd Bomb Squadron, 91st Bomb Group and it ended its ETO service with the 324th Bomb Squadron as a target tow and general liaison aircraft. 41-9023 was finally salvaged on 26 July 1945. (USAF)

4.B-17F 41-9022 *Alabama Exterminator II* which operated in both the 97th and 92nd Bomb Groups and was used as a ferry navigation aircraft in the 384th Bomb Group. (USAF)

Officers on the roof of the control tower at Grafton Underwood on 17 August 1942 watch for the Fortresses returning from the Rouen marshalling yards. With hands in pockets. On the right, is Major General Carl Spaatz, commander of the Eighth Air Force. The officer at the corner with his ight foot on the rail is Colonel Frank Castle, who would lose his life leading the largest 8th Air Force mission of the war in December 1944 and posthumously be awarded the MoH. (USAF)

B-17F 41-24486 *Man O'War* in the 306th Bomb Group which was lost with 2nd Lieutenant James M. Stewart and crew when they ditched in the North Sea on 9 November 1942. (USAF)

B-17F 41-24388, ex-92nd Bomb Group which transferred to the 97th Bomb Group, at Gibraltar heading for North Africa. and Operation *Torch*. (USAF)

B-17F 41-24996 *Chennault's Pappy* which force landed at Exeter on 17 November 1942. (USAF)

B-17F 41-24607 *Jerry Jinx* in the 303rd Bomb Group which went MIA with crew on 23 January 1943. (USAF)

Captain Frank D. Yaussi checks the 500lb GP bombs in the bomb bay of a 91st Bomb Group B-17 at Bassingbourn on 30 June 1943. Yaussi was the first man in the Eighth Air Force to drop bombs on Germany, on 27 January 1943. (USAF)

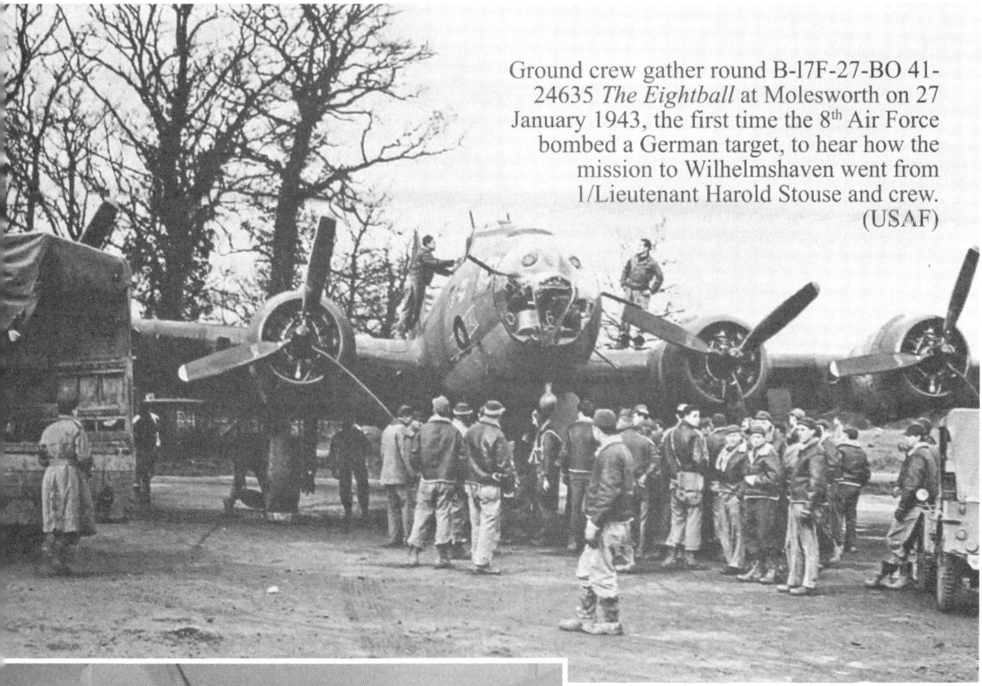

Ground crew gather round B-17F-27-BO 41-24635 *The Eightball* at Molesworth on 27 January 1943, the first time the 8th Air Force bombed a German target, to hear how the mission to Wilhelmshaven went from 1/Lieutenant Harold Stouse and crew. (USAF)

Left: B-17F 41-24435 which served in the 92nd and 97th Bomb Groups and which flew Operation *Torch* commanders to Gibraltar on 5 November 1942. (USAF)

Below: Sack time is over. Its breakfast and briefing and the day's mission lie ahead. (USAF)

Briefing. (USAF)

Set Watches. (USAF)

The 93rd Bomb Group was the first equipped with B-24D Liberators and arrived in the United Kingdom in September 1942 and the 44th Bomb Group - less one squadron – followed in October. B-24D 41-23754 *Teggie Ann*, seen here at Alconbury, was usually flown by the 93rd Bomb Group CO or his deputy. The bomber crash-landed in Turkey on 28 August 1943 while on TDY with the 9th Air Force in North Africa. (USAF)

Ordnance men in the 328th Bomb Squadron, 93rd Bomb Group attending to 1000lb bombs next to B-24D-1-CO 41-23737 *Eager Beaver* at Alconbury late in 1942. This Liberator was transferred to the 446th Bomb Group on 24 February 1944 and it was re-named *Fearless Freddie*. (USAF)

On 15 February 1943 21 44th 'Flying Eightballs' Bomb Group B-24D Liberators attacked Dunki
Their target was the *Togo,* a German fighter-control ship. Their long, straight run had enabled t
German gunners to determine their speed and height. Flak enveloped the formation, and just
the bomb-release light came on, the lead aircraft, B-24D-5-CO 41-23783 *Betty Anne,* which w
piloted by Captain Art V. Cullen and Major Donald W. MacDonald, 67th Squadron CO, took
direct hit. It knocked the roof off the cabin, and blew the cowlings off No.2 and 3 engines, whi
were smoking. For a few moments the noseless bomber flew on, only to fall away to starboa
with the port inboard engine aflame and the right inboard ripped from its mounting. Finally t
starboard wing fell off and a huge explosion scattered debris among the formation, hitting anoth
Liberator whose pilot managed to recross the Channel and force-land at Sandwich. MacDona
died later in a German hospital and Cullen, who was captured, was repatriated in September 194

B-24D-5-CO 41-23807 *Little Beaver.* (Bill Cameron Collection)

The 'Eightballs' taxi out from their muddy dispersals at Shipdham. B-24D-5-CO 41-23818 *Texan II* in the unlucky 67th Bomb Squadron was lost in a mid-air collision with B-24D-53-CO 42-40354 *SNAFU* flown by Lieutenant Fred M. Billings Jr, shortly after leaving the coast of England on 16 February 1943 when the target was St. Nazaire. Both aircraft were engulfed in flames, and seconds after impact both exploded, scattering debris even as far as the Fortress formation flying below them. All ten men in Lieutenant John B. Long's crew were killed while one man survived from Billings' aircraft.

Contrails. (USAF)

Captain Chester 'George' Phillips (middle) a pilot in the 67th Bomb Squadron, 44th Bomb Gro at Shipdham died in one of three explosions which rocked B-24D-5-CO 41-23807 *Little Bea* after leaving the target at Kiel on 14 May 1943. (Bill Cameron Collection) (USAF)

Old Bill was the creation of British artist and *Stars and Stripes* cartoonist Bruce Bairnsfat who painted the nose of B-17F-65-BO 42-29673 in the 365th Bomb Squadron, 305th Bor Group with a rendition of the World War I soldier. On 15 May 1943 pilot 1st Lt William Whits helped by gunner Albert Haymon and bombardier 1st Lt Robert Barrall got *Old Bill* to Chelveston after 20mm cannon fire fr fighters over Heligoland had riddled the Fortress and shot out Plexiglas nose, killing navigator 2nd Lt Douglas van Able a injuring Barrall. Whitson and Barrall were each awarded the D and the rest of the eleven-man crew (which include photographer) received eight Silver Stars a seven Purple Hearts. (via Bill Dona

B-17F-27-BO 41-24605 *Knock-Out Dropper,* which was flown on the Schweinfurt mission by Lieutenant John P. Manning, who led the low squadron in the 303rd Bomb Group formation. On 16 November 1943 the 359th Bomb Squadron Fortress set a new 8th Air Force record for a B-17 when Manning flew it on its 50th mission. *Knock-Out Dropper* was scrapped at Stillwater, Oklahoma in late 1945. (USAF)

Left: On 18 March 1943 Captain Harold Stouse in the 427th Bomb Squadron, 303rd Bomb Group flew B-17F-25-BO 41-24561 *The Duchess* home to Molesworth with the body of 1st Lieutenant Jack Mathis, the lead bombardier on board. Mathis was awarded a posthumous Medal of Honor (the first awarded to an 8th Air Force crewmember) for his actions this day on the mission to Vegesack. *The Duchess* was returned to the ZOI by 1BAD on 6 June 1944. (USAF)

Below: B-17F-20-BO 41-24504 *The Sad Sack,* one of the original Fortresses assigned to the 91st Bomb Group. Along with sister aircraft 41-24505 *"Quitchurbitchin", Sad Sack* was the longest-serving of the Bassingbourn group's original Forts. Both were among the first ten 8th Bomber Command B-17Fs to be returned Stateside on 15 March 1943 for training duties. (USAF)

The crew of B-17F-10-DL 42-3002 *The Old Squaw* which joined the 359th Bomb Squadron, 303 Bomb Group at Molesworth on 8 April 1943, the day that Lieutenant (later Captain) Claude V Campbell's crew made their first training flight. Back Row L-R: Claude Campbell, Miller, Riri and William A. Boutelle, bombardier. Kneeling L-R: Howard E. Hernan, top turret gunner; Wilson Quick; Kraft and Backert. *The Old Squaw* was lost on 6 September 1943 when it was ditched i the North Sea. Lieutenant Robert J. Hullar and crew were rescued. (Howard Hernan)

Mail Call. (USAF)

B-17 41-24606 *Werewolf* in the 303rd Bomb Group which crashed at Dawlish on 13 January 1943. All ten men in Lieutenant G. J. Oxrider's crew survived. (USAF)

Right: Back in a Molesworth hangar on 16 February 1943 after the raid on St-Nazaire, 1st Lieutenant Donald Stockton in the 427th Bomb Squadron, 303rd Bomb Group takes a close look at the damage to B-17F 41-24610 *Joe Btspik,* which was caused by attacks by FW 190s. Lieutenant H. E. Miller, 6 feet 4 inches tall, sits on the hole. *Joe Btspik* was lost with Lieutenant Vincent X. Walsh and crew on the mission to St-Nazaire on 1 May 1943. Seven men were killed. Three were taken prisoner. (USAF)

Left: Captain John C. Bishop (second right), 323rd Bomb Squadron Operations Officer, with 1st Lieutenant Charles H. Silvernail (left, with arm raised) and his crew, back from Wilhelmshaven, 22 March 1943. The manufacturer's frontal armament provision for the B-17F was a single rifle-calibre machine gun which could be moved to one of three sockets in the Plexiglas nose. This was impractical and of little value. In-the-field modifications improved forward firepower, and this Fortress has a .50-calibre Browning in the upper right gun socket and another through a side window for use by the navigator. B-17F 42-5077 *Delta Rebel 2nd* completed its 21st operational sortie on this date, a higher total than any other Fortress in the Eighth Air Force up to this time. (USAF)

B-17F 41-24559 *Ooold Soldjer* in the 303rd Bomb Group, which was lost in a take-off accident and mid air collision with 42-29573 *"Two Beauts"* on 1 April 1943. Eight of Lieutenant K. O. Bartlett's crew on *Ooold Soldjer* were killed and two survived. Six of Lieutenant J. R. Dunn's crew were killed. (USAF)

Coffee and doughnuts were the usual fare for weary Eighth Air Force bomber crews awaiting interrogation. These men at Bassingbourn are just back from the 6 April 1943 mission to Antwerp. (USAF)

B-17F 42-5251 *Pride of the "Kiarians"* (formerly *Bodacious Critter*) in the 306th Bomb Group, which was lost with Lieutenant Theodore Jankowski and crew on 17 April 1943. Three men were killed and seven were taken prisoner. (USAF)

to the 'Travelling Circus'. For almost 1¼ hours the Liberators came under attack. However, the run into the target was good and the bombing successful. Leading the 'Flying Eightballs' were the 67th Squadron led by Major 'Pappy' Moore in *Suzy-Q*. Over the target his gunners claimed six enemy fighters.

On the return leg the *Luftwaffe* stepped up its attacks, sometimes with as many as thirty fighters taking part. In the 'Travelling Circus' formation Frank Lown's B-24 was hit in the No. 4 engine and a hole was blown in one of his vertical stabilizers. Next it was the turn of the twin-engined Messerschmitt Me 110s and Junkers Ju 88s. Their attacks were more nerve-wracking, taking longer to complete before they broke away. Just as the B-24 crews thought they were safe, the German pilots would skid their fighters and fire longer bursts. When at last the fighters broke off their attacks, the crew of *Shoot Luke* saw Lown's engine beginning to smoke and vibrate badly. Lown was formerly *Shoot Luke*'s co-pilot before getting his own crew. The B-24 dropped from formation and Lieutenant John H. Murphy and his crew decided to help Lown home. *Shoot Luke* broke formation and took up position off the stricken Liberator's wing. Unfortunately, the stragglers attracted the attention of a lone FW 190. Its pilot surveyed the situation and made his attack from 9 o'clock with his four machine guns and cannon blazing. Three bullets missed Lown's head by less than eighteen inches.

Shortly afterwards, *Shoot Luke* bucked with a sudden explosion in the rear section. Although hit in the eye by fragments, Sergeant Floyd H. Mabee remained at his waist gun and succeeded in shooting down the fighter. Sergeant Paul B. Slankard, the tail gunner, was blasted through the top of his turret by a direct hit from a 20mm shell. Slankard flew for interminable minutes at 22,500 feet with the upper part of his body protruding from his turret. His left foot, which had caught in the gun controls, was all that had prevented him from being shot, projectile fashion, through the turret roof. Floyd Mabee made his way back to the bomber's tail, pulled Slankard back into the aircraft and applied an oxygen mask to his face. Lieutenant Edmund J. Janic, the bombardier, crawled to the rear of the ship despite severe head wounds and applied sulphonamide to Slankard's wound. Together, Janic and Mabee then dragged the severely wounded tail gunner to a hole in the fuselage where the frigid air entering the aeroplane at a temperature of 45 below zero sealed the wound. The hypodermic needles had frozen and no amount of warming in the crew's mouths could thaw them enough to enable drugs to he administered. Slankard remained in his precarious position for two hours while Mabee massaged his hands to maintain circulation. Janic returned to the flight deck and collapsed from loss of blood and shock. Lieutenant Arch Rantala, the navigator, successfully navigated the two bombers home. Frank Lown landed and thanked Murphy's crew, which completely filled an ambulance, for saving him and his crew from certain destruction.[15]

Vegesack was officially described as 'extremely heavily damaged'. The bombers had dropped 268 tons of high explosive, smack on target and later photographic reconnaissance revealed that seven U-boats had been severely damaged and two-thirds of the shipyards destroyed. British Prime Minister Winston Churchill and Sir Charles Portal, Chief of the Air Staff, recognized the importance of the success achieved on the mission and sent congratulatory messages to Eaker.

On 22 March the bombers attacked Wilhelmshaven. In the 'Flying Eightballs' formation Lieutenant Jim O'Brien and Major Francis McDuff, the 68th Squadron commander, led the 'Eightballs' in *Rugged Buggy* behind five B-24s of the 'Travelling Circus'. Jim O'Brien described the mission as 'hot as my first' and later counted 29 separate holes in *Rugged Buggy*. Despite a thorough going over by Me 110s and FW 190s, it was flak rather than fighters, which claimed *Maggie* and *Cactus*. *Maggie* was flown by Captain Gideon W. 'Bucky' Warne of Elburn, Illinois, the sixth original 67th Squadron crew and *Cactus* was piloted by Lieutenant Virgil R. Fouts of Los Angeles, California, in the 506th Squadron. Two men aboard *Maggie* survived and were taken prisoner. There were no survivors in Fouts' crew. The loss of *Maggie* left *Little Beaver* and *Suzy-Q*, as the only remaining original Liberators in the squadron. Colonel Ted Timberlake, who was leading his Group in *Teggie Ann*, narrowly escaped death when a 20mm shell entered the cockpit and missed him by only a few inches. Four days later Colonel Timberlake assumed command of the 201st Provisional Combat Wing. When elevated to brigadier-general in August 1943, at age thirty-three, Ted Timberlake became the youngest American general officer since the Civil War. On 17 May thirty-six-year old Lieutenant Colonel Addison T. Baker replaced him. Baker was born in Chicago on New Year's Day 1907. He left school in 1927 and worked as a motor mechanic in Akron, Ohio. He enlisted in the AAF in 1929, earning his wings the following year and was commissioned as a 2nd Lieutenant in the Air Reserve. Assigned inactive status and between 1932 and 1940 Baker ran his own service station in Detroit, Michigan and worked for a graphite bronze company in Cleveland, Ohio. He had joined the National Guard in Michigan in 1936 and later transferred to the Buckeye State's

112th Observation Squadron before it was called into federal service in 1940. In February 1942 he was assigned to the 98th Bomb Group at Barksdale Field, Louisiana for B-24 pilot training and the following month was assigned as CO of the 328th Squadron in the 93rd. Before taking over the Group he held the post of Operations Officer. Under Baker, 'Ted's Travelling Circus' became simply, the 'Travelling Circus'.

On 31 March the bombers were sent to the E-boat pens at Rotterdam. Shortly after take-off *Ooold Soljer* and *Two Beauts* in the Hells' Angels' were lost in a mid-air collision near Wellingborough. Fourteen men died. Four out of the six bomb groups which took part were recalled because of strong winds and thick cloud, which all but blotted out the target. Thirty-three bombers hit the dock area, while others attacked docks at Schiedam and the city area of Bocholt. Many bombs missed the target completely and caused 326 Dutch casualties when their bombs hurtled down into the streets of Rotterdam. *Satan's Chariot* in the 93rd, flown by Lieutenant Bill F. Williams, was shot down into the sea sixty miles off Ostend with no survivors. Fighters intercepted the returning 305th formation over the sea and made one pass before their fuel was expended. *Unteroffizier* Peter Crump of 5./JG 26 attacked *Southern Comfort* flown by Lieutenant Hugh Ashcraft and it caught fire between the No. 1 and No. 2 engines. During the latter stages of the fight the radio operator discovered the ship was on fire. 'I was shooting my gun. I saw our rudder hit and then I looked down and saw the fire. At first it was behind the vents, inside the wing and then it started coming out.' As the enemy attack slackened, Ashcraft turned out of formation and swung back toward the English coast. Solid overcast swallowed the plane. The fire, apparently feeding on oil and not gasoline, was now 'very persistent in character'. The rear gunner, who had been with *Southern Comfort* through all her troubles, recalled:

> It didn't bother me so much this time, because I knew what it was. We had plenty of time to arrange everything and I just sat there waiting for the signal to leave. Most of the rest of the crew gathered into two groups, one around the navigator's escape hatch in the forward end of the ship and the other about the door at the rear of the fuselage.

Ashcraft reported:

> We were in the clouds at about 15,000 feet, dropping fast and on instruments. We couldn't see a thing, but the navigator said it was about time we were over the coast. He gave me a heading to fly, but the tail was a little shot up and I couldn't do much. I looked at the

wing and could see the metal buckling and the flames getting around, so I decided all God's children ought to have wings.

As the alarm bell rang, the radio operator, who had been sending SOS signals, was waiting for an answer. He screwed his key down and prepared to jump with the rest. They were all out in less than a minute, each man instantly disappearing into the thick bank of clouds. Ashcraft waited until the last man had jumped – or until he thought the last man had jumped. Then he trimmed the ship so that it was flying level and followed the others overboard through the forward escape hatch. Later it was discovered that the left waist gunner, last man to leave by the door at the rear of the ship, had delayed to change his parachute. When he looked around he found himself in a pilotless and deserted airplane. He left immediately.

Ashcraft remembers the long trip earthward.

It was like flying in a void. Just grey mist. You couldn't see anything. We weren't sure whether we were still out over the water or not. Somebody said there are no atheists in foxholes. Well, there aren't any in parachutes, either. I guess it's the same whether you're down looking up, or up looking down.

The bombardier's main thought was to get back home before his roommates started dividing up his clothes. I could see one of them wearing my bathrobe. I finally hit a tree in an orchard. I looked down and there were a lot of firm-looking people waiting for me. They were all right, though, once they found out what side I was on.

Three of the gunners came down together, one of them with a five-foot rip in his parachute. The waist gunner reports:

We had quite a trip down. Ball turret was a man who was always griping about something. Well, there he was, griping again about the holes in his chute. So I yelled to him: 'Listen, can you swim? Because if you can, you'd better get ready.' The three gunners came down just off the perimeter track of a British airdrome near the coast. The waist gunner, whose face was frozen and whose flying boots had been ripped off when he jumped, was dragged over some bushes and into a muddy creek. A group of workmen pulled him out. 'It was just like a New York subway I didn't know what I was getting into.' The bombardier and the other waist gunner landed in a swamp, the bombardier's chute pulling him along for 200 yards before it collapsed. 'I don't know why I should have landed with my mouth open, but I did and it filled up with sewer water.' The navigator and

> the radio operator came out of the clouds over a broad estuary and dropped into the water. At that moment a new ASR launch happened to be cruising the inlet on a test run. As the two Americans hit the water the launch came alongside the gunner and picked him up. A minute later they also had the navigator in the boat. They got a couple of cash customers on their first day out. 'I didn't exactly cut a path when I hit, but I feel sorry for those poor surfboards and aquaplanes.'

The only fatality among the crew was *Southern Comfort*'s top turret gunner (S/Sgt Steve Gogoyla), who apparently slipped out of his parachute harness as he neared the ground. Three times the burning B-17 gracefully circled Wickham Bishops, a small village, and then crashed in a field; the last considerate act of a gallant lady.

After a three-day stand down, on 4 April Eaker switched to targets in France when the Fortress crews in the Bedford area were briefed for industrial installations in the Paris area, which included the Renault factory in the Billancourt district.[16] It took two hours for the four B-17 groups to complete assembly before a total of ninety-seven Fortresses departed the rendezvous point at Beachy Head. However, only eighty-five Fortresses remained when landfall was made at Dieppe, twelve having aborted through malfunctions. For once the sky was clear and blue and many of the Spitfire escort fighters could be seen quite plainly. Others were simply vapour trails in the upper reaches of the atmosphere. From their altitude of 25,000 feet crews could see the black mass of Paris cradled in the long, curved arm of the River Seine, ninety-five miles in the distance. At 1414 hours the Fortresses were over their target and 251 tons of high explosive rained down on Paris. Flak was moderate and not too accurate and crews were able to pick out the Renault works despite the industrial haze, which covered much of the city. Most of the 81 tons that landed square on the factory were released by eighteen B-17s of the leading 305th formation led by Major Tom McGehee in *We The People*, flown by Captain Cliff Pyle.

Before the last group had left the target a thick pall of smoke reaching to 4,000 feet blotted out the whole area. The groups in the rear of the formation were not as accurate as the 305th had been and many bombs fell outside the target area, causing a number of civilian casualties. So far no enemy fighters had been sighted but five minutes after the target fifty to seventy-five *Luftwaffe* fighters began attacks on the formation, which lasted all the way to Rouen. Four B-17s were shot down in repeated frontal attacks, sometimes by four and six fighters at a time, until the Spitfire escort reappeared to provide withdrawal support. One of the three losses in the 305th was *Available Jones*, which was piloted by Lieutenant Morris M. Jones, who along with six of his crew was taken prisoner after they bailed out near Les Andelys in the French countryside.[17] Edward G. Mescher's ball turret jammed at a position where he could not open his exit hatch. After frantic efforts to free him, self-preservation took hold and his crewmates were forced to abandon him and bail out. Jack O. Luehrs, the radioman, the last man out, witnessed the final moments as he descended by parachute. William H. 'Bill' Johnson, the young engineer from Jarbur, Oklahoma kept his turret going and claimed 'fighter after fighter with deadly accuracy', even after the ship, crippled beyond flying was out of formation and the natural thing do was to bail out. The Forts came home to Chelveston riddled with cannon and machine gun shell holes. The gunners aboard *Dry Martini 4th*, piloted by Captain Allen Martini, were credited with the destruction of ten enemy fighters, a record for a bomber crew on a single mission. In all, American gunners claimed forty-seven enemy fighters destroyed. Pictures smuggled back to England by the French resistance after the raid showed that the Renault works had been severely damaged.

The following day eighty-two Fortresses and Liberators bombed the Erla aircraft factory and engine works in Antwerp. The 306th bore the brunt of head-on attacks by FW 190s, which shot down four of the Group's B-17s. These were the only losses among the heavies this day. *Dark Horse*, flown by Major James Wilson, the Air Executive, carried Brigadier General Frank Armstrong, now commanding the 101st Provisional Combat Wing in the 1st Bomb Wing, who was flying as an observer. Captain John Regan, normally a command pilot, took the co-pilot's seat. During the bomb run the Fortress was hit by 20mm cannon fire from a FW 190 attacking head-on. Captain Robert Salitrnik, the lead navigator, was hit in the leg by fragments from a can of .50-calibre ammunition that exploded. Armstrong administered first aid as he shared a walk-around oxygen bottle with Regan. Wilson got the Fortress home safely to Thurleigh. The critically wounded navigator received four pints of plasma on arrival at Thurleigh and was out of shock the next day but developed gas gangrene on 15 April. Salitrnik died the next day. Armstrong later received the DSC for this mission.

Armstrong had been the 306th CO for a month before being promoted to Brigadier General in February. It has always been claimed that General Frank Savage, the main character in Sy Bartlett[18] and Beirne Lay's 1948 novel, *Twelve o'Clock High*, which became a hit movie a year later, was based on Armstrong, who on 18 November, assumed command of the 315th Bomb Wing (Very Heavy) in the Pacific Theatre.[19] Savage undergoes a steady mental decline as battle fatigue overtakes and finally engulfs this remarkable leader of men. Ultimately, Savage allows the full weight of responsibility to fall squarely on his shoulders and his alone; Savage continues to fly missions when it is not essential or required of him to do so. He insists on leading from the front as if he still has something to prove to his men. He begins to crack and then suffers the final painful mental breakdown at planeside prior to a mission. He is so wracked with mental fatigue that he cannot summon strength in his arms to lift himself up and into the nose of his B-17. This final part of Frank Savage's persona is not based on General Armstrong at all, but the incident, as Lay confirmed, did happen to 'a very fine commander'. It seems that this 'very fine commander' was Brigadier General Newton Longfellow.

Longfellow, who had been given command of VIIIth Bomber Command on 1 December 1942 when Eaker moved to command 8th Air Force HQ, was[20] 'Perpetually overwrought, (he) struggled to overcome its (VIIIth Bomber Command's) difficulties by shouting himself hoarse... (His) nonstop ranting had earned him the nickname "Screaming Eagle". At the end of June (1943) he was sent home, a burned out wreck.' Eaker had to replace his oldest friend. (General Arnold held the opinion that his Bomber Commander was 'especially weak'.) When he did, Eaker recommended Longfellow to the commander of Second Air Force, a training command in the US. Eaker added: 'He is a tireless worker and despite the fact that we almost killed him off here working, or carrying the responsibility for 24 hours a day, seven days a week, I believe he will spring back after a few weeks' rest and do a tremendous job...' Longfellow got the job but was reduced to his regular rank as colonel. Longfellow was replaced by thirty-seven-year-old Brigadier General Frederick L. Anderson Jr, a West Point and Kelly Field graduate, who had served with air units for five years in the Philippines and who since April, had been in command of the 4th Wing.

After a few days' break in missions VIII Bomber Command struck at Lorient and Brest on 16 April. Lieutenant Claude W. Campbell's crew in the 359th Squadron in the 'Hell's Angels' flew their first mission this day, to Lorient. The crew arrived at Molesworth in March and were assigned a B-17 they called *The Old Squaw*, as Howard B. Hernan, the top-turret gunner, recalls it:

> ...was a complimentary term in the state of Mississippi at one time. When the Choctaw Indians occupied Mississippi, the term was one

of respect bestowed on the oldest female in the tribe. She was considered 'good medicine' and was the only woman permitted to attend tribal meetings. Of course, Andrew Jackson drove the Choctaws out of Mississippi in 1830, so maybe it wasn't such a good name after all but it seemed appropriate at the time.

Our crew later had a theme song. We would listen to it on the Armed Forces Network. They would give out censored news, various other programmes and also had a period of time that they would play music if someone wrote in and requested such. They played some of the popular tunes at that time and our crew started sending requests so often that they finally gave us a theme song, which was 'The Campbells are Coming' because we always requested the songs to be for Campbell's crew. One of the crewmembers had left the States with a small radio, which seemed to be turned on all the time. (When we left the States we did not know that the electric in England was 220, whereas in the States it is 110, but we overcame that by putting a 100-watt bulb in the line reducing the voltage.) At any rate this radio would be tuned in to the AI Network and then after that programme was over, we would switch to 'Lord Haw Haw' who seemed to know more about us than people on our own base. He would also play some popular music, which I assumed they thought would make the boys lonesome or have some adverse effect on morale, which it didn't. I suppose they monitored the AI radio network and from it they got our crew's name, etc. Haw Haw would also dedicate a song or two to us and then say they would be over to pay us a visit some night. I suppose subconsciously he got to me as after I would go to bed and sleeping I would always dream of the Germans coming over, trying to bomb our field. It was always the same dream, night after night, until I finished my missions. During these dreams I would always try to get to the top turret of the plane, but would always wake up about the time I got there. I don't know why I should do that as the 'guts' of the guns were in the armament shop and not in the turret.

The combat crews were kept separate from the rest of the base personnel and we lived primarily in the north-east corner of the base in small Nissen huts with twelve men to a hut, making two crews. Most generally, right next door lived eight officers which formed the rest of the two crews. We had a little coke stove, but toilet facilities were a little lacking. We had a couple of flush toilets but no facilities to take a shower, so we rigged up a couple of barrels with a charcoal

> stove underneath to get a little warm water. A dirty body at high altitude was so much harder to keep warm and it always surprised me that better washing facilities for the combat crews were never provided. What a life. Up at 1400 and the only sleep we got was in the afternoons and also, we were only getting two meals a day. At the first opportunity we ventured into Thrapston to buy some bicycles. I purchased a little sports model with 24-inch wheels for £5. T/Sgt John A. Dougherty, the engineer in Pentz's crew who shared our hut, purchased a 26-inch wheel bike. His had more speed but mine had more power so we hooked them together. It was the most contrary thing to ride but we made many trips on it around the base and into Thrapston and for trips to buy fresh eggs. Combat crews were entitled to bacon and fried eggs on the morning of a mission but there were not enough to go around. Sometimes we had powdered eggs and if they had been prepared right you couldn't tell the difference.

On 8 April Campbell's crew made their first training flight and flew three more up until the 15th. Claude Campbell was a good formation flyer and Hernan guessed that four training flights were all that they needed. On 16 April Campbell's crew were detailed for their first mission. At the mess hall a bedlam greeted them as they entered the door. The smoke of burning grease assailed their nostrils and smarted in their eyes as they filed in for their 'real fresh eggs'. Perhaps a slice or two of salty bacon also on the plate and to a table for the first problem: Could they get them down? After a drink of grapefruit or tomato juice it usually became easier but it did not take much to satiate their appetites! Each mouthful became an additional lump of lead in the pit of their stomachs and they were soon ready to board the truck that would take them to briefing. The target was Lorient. William A. Boutelle, the bombardier, wrote of the Lorient mission:

> I'd heard plenty about these raids and while a lot of the stories conflicted, knew a little of what to expect. As we approached the coast of France, though, my knees felt weak and the long time in which I had to set up my bombsight seemed to be flying by: I found myself rushing so fast that I made mistakes. I kept trying to look for the first flak and fighter and work my sight figures too. I settled down and set up my sight and looked up just in time to see the first fighters. There were two Focke Wulfs coming up at 11 o'clock low, so I reported and grabbed my gun, even though they were a mile out of

> range. They soon made an attack apiece from 12 o'clock with no results on either side. I did expend 15 rounds at one as he flashed by with his wings spouting 20mms like Roman Candles. About that time a formation of 10–15 fighters showed up and sat on our right wing, about 2,000 yards away. Then they came barrel-assing in with a short burst for us and all they had for the group below. The tail gunner said it was 'Some show'.

Howard Hernan continues.

> A FW 190 came in at about 2 o'clock high. The pilot could not have had much experience firing at a B-17 because he fired from a long way off. I gave him a burst at about 1,500 yards, a little further than I should have. About the same time he fired his 20mm cannon and they all went off at about 400 yards ahead of us. After he fired he immediately flipped over on his back and down he went. It was the last I saw of him. We came through unscathed but the Group lost two B-17s.

On the morning of 17 April crews throughout eastern England were alerted for a raid on the Focke-Wulf plant at Bremen and a record 115 were assembled. For the first time two large-scale combat wings, with the 91st and 306th in the first wing and the 303rd and 305th making up the second, were dispatched. Each wing formation consisted of three group boxes of eighteen to twenty-one aircraft, flown for mutual firepower and protection. Eight bombers returned early with malfunctions, leaving the remaining 107 bombers to continue across the North Sea. The long over-water flight was uneventful and even monotonous. Some crewmen took advantage of the lull before the storm to catch up on some sleep or letters home. William Boutelle settled down to his note pad and began writing, 12,000 feet above the North Sea.

> As I write this I'm on my way to Bremen, one of the hottest spots in Germany. Yesterday we flew in the leading and highest group. In that position we had a very calm and for the most part, boring flight. The lower and rear groups caught some hell from flak and fighters while we only saw a few puffs of ack-ack and about twenty fighters. Today promises to be a very different story. We're in the highest but last group and have a grandstand view of all the other ships, of which I can count over 100 right now. We should really see a show today. I'll see it all I hope.

Shortly after leaving the English coast the mass of aircraft had been spotted by a German reconnaissance aircraft and the Americans' approach was radioed to fighter controllers along the enemy coastline. The German defences did not know where the bombers were headed but, just after the B-17s passed the Frisian Islands, *Luftwaffe* fighters were vectored towards them. However, the FW 190 pilots waited until after the bomb run before commencing their attacks. The reason was not long in coming, as Howard Hernan explains:

> Of all the missions I would fly I never saw flak as bad as on this mission. At briefing we had been told that there would be 496 batteries around Bremen. The Germans put up a box barrage. The 88s gave off black smoke when they fired and the 105s were grey. It was just like one black cloud. The windshield was broken out and flak holes appeared in the radio compartment. I tied a pillow into a hole in the window and Campbell flew on from the co-pilot's seat. We were flying number two off the lead ship on the right-hand side and so close were we that our wing tip was in the lead ship's waist window.

Captain Bob Morgan considered that the first Bremen raid on the Focke-Wulf plant was about the most effective and successful raid ever made from the standpoint of planning, efficiency, damage done and losses.

> We were briefed for that raid as well as, or better than, for any other. The Germans had 178 flak guns to be turned on us. We went in from the southwest to the northeast on a heading, so they could never get more than 72 guns on us. We found the plant and turned off to the right and made a complete turn and came out. That is the long way around but if we had come out the other way we would have had to run through the other 106 guns. The raid was well planned. We assembled over England below 5,000 feet and went out below 5,000 feet until we got ready to turn and come in. We began to turn and climb and when we reached the German coast we had our altitude. We tried to make them think we were going to Wilhelmshaven and it seemed to work. The weather was pretty overcast below. It looked as though Wilhelmshaven was open and Bremen would be overcast, so I thought we might go back after Wilhelmshaven instead. But a few seconds later I found the target by flak; I looked over to the left and there was one black cloud sitting there and it was flak. I figured that must be Bremen. Sure enough, we could see Bremen when we turned.
>
> We went in from the southwest to the northeast. German fighters

could be seen coming up from the ground and I have never seen so many at one time. I had to forget about the fighters because we had started the run. We were the high Group. We made the run. The flak was pretty bad, bursting all around us. The boys in the low Group really caught hell from it.[21] They had set up a barrage and it worked well but the bombing was successful. There were three factories there and two were completely destroyed and the third about 60 per cent destroyed. We lost sixteen bombers, all in the low Group. This was the greatest loss we had sustained to that time. When we turned off the target the fighters began to hit us. They had 109s, 110s, 190s and Ju 88s. But we found out that if you kept your Group weaving, when the attacks came, you could nose down and turn into the attack and they wouldn't hit you. They didn't hit our Group at all.[22] We came out by water and came home.

Here is a navigator's story of the action that day.

Up ahead, finally, I made out through the haze and cloud something that had possibilities of being a city. We spotted the target. Just about then somebody on the ship called out that there was a group of B-17s on our left and another on our right. But they were moving just a bit too fast for Fortresses and somebody from the cockpit called out the disconcerting news that they were enemy fighters flying up ahead in formation, evidently getting in position to attack us head-on. By this time the bombardier was on the bombsight and we were settling down on our bomb run. And then the flak began to come up at us. It came up so thick and fast that it looked as though we had run into a thunderhead...At the same time we were hit by fighters coming head-on into us. Just before our bombs went away our No. 4 engine was hit and oil started pouring all over the place. Vibration caused by the wind-milling propeller seemed to be about to shake the ship to pieces. When the bombs finally went, none of us felt them give the ship the jar they usually give it, as we were already bouncing around like a stovepipe hat in a March gale.

The sky was literally swarming with fighters. The pilots made old *Queenie* hurl herself around the sky in evasive action dodging the oncoming pursuits until we must have looked like a small plane doing acrobatics. The pursuits came in so fast that at times the navigator and I had to be content with taking shots at every second or third plane making a pass at us. And the way we were thrown around in that nose from the evasive action made us feel like a pair

> of dice. All this time I was trying to navigate us out of that place by the fastest route possible. I'd get a checkpoint and then grab my gun and start spraying lead out like a hose. They had every kind of plane in the *Luftwaffe* up there trying to knock us down. Bombing was excellent. As the English say, we really pranged the target. Not one of our bombs was off the target area.[23]

At interrogation, gunners put in claims for sixty-three fighters destroyed but in reality only about ten fighters were actually shot down. Howard Hernan sums up the problem.

> I know that gunners made many claims and probably a lot of us got credit for planes that were not actually shot down. I think this was true on both sides. In order to claim a fighter you had to have two other witnesses. Heaven knows how many men were shooting at the same plane. Intelligence would ask what the exact location was and it would sometimes take up to forty-five minutes longer to sit in interrogation if you were claiming a fighter. By this time we were absolutely worn out, hungry, trying to get warm, and it just wasn't worth the effort. After all, we weren't there to shoot down fighters. Our primary concern was the bombing of the targets. Eventually, intelligence told us that we were claiming too many fighters. From then on I never claimed another fighter, even if I knew I'd got it.

Half of the Focke-Wulf factory was destroyed but Albert Speer, the German armaments minister, had issued instructions for dispersed fighter production some six months previously. Crews received a much-needed boost with the news that, despite the continuing losses, the 8th Air Force was to be expanded. In February the Casablanca Conference had approved additional aircraft for VIII Bomber Command.[24] Eaker's successful strategy meant that now they were to be used for daylight bombing.

Whilst the new groups continued training, Eaker scheduled another attack on St-Nazaire for May Day. Thick cloud over the target curtailed bombing attempts and the 306th flew back, unaware that it was off course through a navigational error. What was assumed was Land's End turned out to be the Brest Peninsula and as the formation began to descend it was bracketed by accurate barrage of flak. Altogether, the Thurleigh group lost six aircraft. Lieutenant Lewis P. Johnson's aircraft was hit several times and caught fire. Staff Sergeant Maynard Harrison 'Snuffy' Smith the thirty-two-year old ball-turret gunner, son of a small town judge, from Caro, Michigan, who was on his first mission, hand-cranked his turret back into the aircraft and discovered that the waist gunners and the radio operator had bailed out. Smith could have bailed out but he elected to remain in the aircraft and fight the fire with a hand extinguisher. The aircraft did not show any signs of leaving formation, so Smith assumed that the bombs were still aboard and went aft to treat the badly wounded tail gunner. Then he jettisoned the oxygen bottles and ammunition in the radio compartment and manned the two waist guns during an attack by enemy fighters, stopping to dampen down the fires and treat the tail gunner. After Smith had thrown out all excess equipment, Johnson, who was on his twenty-fifth mission, managed to bring the bomber home and put down at Predannack near Land's End. On the crew interrogation report he wrote – 'This is a hell of a way to finish'. On 15 July 1943 'Snuffy' Smith received the Medal of Honor from Secretary of War Henry L. Stimson.[25]

On 4 May Eaker dispatched seventy-nine B-17s to the Ford and General Motors plant at Antwerp, escorted by twelve Allied fighter squadrons, including, for the first time, six squadrons of P-47s. Howard Hernan in the 'Hell's Angels' recalls:

> The Spitfires and Thunderbolts did a wonderful job of working the Focke-Wulfs over and it was a very successful mission. We flew on Captain William R. Calhoun's wing and Clark Gable flew with him and handled the radio hatch gun. Claude Campbell, my pilot, could see the Hollywood film star grinning at him over enemy territory. One of our B-17s, piloted by Lieutenant Pence, was shot up by a FW 190 that jumped the group as we reached the English coast and the co-pilot got shot in the leg and never flew again; the radio operator got hit over the eye and in the leg. Next morning I looked over Pence's 'plane. It had nine holes in it and I measured them. The spread was 9 feet, although they had been attacked from head-on. Captain Gable visited the co-pilot every evening at a nearby hospital to see how he was getting along.

On the night of 12 May the 94th, 95th and 96th received orders to participate in a maximum effort starting at 1300. The news came as something of a shock at Bassingbourn, Alconbury and Grafton Underwood because the ground echelons had only arrived in Britain two days before. Remarkably, the three groups managed to prepare seventy-two bombers for the mission, to airfields at St-Omer but at such short notice problems were bound to occur. The 96th failed to complete assembly and aborted the mission. One B-17 got into difficulties and ditched in the Channel, where the crew was rescued by Air Sea Rescue. Thirty-one B-17s in the 94th and 95th continued to the target but the bombing was 'poor'.

Notes

1. Becker had scored his first kill on 16 October 1940 when he downed a Wellington of 311 Squadron RAF and in 1941–42 he had developed into one of the leading *Experten* in the *Luftwaffe* night fighter arm. He not only shot down forty bombers in 1941 but also taught the new and young crews from his experiences. To them Becker was an inspiring fatherly figure.
2. Most of the night fighter aircrew were sceptical about this new gadget – they liked to rely on the 'Mk I Eyeball' – but Becker took the lead and had one of the still experimental sets installed in his Do 217Z night fighter at Leeuwarden aerodrome. Guided by the revolutionary radar, he shot down no fewer than six RAF night bombers between 8/9 August and 29/30 September 1941. Most of his colleagues and the *Luftwaffe* High Command were now convinced that the AI radar was an invaluable new asset in the night battle against the British bombers and the *Lichtenstein* went into mass production shortly after. In the course of 1942, most of the *Luftwaffe* night fighters were equipped with the AI.
3. All ten of Tribbet's crew were taken prisoner. All ten men in Benson's crew perished. Lyn Mokler's crew were one of the original crews in the 364th BS, having arrived in England in October 1942. He did not like aeroplanes having nicknames so they just called their plane '590' after the serial number. Mokler was the first pilot in the 305th BG to finish his twenty-five missions and on 17 October 1943, by now a Major at HQ 3rd BD, was over-flying Elveden Hall in a RAF Miles Master trainer. While performing a climbing turn he suffered complete engine failure. At only 200ft of altitude with no hope of recovery, the Master crashed into a spinney killing Mokler and seriously injuring his passenger, Captain R. J. Yonkman. '590' was one of five 305th BG B-17s lost on 19 May 1943. Of the Harvey J. Kohler crew on board, only three survived. *John Burn One-Zero-Five; The story of Chelveston Airfield and the 305th Bomb Group in pictures* by William Donald (GMS 2005).
4. 1st Lieutenants Robert H. McPhillamey and Wilbur E. Wockenfuss and seven others survived to be taken prisoner. Robert Perkins Post was among the dead. *Maisie*, which other crewmembers called 'old 777' (after the last three digits of 41-23777's serial number) flown by Captain Howard Adams and Stanley McLeod, who was from Oklahoma City, was also shot down. Adams was killed and only two men on board survived.
5. The B-17 landed with a gaping hole where the rudder should have been, a shattered nose section, a wing spotted with ragged shrapnel wounds and its fuselage riddled from nose to tail with flak and cannon-shell holes. One shell had crashed through the fuselage directly behind the tail gunner's position,

leaving a gash the size of a grapefruit. One by one, the crew climbed out – uninjured. They reported they'd made a pretty good bombing run.

6. 'The hydraulic and power lines in the tail turret were shot out, as were the primers, intakes, carburetors, oil coolers and oxygen regulators. The undercarriages wouldn't work. The tyres were punctured. There was a 15-inch hole in the right tail-flap. There were 47 .30 calibre holes and five 20mm holes in the rear fuselage; 16 .30s and four cannon in the left fin; five .30s and one cannon in the stabilizers; nine .30s and four cannon in the right wing; three .30s in the right aileron; 12 .30s in the top fuselage; 36 .30s in the left wing and 27 .30s in the bomb-bay doors. And all gun barrels were 'burned out'.
7. Either Uffz Heinz Hanke of 9./JG1, in a FW 190, or Uffz Wennekers of 2./JG1, in a Bf 109, had claimed the apparently doomed B-24 as their first victory. Bud Fleenor and his crew went down in the Channel on 16 April in *Missouri Sue*. The bombardier had bailed out over France.
8. Twenty years to the day at an Air Force Association Dinner in New York City, Walter Cronkite, Gladwin Hill and Paul Manning were awarded a special citation for their participation in the raid. Paul Manning, twice nominated for a Pulitzer Prize, went on to cover the B-29 missions over Japan.
9. The 303rd and 305th Groups turned south and successfully bombed the Wilton Feyenoord docks near Rotterdam. The twenty-one B-17s in the 306th BG aborted the mission and twenty returned to Thurleigh with bombs on board. Captain William Friend's B-17 was badly damaged and set on fire by *Uffz* Flecks and *Uffz* Meissner, both of 6./JG1, and fell out of formation. The crew probably jettisoned the bomb load while under fighter attack: nine bombs hit two schools and two houses at Den Briel near the Hook. Four Dutchmen were killed and between sixty and seventy children were killed. The fire took hold and Friend gave the order to bail out over the sea. Seven parachutes were counted yet no survivors were ever reported.
10. IV./NJG1, led by *Hptm* Hans-Joachim Jabs and *Hptm* Rudolf Sigmund. On 3 October 1943 Sigmund. *Kommandeur* III./NJG3, was KIA when he was hit by flak over Kassel. He had twenty-eight victories.
11. *Hptm* Jabs of IV./NJG 1 and his three wingmen finished off a straggler, which had repulsed at least thirty attacks before finally going down. *Hptm* Lütje then claimed a B-17 at 1131 hours and, shortly after, four Me 110s had finished off another. These were probably B-17F 42-5370 flown by Lt Harold H. Henderson (9 KIA, 1 PoW) and B-17F 41-24512 *Rose O' Day* captained by Lt Ralph A. Felton Jr (seven KIA three PoW). Both crashed in the sea west of Texel and Den Helder respectively. The battle raged on for another ten minutes and B-17F 41-24464 *Excalibur* captained by Lt Brill finally fell victim to a Bf 110, probably of IV./NJG1 flown by Lt Kostler. Brill succeeded in ditching the heavily damaged bomber in very rough seas forty miles west of Texel and although it broke in two, the crew managed to get out safely and

enter their dinghies. In a six-hour struggle with the high seas, three of the crew drowned before the seven survivors were picked up by an ASR Walrus.

12. Both III and IV./NJG1 lost a Me 110. The attacking Fw 190s of II./JG1 and JG26 suffered no losses.
13. Appointed *Staffelkäpitan* of 8./NJG1, by the end of 1943 Dieter Schmidt-Barbo had nine kills to his credit. During 1944 he proved an expert night fighter pilot and claimed three kills on four nights: on 22/23 April (his 19th to 21st kills); 3/4 May (23rd to 25th); 22/23 May (27th to 28th) and 28/29 July (33rd to 35th kills). Barbo was awarded the Knight's Cross on 27 July 1944, after thirty-two night victories. As *Oblt* Schmidt-Barbo, he left 8./NJGl for 9 *Staffel* of the same elite night fighter wing, again as *Staffelkäpitan*. By the war's end he had risen to *Hauptmann*, flown 171 operational sorties and claimed 40 RAF aircraft, all at night.
14. Contrary to popular belief, *Memphis Belle* was not the first to complete an 8th Air Force tour but its twenty-fifth mission on 17 May 1943, to Lorient, was duly recorded (using a 'stand-in' B-17F) in 16mm colour and used with great effect in the documentary. Everyone it seemed wanted to meet the famous men of the *Memphis Belle*. On 26 May they were introduced to HM King George VI and Queen Elizabeth at Bassingbourn and on 9 June General Eaker paid them a visit and then bade them a Stateside farewell to take part in a bond tour of US cities. When the tour was completed in December, Bob Morgan got married, but not to Margaret Polk, his Memphis belle, but Dotty Johnson, a hometown girl he met on his war bond tour. What finally emerged in April 1945 was a colourful and exciting thirty-eight-minute masterpiece that gave American cinemagoers a timely reminder of the grim reality of the war that was being fought at high altitude in the skies over Europe. By this time a tour of missions had risen to thirty-five and the chances of completing them were even more remote than they had been in 1942–3. Britons saw the film for the first time in the winter of 1944–5.
15. Lown was shot down on 16 April over Brest and taken prisoner. Slankard eventually recovered from his terrible wounds.
16. On the night of 3/4 March 1942 the RAF had destroyed the plant but the Germans had rebuilt it in nine months using slave labour and had even managed to increase production.
17. The B-17 flown by Lt Herschel B. Ellis also crashed there with the loss of two men KIA and eight men bailed out to be taken prisoner.
18. Bartlett, who as a major had been General Spaatz's aide, was working as a screenwriter at 20th Century Fox Studios when he approached Lay to write a screenplay about the air war.
19. Armstrong retained command of the B-29 wing until January 1946. According to Wilbur H. Morrison in *Fortress Without A Roof*, after 'Possum' Hansell left England in October 1943 to become the air member of the Joint Plans

Committee of the Joint Chiefs of Staff in Washington, DC, he discovered that Armstrong had told members of the 101st Combat Wing that General Hansell had supported suicidal missions, which led to high casualties. Armstrong gave the impression that if he had been at the helm he would have rejected missions against such heavily defended targets until VIIIth Bomber Command was stronger. In the Pacific war, Armstrong joined former 8th Air Force generals, Curtis F. LeMay and Possum Hansell, who was given command of XXI Bomber Command in August 1944 and all took part in the final downfall of the Japanese Empire. Notably, Hansell and LeMay continued the same unescorted daylight precision bombing doctrine they had pursued whatever the odds in England.

20. According to Geoffrey Perret in his book *Winged Victory*.
21. A German reconnaissance aircraft had spotted the mass formation shortly after leaving the English coast and the Americans' approach was radioed to fighter controllers along the enemy coastline. The German defences did not know where the bombers were heading but *Luftwaffe* fighters were vectored towards them just after they passed the Friesian Islands. However, the flak barrage was so intense that the FW 190 pilots waited until after the bomb run before launching their attacks. Worst hit was the 306th, which lost ten bombers. One aircraft came home with a parachute harness tied to control cables, which had been shot away by cannon fire. Gunners claimed sixty-three fighters destroyed but only about ten were actually shot down.
22. The 401st BS in the 91st BG, flying as the low squadron in the 1st Bomb Wing formation, lost all six aircraft.
23. *Target Germany*; the US Army Air Forces official story of the VIII Bomber Command's first year over Europe, 1944. Possibly the aircraft is 42-5125 *Q-Queenie* in the 305th BG, in which case the navigator was W. M. Smith. 42-5125 was lost with 2nd Lt Grant B. Higgs' crew on 16 June 1943. Eight crew were KIA and two were taken prisoner.
24. During mid-April 1943 four new Fortress groups – the 94th, 95th, 96th and 351st – were dispatched to Britain, to be joined by three more B-17 groups in May. All but the 351st had B-17Fs with long-range 'Tokyo tanks' built into their wings near the tips to hold an additional 1,080 gallons of fuel.
25. See *First Over Germany: A History of the 306th Bombardment Group* by Russell A. Strong (1982). The raid was a special one for Captain Cliff Pyle, who was flying his twenty-fifth and final mission with the 305th BG. The 305th lost two aircraft but Pyle and the crew of *We The People* came through safely. Within ten days of this mission he was attached to the 1st Bomb Wing with the title of 'President, Tactical Advisory Board'. The board's primary function was to advise the commanding general about combat tactics and to monitor the preparation of the Tactical Doctrine, later known as 'Standard Operations Procedures'.

CHAPTER 4

Maximum Effort

There is a clearly understood working agreement between crew and pilots that permits maximum effectiveness with the least expenditure of work, time and effort. Only crews that gain such ability survive long, for the Nazis are quick to take advantage of any slip. But how does food affect these things? Surely food alone doesn't make the difference between a lost crew and a safe one? No, not food alone. Yet it is a fact that the losses in a large group of men will be smaller if they are properly fed. And the phrase, properly fed, deals with more than cooking alone.

The crews of the Little Beaver and the Suzy-Q eat apart from the squadron mess. They have fostered a feeling of oneness among themselves to a point where they not only live together but they eat together, fight together and when the time comes, if it must, they will die together. Part of that feeling, that esprit, comes from their crew mess.

The private mess they operate began because of the dislike of these men to 'foofaraw'. They didn't want to wear their blouses to dinner in the officers' mess. They came to England to fight a war.

When they landed as part of the early contingents of First Wing, they were ready to fight their way into the country. They alighted from their planes at an air-transport base with guns loaded at ready in their holsters. Lieutenant Chester Lucius Phillips, who through the subtle alchemy of nicknames is called George, phrases it thus: 'We thought the war was right here in England instead of two hours flying time across the Channel.'

These men wanted to grow beards and wear torn, comfortable uniforms like the men pictured at their posts in the Pacific.

'We didn't want to wear blouses and pinks and get all dolled up. To get away from that we just had to learn to cook, so we did,' Phillips explains it.

In the Nissen hut where the crews of the Little Beaver *and the* Suzy-Q *await their dinner, there is a cheery odor of broiling pork. Through the pleasantly smoky atmosphere comes the crackle of spattering grease as the potatoes fry merrily on top of the little stove, behind the broiling meat. Coffee will be prepared later with Nescafe. The men are ready for their meal. And they are not wearing their blouses. It is important to them, this manner of eating.*

Major John M. Redding and Captain Harold Leyshon of 8th Air Force Public Relations

At Station 115 late in the afternoon of 13 May 1943 the weather was typical for an English spring day, clear but cool. 2nd Lieutenant Robert L. Fisher, a navigator in the 68th Squadron in the 44th Bomb Group, left the officers' mess after the evening meal and upon seeing the late spring sun still well above the western horizon, he borrowed one of the bicycles that had been conveniently left leaning against the mess, to make a trip to the *King's Head* pub just off the west end of the runway in the little village of Shipdham. Cycling down the lane bordered by a mixture of hedgerows, trees and rock walls, Fisher could see from a section that ran close to the perimeter taxi way connecting the dispersal parking sites of the Liberators, the late afternoon activity about the bombers. Ground crewmen were working on and about the B-24s; some planes had cowling off engines on which work was being done; at other aircraft, refuelling trucks were putting fuel in the 'big birds'; at others, armament trucks were delivering the assigned loads to be put into the bomb bays of the ready aircraft. And he thought, 'Already with the sun still up today, tomorrow's mission begins.' Fisher felt personally involved with what he saw because before mess he had checked the squadron assignment board for crews for the next day's mission and knew that his crew was on it.

Some of the zest for a cycle off base and a pint at the nearest 'local' was lost. After a quick one at the 'King's Head', Fisher cycled back to base to return the 'borrowed' bike to the mess and to find the lounge almost deserted even though the evening's darkness had just settled in.

Word must have got around, so off he trundled to the Nissen hut where he bunked with seven other crew officers – the officers of two crews having been assigned one open-bayed hut as quarters. In the centre of the hut there was a small coal burning heater with a stove pipe going up through the sloping ceiling. The hut was made of one layer of corrugated iron formed into a tunnel shape and set upon a concrete floor. The eight beds were set four on a side with the feet to the walls and the heads set out toward what could be thought of as the centre aisle, which started at the door at each end of the hut and proceeded past the centre spot of the coal stove. This was the natural point of congregation of the hut members on cold nights. Along each side of the hut, there was a shelf and pole fixed so that they had a place for personal items and a place to hang clothes. Footlockers and denim clothing bags were placed under the beds. And that was home! When Fisher got there, he found it was dark, all the others having already turned in. He slipped in and got ready for bed in the dark, placing clothes and boots so that he could find them easily in the morning – whenever that would come. After settling down between GI wool blankets laid across the horsehair 'biscuits' that passed for a mattress, he heard 1st Lieutenant David W. Alexander, his pilot, in the next bed whisper from only a distance of several feet, 'There's one on for tomorrow and we're up for it.' Fisher told Alexander he knew and stretched out to sleep. He knew. He had done five; this was to be number six and like all other crewmen he lived with that ever present knowledge.

That night the ticker-tape machines started clattering out orders for the B-17 and B-24 bomb groups in East Anglia. Jim O'Brien had just returned to Shipdham from a sortie 300 miles out to sea shadowing the German battleship *Tirpitz*, as the 'Flying Eightballs' were assisting RAF Coastal Command with raids on German shipping and naval forces. On 7 May the twenty-four-year-old pilot was promoted to major and given command of the 68th Squadron, replacing Major Francis McDuff, who was rotated home. O'Brien had no sooner found out what a squadron commander was supposed to do when word came recalling all crews for a maximum effort on Bordeaux. However, at 0200 the Field Order was changed to remove the bomb bay tanks and load up with 4,000lb of the new-type incendiary clusters for a raid on Kiel. He would only find out why at the briefing the following morning.

In the spring of 1943 it was not yet practical or possible for the 8th Air Force in East Anglia to despatch its bombers further than Bremen or Kiel, a round trip of approximately 800 miles. However, for the 14 May mission Eaker could call upon more than 200 B-17s and B-24s, which meant that he could diversify his attacks with a multiplicity of options, further improved by the debut of twelve B-26 Marauders in the 322nd Bomb Group. At Polebrook the 351st Bomb Group was also making its bombing debut. 2nd Lieutenant Jack Howell, navigator in 1st Lieutenant Joseph A. Meli Jr's crew in the 511th Squadron, recalled:

> Our squadron had spent the past few days making sure our airplanes were ready for action when the call came on the morning of 14 May with reveille at 0500 followed by breakfast in the mess hall.

> Apprehension was thick in the air as we moved through the line and sat down to eat. There was not much conversation when we were called to the briefing room at 0630. There we learned of our first strategic bombing mission: knock out a German airfield in Belgium. It was our turn and after only twenty-five bombing missions we could go home and let someone else take over.

In April Howell had carried the responsibility of navigating a new quarter-million dollar airplane, Uncle Sam's finest, across the Atlantic to East Anglia. Born Jack Howell on 3 January 1920 he was the second of four boys. Late in November 1942 Jack had received word that his father, owner and operator of the first restaurant in Florida to have air conditioning, had died. He was only fifty-eight, so it was a bit of a shock. Jack was given ten days to attend to the funeral before getting back to the business of preparing for war while Nana, his mom, known to everyone as Bud, who worked at the restaurant with Dad, took over the running of the business. Jack Howell found England quite different from Florida.

> It is a bit farther north and cooler than Florida and the days are longer too. The sun rose before 5am that time of year and did not set until after 9pm. The countryside was full of young, pretty English girls eager to show us around. Clark Gable, the movie star himself, was assigned to our squadron. He came to document the 'daily life of the American flying fighter'. Gable used movie clips he took to produce the movie *Combat America*. I heard he put together a pretty good film. Major Clint Ball was our commander, so 'Ball' was part of each of our airplane's name.[1] Mine was *Spare Ball* and it turned out to be a bad omen.

At Shipdham long before light on the morning of 14 May the enlisted man in charge of quarters opened the end door of Fisher's hut, gave the time and said that breakfast was in half an hour and briefing an hour later. Someone put on the overhead bare electric light and they all began to grope for clothes and boots with no talking except for an occasional word or grunt. They straggled out of the hut into the chill night air to walk the country lane from the living site to the mess site in groups of ones, twos and threes. At the mess there was a short line of men at the cooking range waiting for the cook to finish a batch of whatever he was cooking; most times it was dehydrated eggs that usually came off the grill looking like pancakes. In fact, the first time Fisher had dehydrated eggs, he thought that they were pancakes and he completely spoiled a breakfast of something that had started out marginally edible by pouring a big serving of Karo syrup on it. On rare occasions they were given fresh eggs, but these were very rare, indeed.

As he did his job, the cook did not look at the men and rarely spoke and then in a low mumble. And from all the times Fisher ate early breakfasts before missions, he got the impression that he would like this whole line of drowsy, sleepy-eyed men who were responsible for him being up and working this early, to go away and leave him alone. And indeed, many did – permanently.

There was little talk at breakfast, each man seemingly occupied with his own thoughts, but in retrospect, they were probably all occupied with about the same pattern of thoughts a blankness of feeling, unformed questions of what the day would hold, a turn off of everything except the present. When the men finished breakfast, they went outside to where shuttles of GI trucks stopped to give them and the enlisted men who had eaten in a nearby mess hall, a ride to the technical site near the runways where the group briefing room was. By this time the total black of the night had been broken by a translucent greyness on the eastern horizon, the start of the long dawn of the northern latitudes.

As the groups of men arrived at the briefing room by separate trucks, they went inside exchanging the half light of the dawn for the chill and little better lighted, atmosphere of the briefing room, the officers taking the chairs near the front and the enlisted taking those toward the centre and rear. By this time they were all more awake and there was a level of conversation going on between all the men. They sat in the folding camp chairs and wore various combinations of uniforms and flying gear and caps or helmets as each felt inclined.

Enough of them smoked to cause a blue haze to form in the upper reaches of the dimly lit room. The only well lit area of the room was the rostrum and the rear wall covered by the large briefing map of the European Theatre of Operations – from the British Isles east to Russia and from the northern reaches of Norway to Italy. Before the flying crews had arrived, someone from group operations had placed the route of the day's mission on the map with yarn and map tacks. The map was then screened off from all eyes by a pull curtain made from white sheeting. And that's what the crews viewed as they all waited for the briefing to begin – a white sheet covering the mission for today! And as usual, remarks and speculation, many of them to ease the tension of the speakers, were rampant. On the rostrum and to the side of it, the group operations officers were also waiting and making last-minute revues of briefing information: operations, weather, intelligence, navigation and bombing.

And through all this subdued activity there seemed to be a growing feeling of anticipation.

Major O'Brien had cancelled the recall of Lieutenants Tom Cramer and Bud Phillips because the 68th Squadron could put up six B-24s without calling on either of them. This was provided that O'Brien flew with his usual co-pilot, 'Mac' Howell, who was from Topeka, Kansas, to check him out as first pilot for combat flying. Lieutenant Ralph Ernst who was from Enderlin, North Dakota, would fill in as radio operator. O'Brien said he showed up 'not so much as the squadron commander but as co-pilot of *The Rugged Buggy* in a "tail-end Charlie" slot; what a glorious way to go!'

A few of the 'Eightballs', including Bill Cameron and Major Howard 'Pappy' Moore, who were on forty-eight-hour passes, managed to get back to Shipdham for the briefing but were too late to be considered for the raid so Everett W. Wilborn Jr, from Port Lavaca, Texas, took the co-pilot's seat in the *Beaver* piloted by Captain 'George' Phillips. 1st Lieutenant Tom E. Bartmess from Houston would fly as his navigator. Staff Sergeant Edward V. Phillips, one of the gunners, who was from Fort Worth, made it four Texans on the crew. *Suzy-Q* was undergoing maintenance in Northern Ireland, so 'Pappy' Moore's regular crew were reassigned *Miss Delores* or *Q for Queenie*, as she was known, because of her call letter. Lieutenant Robert Brown, *Suzy-Q*'s usual co-pilot, who was from Norwalk, California, took the pilot's seat and Lieutenant Hartley 'Hap' Westbrook from Coon Rapids, Iowa, would fly co-pilot. Captain Bob Bishop, the navigator from Knoxville, Tennessee, plus seven others, all from the *Suzy-Q*, completed the scratch crew of *Miss Delores*. Gilbert 'Gibby' Wandtke, the engineer, was not happy about the change in aircraft. He had been jilted by a Delores in the States and claimed that *Miss Delores* would probably take them over the target but would not bring them back!

Someone in the rear of the room gave the command, 'ATTENTION' and all in the room 'popped to'. Down the aisle to a seat waiting for him in the front row moved Colonel Leon W. Johnson the group commander, saying as he did, 'Seats, gentlemen'.

The men sat, the room was quiet – anticipation was replaced by rapt attention. One of the briefing officers pulled the white curtain back to the edge of the rostrum, uncovering the wall map. The group operations officer stood with pointer in hand waiting to begin the briefing. The moving curtain first uncovered the British Isles and as it did the men could see the red yarn string that began at the base and departed land on the northeast coast of East Anglia and extended out into the North Sea.

As the curtain moved the route was further seen to turn east toward Germany, enter the northwest German coast east of the Island of Heligoland and thence feint south-eastward before turning north to the target – *Kiel*. The operations officer hadn't spoken yet and before he could, some wag in the rear of the room was heard to comment, not too loudly, 'This will only lead to bloodshed'. Fisher felt that probably all of those who heard him were thinking, 'Hopefully, not mine!'

The group operations officer named the target, the Krupp Germania and Deutsche Werke submarine building works, and told of its importance as a construction and repair facility for submarines that had been making havoc with the North Atlantic convoys bringing supplies and men to Britain as a major support to the war effort. He said that the 44th would be in addition to a force of several groups of B-17s who would bomb first with 500lb high-explosive general purpose bombs. The 'Eightballs' would follow, carrying in some aircraft the same type 500lb high-explosive general purpose bomb, but in others, magnesium incendiary bombs – the first time the American force had penetrated Germany to bomb with incendiaries. All this had an impact on the men, especially the part that they were to be the only B-24 unit on the mission and the idea that they were to be on the end of the bomber force. 'Yes, somebody had to do it' thought Fisher, 'but there it was – the 17s stir them up and we catch it!'

A total of six B-17 groups with 136 aircraft and the twenty-four Liberators of the 44th would head for the shipyards at Kiel. The 94th and 95th were detailed to bomb the Ford and General Motors plant at Antwerp. The 96th and the 351st were to hit the airfield at Courtrai-Wevelghem in France. On previous missions the Liberators had bombed through the lower flying Fortress formations. To prevent this recurring, higher headquarters decreed that the Liberators had to reduce their speed and fly behind the Fortresses, although it was said that in so doing the B-24s 'would drop out of the sky'. The B-24D's cruising speed was 180–185mph indicated airspeed, while the B-17s cruised at 160mph indicated. The Liberator pilots would have to fly a constant cruising speed of 180mph while maintaining a height of only 500 feet to avoid detection by enemy raider, a task made more difficult because they would have to zigzag continually 20 miles in one direction and 40 miles in the other to remain behind the slower Fortresses.

The 44th intelligence officer projected maps and photographs on a film screen and pointed out the IP (Initial Point) or last turning point before hitting the target. It was at this point that the bomb-run began and all evasive action for flak or enemy fighter attacks would cease, giving a nice stable platform for the bombardiers to sight from and thus creating the time of greatest vulnerability of the bomber force to enemy action – a nice predictable target for enemy anti-aircraft gunners and fighters. He suggested some points on the ground that bombardiers might use for identification from the IP to the target and of course, indicated the aiming point in the target area. Then the weather officer told what the expected weather at base, en route, at the target and at base on return was forecast to be – today, clear all the way, a rarity in Europe. He reminded the navigators that they would be given predicted winds aloft charts to be used in computing flight plans in their specialized briefing to follow this generalized one. Then in turn the group navigator and bombardier each gave very brief remarks as each would have a later specialized briefing. Then the group commander stood up and made some short, terse comments on the importance of this mission and the fact that it was the first time that American bombers were carrying incendiary bombs into the heart of Germany – the quiet direction of a commander sending his force to combat the enemy.

Finally, the Protestant chaplain was called on for a prayer and he ended his prayer in a pattern he used for all briefings, '... and may there happy landings be; here and in eternity.' And as usual, Fisher had an almost reflexive selfish thought that concentrated on a happy landing back here at the base, leaving the one for eternity for some indefinite time in the future. Then he went to the navigators' briefing, got the winds aloft chart, the route laid out by the group navigator from the field order received by teletype the night before and computed the flight plan and drew the route on his maps. Any special comments the group navigator thought necessary were made then and they all left to get their special flight equipment and go out to the aircraft. The other specialists on the crew were at their own meetings, the radio operator to re-affirm frequencies and procedures, the bombardier to clear up any last minute details on bombing procedures. As they completed the specialized briefings, they went individually to the special equipment building to pick up their own parachutes, escape kits (maps, money, small compasses etc.), flying boots and altitude flying suits.

Outside the special equipment building, again GI trucks were shuttling the men to their aircraft parked at dispersal sites all around the perimeter taxi way. When Fisher arrived at the aircraft, the sun had come above the horizon. The morning was clear with no chill in the air. He stowed his equipment in the nose compartment of the aircraft and got out to savour the open air for the time left and because the rest of the crew was there. The two pilots were talking together in low tones. They asked some questions about the flight and Fisher filled them in from the flight plan. Then Alexander announced it was time to get on board and get ready. Fisher climbed into the nose compartment by way of the nose wheel doors, put on his parachute harness and stowed the chest pack of the chute on the side of the compartment in a spot that he hoped would keep it most secure from being unintentionally spilled. He opened up flight log and maps and placed them on the small navigation plotting table on the left and rear of the compartment. Ammunition had been dumped into the nose for the two flexible .50 calibre machine guns he was to man out of the left and right side of the nose and the one mounted directly in front of the bombardier's position firing directly ahead that he would man when he wasn't engaged with the bombsight. Fisher broke the belts of ammunition up into lengths of twenty to thirty because it had been found that longer lengths would not feed easily and too often could cause the gun to jam. About the floor of the compartment he distributed the lengths of ammunition so that they would be within easy reach any time they were needed. The guns would not be loaded and charged ready for action until they were at altitude and heading out from the coast on departure over the North Sea.

Launch time at Polebrook was 0730, as Jack Howell on *Spare Ball* in the 351st at Polebrook recalls.

> The engines of the day were problematic and required a lot of maintenance and babying but once you got them going they would blast your ear drums out all day long. Waiting for the signal were lines and lines of Fortresses, engines rumbling their passive idle. At the signal of a flare gun, the pilot pushed the throttles forward and brought the mighty engines to a full roar. Twelve hundred horsepower each pulled their burden to its destination. The heavily laden bombers would begin to roll down the runway gaining airspeed before climbing slowly skyward. After taking off, the airplanes would circle the airfield while the rest of their squadron formed up with them before heading out to make some holes in the ground. The P-47 escort fighters had a much shorter range and could not fly to the target zone with us. This added to our uneasiness, but we had confidence in our Forts; nothing else in the air could match our firepower. Just after our escort turned back, the pilot announced flak ahead. Nothing amplifies the feeling of helplessness like having to fly through flak. It was like walking through a minefield.

> The Flying Fortress was vulnerable from practically all sides, but not necessarily due to the lack of defensive firepower. The 17's weakness was its thin skin and non-existent armour plating. Our bird had a maximum ceiling of over 37,000 feet and carried a crew of ten but was not big enough inside for a six-footer to stand fully erect. In fact it was a bit cramped and since the Fort was not pressurized, each crewmember had to don an oxygen mask as we climbed through 10,000 feet. What's more, the higher you climb the colder it gets and 30,000 feet up the temperature drops to a very cold 50° below zero. We had to wear several thin layers of clothing to guard against the cold. Frostbite became a common hazard as this was before the electrically heated long johns. It was also quite windy inside the aircraft, more so when the bomb bay doors were opened. It was enough wind to register as a hurricane. On maximum fuel the range of a Flying Fortress was 4,400 miles, or from Jacksonville to Seattle and back to Denver, but the normal range fuel load was 3,300 miles when it carried a bomb load. Using this fuel load the B-17 could carry 4,800 pounds of bombs. On short runs she could carry as much as 8,000 pounds of bombs but could only fly 180mph. With an empty bomb bay she could make almost 300mph but still not fast enough to keep the Nazi fliers from buzzing us like mosquitoes. And nothing protected us from the anti-aircraft fire.

At 0900 hours twenty-one Liberators began taxiing out at Shipdham. As the Rugged Buggy taxied out behind Lieutenant George Jansen's ship, *Margaret Ann* 'Mac' Howell said, 'If I get back from this trip, I'm going to get stinking drunk.'

Dick Castillo, the rear gunner, commented. 'Come on, let's quit kidding, this will be just as tough as any we had ever flown.'

Jim O'Brien thought too about Howard Moore's remark at briefing. 'I wouldn't go on this mission if I were you.'

Fisher continues:

> By this time all four engines had been started and the big aircraft was vibrating as something alive and eager to be on the move. Other planes had begun to taxi past our dispersal site and Alexander released brakes and we moved out slowly to be in position to take up the assigned location in the group; the nose compartment dipped and bobbed as he applied and released brakes causing the nose-wheel oleo strut to compress and expand; at the same time there was an accompanying squeal of the main wheel brakes as if they were

complaining of the heavy load applied to them. After our flight's assigned leader passed the entrance to our dispersal site, the pilot again released brakes and we moved in behind the flight leader with more nose dipping and brake squealing. We were then part of the parade of aircraft on the perimeter track moving slowly toward the take-off position. Because of the curvature of the taxiway, I could see the group lead aircraft already at take-off position on the eastern end of the east-west runway, the aircraft ahead of us waiting to take their position on the runway and at times a portion of the line of aircraft behind us – seventeen aircraft, poised and waiting to go to war.

The bombardier standing in front of me pointed and at the same moment I saw a green flare arc into the sky from the top of the control tower. Looking at the group lead plane I could tell that he had applied take-off power while holding his brakes; the nose-wheel oleo strut was compressed giving the aircraft some small resemblance of a sprinter with his feet in the chocks waiting for the starting gun. Then with the green flare signal he released his brakes; the nose rose a bit and the plane began to roll and gained speed seemingly so very slowly as he used runway – so very rapidly. Then far down the runway the plane almost grudgingly separated from the runway and slowly began to climb; as it did the heavy landing gear just inboard of number two and three engines began to come up, one markedly slower than the either. And this take-off picture was repeated until it was our turn to take the runway. During those early missions, I saw nothing amiss about taking off in the nose of the aircraft; so, the bombardier and I watched the process from that vantage point. While waiting and watching the others, I had a view of the operation from over the gun sights of the swivel guns mounted in our compartment and remember thinking, This is going to be my view of the war, over the post sights of the guns; navigation may be what is supposed to be my specialty, but shooting just may be a great deal more important at times. And I remembered the pilot had said on several occasions that when on missions he looked out and saw enemy fighters coming at us from some position ahead of us he couldn't do anything but fly the aircraft, but he 'wanted to hear those guns firing in the nose; and keep on firing!' – a sense of priority with which I was in tune.

Alexander taxied the aircraft onto the end of the runway to take-off position and then it was our turn. What the other aircraft had done was repeated by ours, except this time as the plane rolled down

> the runway, gaining flying speed ever so slowly, I was watching the runway disappear beneath the nose only 3-4 feet away from my own feet and I was feeling and sensing the power and weight of the aircraft, all of it behind us and its effort to force us into the air. I felt more than a little awed with the process. It was at such moments that I sometimes had an ill defined feeling of being a part of something that was not nice to do, but had to be done and I and others had by some process been chosen to be a part of it – a mixed sense of elation and dread.
>
> And then we were in the air and after proceeding for a short distance straight ahead Alexander began a slow turn to cut off the flight leader so that he could come into formation position with him, just to the rear and below his right wing. This accomplished, the flight joined the group as it circled and the whole group climbed in the clear sun lit spring morning to depart the English coast at the exit point.

For twenty minutes the Liberators circled Shipdham airfield and gained altitude before falling into formation. Assembly completed, they headed out over the North Sea to rendezvous with the B-17s. Lieutenant Alexander cleared the crew to test fire the guns. Robert Fisher grabbed a belt of ammunition from the floor for one of the side guns, inserted the first round in the breech, slammed the plate closed, hand charged the gun, pointed it toward the sea and away from the formation and squeezed the trigger for two short bursts. Then he repeated this on the other gun.

> While I was doing this I could both hear and feel the test firing being done in the other guns of the aircraft, the double 50s of the turrets being heard as a deep almost guttural, 'BRRRRLP' and their reverberations being felt in the airframe. The single 50s sounded with a more staccato sound. Even the ones at the waist position between the wing and the tail firing to the left and right of the plane could be heard in the nose compartment above the sound of the engines and the rush of the slipstream. All the gun positions checked with operable guns, no jams, at least not at this altitude and we hoped the same would be so for the 30 degrees below zero temperature expected at the altitude of 25,000 feet.
>
> The B-17 groups were joined at approximately the briefed rendezvous point and the mass groups continued to climb to altitude. In the climb the discrepancies in operation between the B-17s and the B-24s became apparent: at the lower and medium altitudes the B-17s

> were much faster than the B-24s and over the North Sea the 17s stepped out ahead of this lonely little group of 24s. By the time we got to the area of Heligoland the 17s were far ahead of us and continued to be so at the entry of the German coastline. But on the other hand, above 20,000 feet the B-24 was faster than the 17 and when we entered Germany, we were flying at 24,000 feet and beginning to catch up, but there was such a lot of space between them and us that I had something of a lonely feeling.

At around 1035 a dozen B-26Bs swooped low over the Dutch coast and continued over the outskirts of Amsterdam at rooftop height. They bombed a generating station at Ijmuiden with delayed action mines and then departed as quickly as they had come. It was a curtain raiser for a vast armada of aircraft, the like of which had never before been seen on German radar screens during daylight hours. About an hour after the B-26s departed, the 1st Wing formation flying without escort was picked up. Major James J. Griffith Jr, CO of the 407th Squadron in the 92nd, flying as Air Commander with 1st Lieutenant Earl A. Shaefer, led the mission. Seven B-17s of the 407th Squadron participated in the mission; one turning back fifty miles west of Suderoog Island due to mechanical failure. The *Jägerleitoffiziers* (JLOs or GCI-controllers) in the 'Battle Opera Houses' did not yet know where the American Wing formation was headed. The B-17s and B-24s flew in the general direction of Germany. However, as they approached the German coast they flew in a north-easterly direction, skirting the Frisian Islands. They followed this general route as if making ready to attack either Wilhelmshaven or Bremen. During this part of the mission the combat crews reported several formations of enemy aircraft flying between the American formations and the German coast as if to protect these cities from attack. Very few enemy aircraft ventured to interfere with the mission during this period. Instead of attacking where the Germans anticipated, at 1145 the formation suddenly turned south for the base of the Danish Peninsula and the American formations flew on in the direction of Kiel. Five minutes later, when the Americans' destination became apparent, the German controllers scrambled about 125 fighters. Most of these were single-engined aircraft but there were some twin-engine fighters among them. Combat crews were hard put at times to fight off some of the more persistent enemy attackers. The attacks lasted over a period of about forty-five minutes.

Howard Hernan in the 'Hell's Angels' formation recalls:

> The fighter opposition was intense and the flak heavy. We flew at

> 32,000 feet in the high squadron, high group; the highest I had ever flown. Most of the 88mm flak was below us. The Germans did shoot up some 105s but Captain Ross C. Bales, Captain Campbell's roommate, flying in *F.D.R.'s Potato Peeler Kids,* was shot down twenty miles offshore. All of a sudden he started drifting out to the right, almost in a complete circle. With Captain Bales was Mark Mathis, whose brother Jack had been killed over Vegesack. Nine 'chutes came out of the *Potato Peeler*. Bales appeared to have all his engines turning over, although one or two could have been wind-milling. He came around and made a water landing in the midst of all the 'chutes. We never heard anything from them again.[2]

Also, *Hell's Angels* in the 91st and a Fortress in the 92nd flown by 1st Lieutenant Lowell Walker were lost. Walker's ship was last seen circling down under control toward Amrum Island with one engine out and a stabilizer shot off. All nine crew were rescued and taken into captivity. Kiel was bombed at 1205 with 'good' results.

At about the same time the 96th and 351st were approaching the airfield at Courtrai-Wevelghem in France. Just over twenty-five minutes later they returned east over Ypres to be met by *Luftwaffe* fighters, which became embroiled with the bombers' escorting fighters. Fifty Fortresses won through and bombed the hangars, dispersal areas, runways and workshops at the airfield and put it out of action. The B-17s then flew north and headed for the coast between Ostend and Dunkirk. By 1255 most of the German fighters that took part in the first attack were forced to land and refuel. So far the overall plan seemed to be working, with the German fighter controllers at full stretch having to meet the incoming B-17 and B-26 raids. At 1300 hours German radar picked up the 94th and 95th, led by Brigadier General Fred Anderson, a fiercely aggressive air leader, near Ostend, heading for the Ford and General Motors plant at Antwerp. Captain Franklin 'Pappy' Colby in the 94th (at forty-one years of age the oldest pilot in the 8th Air Force) recalls:

> At the IP we were supposed to meet our supporting fighters but we were 20 minutes late. Finally, we saw about 30 fighters at 2 o'clock and I heaved a sigh of relief, thinking our friends had waited for us. Suddenly they attacked and at about the same time heavy flak started exploding dead ahead. We took violent evasive action and then I discovered that the leading three-ship element of our low squadron had drifted left, out of the group formation. I decided to stay with the group and it's lucky I did because flak started exploding right

> behind him where we should have been. I heard our guns hammering and saw little white smoke puffs just ahead of the left wingman. They were exploding cannon shells from German fighters. We dumped our load of five 1,000lb bombs as carefully as possible and swung out over the coast for home. Flak followed us until we were out of range but the fighters eased up. My tail gunner saw a B-17 that hit the ground and exploded. There were no parachutes. Later, recon' photos showed a heavy bomb concentration on the Ford factory and the nearby canal locks and the western end of the General Motors plant also caught it.

The 'Flying Eightballs' meanwhile, were having problems. They should have avoided the Friesian Islands but the constant zigzag course they had been forced to adopt caused them to stray and they overflew the islands at 19,000 feet to be greeted by sporadic bursts of flak. Jim O'Brien's attention was diverted momentarily to *Victory Ship* flown by 1st Lieutenant 'Tommie' Holmes, which took a burst of flak and appeared to have flames coming out of the bomb bay. Despite this Holmes managed to maintain height and re-cross the sea to England and he put down safely at Shipdham.

Suddenly, two explosions rocked *The Rugged Buggy*. 'The manifold pressure on the two left engines dropped to 15 psi' recalls Jim O'Brien 'and there was a sudden drag to the left which Howell and I struggled to correct. I had thoughts of feathering the two left engines but that would have been a sure give-away to German fighters waiting to come in for the kill.'

The interphone was put out of action in the blast and all communication with the four men in the rear of the aircraft was lost. Unbeknown to O'Brien, flak had also blown a hole in the tail, knocking Dick Castillo out of his rear turret and amputating his foot in the process. Three crew members in the tail came to his aid and quickly realizing the extent of his injuries, pushed him out of the aircraft, pulling the ripcord on his parachute pack for him before they, too, bailed out. Sergeant Van Owen drowned in Kiel Bay although he was wearing a Mae West. Despite the crew losses *The Rugged Buggy* continued to the target. Crews had been briefed to bomb from 21,000 feet but the constant zigzagging now brought them over Heligoland Bay at 18,000 feet. As they turned into the strong wind for bombing they were down to 160mph – almost stalling speed.

Robert Fisher continues:

> Just a short time after entering Germany there was a cry on

interphone, 'Fighters at 2 o'clock high!' They were coming in from the sun and as soon as I could see the first one and began firing when I felt he was something less than a thousand yards range, I realized there were others coming on behind him, groups of threes, sometimes six in a stream making a high frontal attack on the formation. After the first frontal assault the enemy broke up to attack from all quarters and it seemed as if all the guns of our plane were firing at the same time and all the gunners were calling off the positions of the attacking aircraft I fired on the nearest attacking aircraft, jumping from it to the next one in line as I felt the need to deal with as many enemy as possible; a matter of 'share the wealth'. There were Me 109s, FW 190s and at one time I couldn't believe my eyes to see what I still believe to have been a Ju 87 Stuka dive bomber and thought at the moment, 'They're putting up everything they've got.' I also fired at this aircraft and he turned away without completing his attack, which was alright with me! The very concentrated enemy aircraft attacks and flak from 88mm guns continued to the IP, the target and even beyond. I remember nothing, much more than turning from one gun to the other and firing at aircraft making head on and quartering attacks: the action was so rapid that I had no time to watch a fighter after he had either broken off his attack after a partial pass or flew past the traverse of my guns in passing through the bomber formation or underneath our plane's belly. The fighter attacks, the fleecy black puffs of smoke from flak floating past the aircraft, the incessant interphone chatter of gunners calling off positions of attacking fighters, the sound of bursting flak, 'crump,' near the plane and even the gravel-like noise of shrapnel hitting and piercing our plane's thin skin and the sound and feel of all the guns of our plane firing, was my world.

Just after the turn at the IP, the flak intensified and continued through the bomb run over the city of Kiel. By this time our faster speed at altitude had allowed our formation to overtake the last group of B-17s who were flying just ahead and below us by several thousand feet. The explosions, smoke and dust of the bombing done by the B-17s could be clearly seen in the bright sunlight of this almost cloudless day; much of the dockside area of Kiel was covered with a pall of smoke rising thousands of feet into the air. At the bombs away point the bombardier released our bombs as did all the other bombardiers in the group. We were surprised to see the incendiary bombs drop out of the bomb bays and then, not drop as the general

> purpose high explosive bombs, but each package of incendiaries to come apart and thousands of individual sticks of incendiaries filled the air almost like a cloud of confetti and floated down onto the target area. Indeed, some of this deadly confetti floated down through the group of B-17s we had overtaken and some of the individual sticks actually bounced off the surfaces of a plane.

In *Spare Ball* in the 351st Jack Howell sat at a table in the nose behind the bombardier and he would man the left cheek gun when they came under attack. He wrote:

> The sky was dense with Fortresses and Liberators as we maintained tight formations heading toward our targets, all trailing the tell-tale contrails in the bright blue sky, now being blackened by airborne flak explosions all around us. The ones you don't hear are the ones you have to worry about. The shock of a near miss would rock the airplane and bang me against a wall. There were a few short and very tense minutes after we cleared the ground fire and scanned the skies for attacking *Luftwaffe*. There! Jerries at 5 o'clock! Wave upon wave of Messerschmitt 109s and Focke-Wulf 190s peeled out of formation as they began their attack. There must have been hundreds of them. We were so slow they were flying circles around us, buzzing us like a swarm of bees. The fliers of the Third *Reich* were not new to this game, as they brought with them the sharpened skills of years of experience. The roar of those four big radial engines being pushed to their limits was not enough to drown out the screaming engines of the German fighters as they made pass after pass. Turbulence would sometimes toss the mighty Fortress about, slamming the two waist gunners together. More screaming enemy attackers brought more bullets pinging through the airplane. Swinging my Browning .50 calibre machine gun into action and leading the attacker a little would sometimes bring smoke and fire as a Bf 109 or FW 190 spiralled away, a kill we would later display by painting a white swastika on the nose. At every chance, the Jerries would attack from the front and rake down the back of the airplane yielding devastating results. Out of 200 bombers going out, about one third would not return, a grim record of which was kept on an outside wall of the mess hall. This brought about a very impersonal atmosphere at the air base, causing people to keep to themselves so as not to lose too many friends. Even with such a high loss rate, many Fortresses and Liberators returned to base with heavy damage: missing an engine,

> half the tail section gone, heavy wing damage and we wondered at how they could still fly. Our bombers earned the reputation of being sturdy and reliable aircraft.

Jim O'Brien continues:

> The bomb bay doors opened and the 44th let go its clusters of matchstick incendiaries. The clusters did not hold together for more than 200 feet. As soon as they hit the slipstream they were all over the sky in a negative trajectory, flying back through the formation and bouncing off wings and propellers. Nothing worked better for the Germans at this point, as the formation scattered to avoid these missiles. Meanwhile, we had dropped our own clusters of bombs and had plenty of trouble. The cockpit smelled of gasoline and our unspoken thoughts as Howell and I looked at each other were of fire and explosion. We had now separated from the rest of the group after leaving the target and I noticed at least two other stragglers off to the right.

One was Captain John W. 'Swede' Swanson from Warsaw, Missouri in *Wicked Witch*. Flak had damaged the No. 2 engine before the target was reached but Swanson maintained formation and salvoed his bombs. Enemy fighters making head-on attacks finished off *Wicked Witch*. Swanson and three others were the only survivors from the nine-man crew. *The Rugged Buggy* was set on fire after incendiary bullets ignited the intense petrol fumes. Ralph Ernst, the radio operator, managed to put out the fire temporarily between extinguishers but he and the rest of the crew had to bail out as the B-24 would explode at any moment. Ernst and his pilot both landed in farmyards and were captured. Mac McCabe was killed when his torn parachute failed to work properly.

The cargoes of incendiaries had required a shorter trajectory and a two-mile longer bomb run than the B-17s. Flying a scattered formation, the B-24s were exposed to fighter attack. Three more Liberators, all in the 67th Squadron, which brought up the rear of the formation, were lost in quick succession. The first to go down was Lieutenant William Roach and his replacement crew flying in *Annie Oakley*. There were only two survivors.

Miss Delores was hit by flak over the target. One burst hit 'Gibby' Wandtke and he fell from the top turret with shrapnel wounds. John Susan, the radio operator, manned the turret. Unfortunately, Susan's guns would not fire between the twin fins and tail gunner Roy L. Klingler was dead. Six German fighters continued to fire at the ailing bomber from the rear. Two other gunners, George R. Millhausen and Richard Cate, were killed. Just after Haldon R. Hayward the bombardier, dropped his bombs, Bob Bishop spotted a fighter boring in and shouted at Hayward to dock. A shell exploded on the Plexiglas nose and Hayward was struck in the face by fragments. Bishop had the paint stripped from his steel helmet by the blast. As *Miss Delores* fell behind, the left wing caught fire. Brown gave the bail-out order but, unknown to the crew, the flak bursts had also knocked out the intercom. Wandtke, although wounded, made his way aft via the open bomb bay at the height of the battle to warn the gunners to abandon ship. Bishop parachuted into the sea and was hauled aboard a Danish trawler. A fisherman pulled John L. Susan by his shroud lines from the sea after going under for about ten feet. Brown, Westbrook, Hayward, Wandtke and August Ullrich, the assistant radio operator-gunner, were also rescued.

The third 67th Squadron Liberator lost was *Little Beaver*, which was shot down after leaving the target. The flight deck became a mass of flames when a 20mm cannon shell exploded in the nose and ignited the hydraulic fluid accumulators and George Phillips and Wilborn were killed. Only four men from the eleven-man crew survived after three explosions rocked the ship. The aircraft went into a flat spin. Mike Denny, the engineer, put on his parachute and then tried to extinguish the flames but his efforts were in vain. Denny could not open the bomb bay doors, so he bailed out through one of the waist windows. Tom Bartmess bailed out of the aircraft, followed about three minutes later by 'Chubby' Hill the bombardier. Bartmess landed in the water but got tangled in the shrouds of his parachute and drowned. Hill landed on dry land suffering from blows on the forehead caused by the opening of his parachute and the landing. He also had a bruised back and was in shock. He joined Dale Glaubitz, the assistant engineer, and Charles Forehand, one of the waist gunners, as the only other survivors.

Robert Fisher continues:

> After the target our group got some relief from fighter attacks, but not so for the B-17s flying at their lower altitude. By the time we exited the German coast some of the realization sank through of what I had heard on interphone about the number of fighter attacks from all quarters; fighters shot down and losses suffered by our own group and the B-17s. It had been heavy. The floor of the nose compartment was littered with ammunition belt linkage and expended .50-calibre casings from rounds fired by the bombardier and myself. The air smelled of burnt gunpowder and scorched machine gun oil. The formation consolidated and among the survivors there was visible

damage from flak and fighters. And the long flight back across the North Sea was a time of realization, at least in part, of what we had experienced in such a short time and a time of recognition that for others the total experience had come to an end. Over the North Sea the planes were checked for damage; ours had some minor flak damage, but the aircraft on whose left wing we were now flying did not come off so easily; there were some obvious large holes in it and the left landing gear tyre looked to have been gashed by either flak or fighter fire.

The much reduced formation let down and approached the base before breaking up to enter the landing circuit. The aircraft with the damaged tyre waited until the last in case his landing might close the runway. When our aircraft taxied back into the dispersal site and the engines were cut, there was a great feeling of relief to be at last back on firm and friendly soil – six hours and five minutes, take-off to touchdown; life to death to life. The crew crawled out of the aircraft and soon we were working to retrieve the parachutes, other items of personal equipment and the guns out of the plane, the guns to be taken to the squadron armament shop for cleaning and the other gear to be returned to lockers until the next flight. The escape kits, which had been signed for because they contained scarce items of money, had to be returned to intelligence to be issued on the next mission. The crew often worked in pairs on this phase, one man inside the aircraft handing out the heavy and damageable items to another standing by outside. It was while this was going on that the last plane landed. The pilot made what looked like a normal approach westward into the early afternoon sunlight, but at the point of touchdown held his left wing high to prevent that wheel from touching; the right wheel touched and with what airspeed he had he held the left wing up and that wheel off the runway as long as possible. Finally, with the loss of airspeed and lift on the left wing he could hold it up no longer; it came down; there was a loud flapping noise from the tyre, smoke and dust rose from the gear and the aircraft began to turn to the left; a great surge of power applied to the left engines held the plane on the runway until it could be braked to a stop. Long before all this was completed the ambulances stationed along the runway were racing to give aid if they were needed: They were! The plane had several wounded, one of which would die the next day and one was a gunner from our crew who had been 'loaned' to that crew in order to gain experience with an experienced crew. He shot down one enemy fighter and received a head wound.

The truck to take us and our gear to debriefing arrived; we put our gear and guns into the bed of the truck and climbed in to sit on the pull down benches. There we sat facing the ones opposite, two lines of young, but tired faces, at least temporarily lined by the sweat and grime patterns made by the hours of wearing oxygen masks, goggles, helmets and earphones, each making its characteristic impressions. At the armament shop pairs of crewmen carried each of the guns into the shop. Then we were off to the debriefing area where the rest of the gear was off-loaded for storage.

Outside the briefing room there were groups of crewmen, either waiting to go in for debriefing or waiting for transportation having completed the process. Before we could go inside, we all had our attention taken by a lone B-24 circling the base a little higher than traffic pattern altitude with its gear up; it obviously wasn't ready to land. Then on one more pass over the base men began to jump from it and almost immediately after each was in the air, clear of the airplane, his parachute was seen to blossom, except for one. He fell well past the others and his chute did not open; he was much below traffic pattern altitude and there was a low, but audible gasp from some of the watchers – and then his chute opened; and the next thing he was on the ground – last out, first down. I heard later that before the war he had made some jumps in civilian life and did what he did this day as a matter of show off. I couldn't understand it, especially following such a mission. The aircraft turned and left the base. We learned later that the pilot had elected rather than crash-land his plane, to jump his crew and head the plane out over the North Sea having jumped from it himself after making sure it would clear land and human habitation. The story told later was that after his co-pilot had jumped and before jumping himself the pilot realized a great kidney pressure and was attempting to figure out how to fly the aircraft by himself and at the same time use the relief tube when he suddenly thought, 'What the hell!' He stood up, relieved himself against the instrument panel, turned around and stepped out of the aircraft through the open bomb bay doors.[3]

In debriefing the crew sat down at a table headed by a debriefing officer, one from intelligence or a group officer conscripted temporarily for this duty. With his form in hand, he asked questions covering all phases of the flight from take-off to landing, deviations

> from briefed mission, flak action, fighter opposition, fighter kills claimed and confirmed for other gunners or aircraft, bombing conditions and results and losses to our own force. He directed most of the questions to the pilot, with the other members of the crew answering or supplying information if the pilot did not know. The room was buzzing with comments made from all the debriefings in progress: claims of fighters shot down, descriptions of our own losses; the fight was being refought – verbally. Someone said, 'There were so many fighters, they were squabbling over who would have first chance at us!' And someone else; 'they had to queue up; there was a waiting list of those eager to attack.'
>
> After de-briefing we went outside to again wait for transportation by shuttle trucks back to the group mess site and the living sites where it had all begun early that morning. A Red Cross mobile van had parked outside the briefing room and the Red Cross lady was dispensing coffee and doughnuts. Several of the gunners went and got some, bringing several extra doughnuts back for others in the crew; they were heavy and doughy, but helped pass the time.
>
> A truck rolled up and we all climbed on board to be jostled for a few more minutes. 'And that was number six,' I thought, 'with nineteen to go.'[4]

Bill Cameron would miss 'George' Phillips and Bob Brown, who was one of his best friends. He once woke old George and 'Gentleman' Jim Devinney at 5am for a practice mission, not realizing they had a couple of girls in the sack with them and was met by a barrage of .45 gunshots over his head in the dark. Cameron hit the floor of the hallway and crawled out! He was the type who got into trouble trying to do the right thing; like getting transportation for the girls at 4am when all his buddies went to bed and left them there.

> A favourite stunt was to drop .45 calibre ammo' in the little potbellied stove, secretly of course. That used to stir things up. I once let go a smoke bomb ... almost ruined our clothes and bedding with the stench. On one occasion it was decided to strip me of my clothes.The girls thought it was very funny but I got as mad as hell (this about 3am) and almost had a fist fight with Bob Brown. He would have killed me. They were quite a bunch and when they were gone there was no one who ever quite took their places.

Spare Ball made it back to Polebrook but the 351st lost *Annihilator* and another Fortress that both went down at Courtrai. In four hours VIII

Bomber Command had attacked four targets, losing eleven aircraft and claiming sixty-seven fighters shot down. Not all of the bombing was accurate but for the first time Americans had shown that they were capable of mounting multiple attacks on a given day. The 'Flying Eightballs' were awarded a Distinguished Unit Citation for their part in the Kiel raid; it was the first made to an 8th Air Force Group.

On 15 May Eaker sent the 1st Wing to Wilhelmshaven while fifty-nine B-17s of the 4th Wing were allocated Emden. At Wilhelmshaven thick cloud obscured the target and the Fortresses were forced to seek alternative targets at Heligoland, Dune and Wangerooge Island. Heligoland was covered in only 4/10ths cloud and the flak was inaccurate. However, numerous enemy fighters put in an appearance and they shot down six Fortresses – three of these in the 306th, a B-17 in the 92nd, one in the 303rd and *Spare Ball* in the 351st – as Jack Howell recalls:

> Flying in close formation was our best defensive strategy, but enemy fighters would swoop right through us, prompting our pilots to jockey the big bombers around, trying to avoid their fire. This would weaken the integrity of our defence and scatter the airplanes making them easy prey. During this tussle over the target zone we ended up under another Fortress unloading his bombs and one of the 500 pound monsters knocked the number four engine clean off the wing. Fortunately, the bomb had not fused itself and did not explode. Things really started to get worse after we dropped our bombs and turned for home when the attacking pass of a FW 190 caused our number two engine to catch fire. It was just a matter of time now because we could not hold our altitude and we were no longer keeping up with the squadron each now two tons lighter, running wide-open throttles back to Jolly Old England. They were already too far ahead to be of any help; all they could do was watch. The rest of our luck ran out when five FW 190s jumped us. They cut us to shreds. Bullets ripped into my left side and through my leg. It felt like being hit with a sledgehammer. The co-pilot signalled back to jump before the airplane began to spin. It was all I could do to get myself out. The crippled airplane was slowly rolling onto its back beginning its death spiral. As if to seal our fate, we were no longer over dry land but over the frigid waters of the North Sea.
>
> The tail of the great airplane passed by as I pulled the ripcord. With a sudden jerk the parachute opened, arresting my plummet toward the surface. Swinging gently side to side, floating slowly earthward,

I could see my squadron in the distance heading for home in the smoke filled skies with the Germans in hot pursuit. Besides my own I saw only four other parachutes. Within seconds, it seemed the mighty bomber crashed into the sea. All the noise of battle in the air had faded and it had become unbelievably quiet. With a splash I hit the water and it was deathly cold. It was not easy unhooking my harness and being a bit disoriented I was not sure which way the shoreline was. Our flight suits were designed to keep us warm at altitude; not in the drink. I began to pray for someone to find me. Ending up in a German PoW camp would be better than becoming a human ice cube. I swam as best I could but with my side and leg being torn up and all of that clothing I had on becoming heavier, it was hard enough just to keep my head above water. From where I was the North Sea looked as big as the Atlantic Ocean and in vain I strained my eyes to spot an airplane or boat... anything! The freezing cold water was stinging and it was becoming harder to move my arms and legs. I noticed myself going numb from the cold and realized I did not have much time left. I had to really work to keep my head above water but it was harder than ever. The next thing I knew I couldn't feel my arms or legs any more. I was still moving them, wasn't I? It seemed strange how I noticed the water above my head as I slid beneath the surface. It almost looked surreal. My lungs ached for breath. I had to inhale.

'Someone tell Mom I love her.'[5]

In the 305th *Old Bill*, immortalized by artist Bruce Bairnsfather and flown by Captain Bill Whitson, was hit by a swarm of FW 190s that came diving and rolling in for a head-on attack. Whitson was wounded in both legs and the oxygen line to the flight deck was severed. Whitson then struggled to the rear of the ship to assess damage and gather some 'walk-around' oxygen bottles. On his return to the cockpit, he found co-pilot Harry Holt in the early stages of oxygen starvation and used one of the 'walk-around' bottles to revive him. Holt recovered and Whitson again left the cockpit in order to receive medical attention to stem the flow of blood from his legs before he returned shortly after to regain control of the ship. Sensing a kill the fighters reformed for another head-on attack, sending 20mm shells through the nose and inside the fuselage, causing explosions throughout the interior of the ship. Navigator Douglas R. Venable Jr was killed and Holt, bombardier Robert Barrall, top turret gunner Albert Haymon and radio operator Fred Bewak were wounded. Whitson, now flying on three engines, no hydraulics and a warped wing, had little chance of keeping up with the formation. Now an easy target and limping, the fighters pressed on with their attacks and Whitson was forced to dive for cover towards the clouds 5,000 feet below.

With Whitson exhausted and near the end of his tether, top turret gunner Albert Haymon already wounded in the head and arm, hauled himself into the co-pilot's seat, replacing Harry Holt who had been taken away to receive attention to his wounds. Breaking out below the clouds, Haymon noticed a lone Me 210 fighter banking around to attack and he alerted the rest of the crew. Also receiving medical treatment, Robert Barrall hurriedly clambered back into the nose in order to man the cheek guns and as the fighter closed in he was able to score hits in an engine which exploded, sending the fighter hurtling into the sea below. On their eventual return to Chelveston, Whitson now without brakes or flaps, overran the end of the runway and ground-looped the plane on the grass and as they came to a halt Whitson collapsed on his control column suffering from exhaustion due to blood loss. Bill Whitson and Robert Barrall were later awarded Distinguished Service Crosses, and all the rest on the crew Silver Stars and eight of the ten, Purple Hearts. *Old Bill* never flew again.

On 16 May the Fortress groups were stood down while all available B-24Ds in the 'Flying Eightballs' and the 'Travelling Circus' were secretly flown to Davidstowe Moor in the West Country. Eaker planned to send the B-24s to Bordeaux while the 1st Wing bombed Kiel and the 4th Wing went to Lorient.[6] At 0900 on 17 May Colonel Leon Johnson, General James Hodges and the crew of the revamped *Suzy-Q* led twenty-one B-24s, followed closely by eighteen B-24Ds in the 'Travelling Circus'. The Liberators flew a 700-mile arc over the Atlantic to minimize the chances of enemy detection. Four Liberators were forced to abort with mechanical troubles. Despite four new Twin Wasps, *Suzy-Q* had one engine stopped when the formation started climbing to bombing altitude. To counteract the fall behind in schedule, Ed Mikolowski, the lead navigator, skilfully prepared a new course, which bypassed the original curved route. Mikolowski's alternative course brought the formation to the Bay of Biscay almost on schedule and over Bordeaux at 1228. *Avenger II* piloted by 1st Lieutenant Ray L. Hilliard was forced to head for Spain after developing engine trouble shortly before the attack began. Bordeaux had hitherto been left untouched by the 8th Air Force and the German defences had become complacent. The Americans could even lapse jamming of German-controlled radio. Thirty or forty barrage balloons had been positioned over the 12 feet thick concrete U-boat pens on the tideless Gironde Estuary to prevent a low-level attack but these did not deter the two Liberator groups bombing from 22,000 feet. Mikolowski said later:

> Suddenly, through the haze and mist we saw a break in the coastline. Although it wasn't very plain, it stood out well enough to be recognized as the estuary that curves crazily from the Bay of Biscay to Bordeaux, 30 miles inland. When we reached our IP on the bombing run a few minutes later, it was the bombardier's baby. 'Gentleman' Jim DeVinney took over. It was the finest piece of precision bombing I ever hope to see. The lock gates at Basin No. 1 collapsed and water gushed out of the basin into the river. There were hits on the bottleneck of the railroad yards and strikes on the Matford aero-engine factory. It was beautiful!

The only casualties during the attack were two crewmen slightly wounded and Tech Sergeant Harry C. Hogan, left waist gunner in Captain John Diehl's *Black Jack* who was sucked out of an open window after his parachute had accidentally opened. He was thrown against the tailplane and pitched into the sea with his parachute in shreds. Six hours after the raid a photo-reconnaissance aircraft brought back pictures revealing that the 480-yard-long pier and two U-boats, which had been in the port during the attack, had vanished. Liberator crews were jubilant, attributing much of their success to the fact that they had not had to fly behind the slower Fortresses.

Fifty-five Fortresses in the 4th Wing, which had been dispatched to Lorient, pounded the U-boat pens and the power station, which served them at fifteen-minute intervals. Bombing was described as 'excellent' but six B-17s, including *Midnight*, piloted by Ed Spevak, the 94th's first combat loss, failed to return when it was hit by flak at the target. An engine caught fire and the B-17 fell out of formation. Fighters attacked and set another engine on fire. *Midnight* was engulfed in flame and smoke in the tail and Spevak gave the order to bail out. 'Pappy' Colby's crew counted eight parachutes. Walter Minor, *Midnight*'s tail gunner, was hit just as he was leaving the burning aircraft. He floated down and saw a wing tear free from the fuselage and continue separately to earth. He and another crew member were picked up by the French Underground and were returned to England via the Pyrenees, Spain and Gibraltar. Ed Spevak and Don Nichols, the co-pilot, also evaded capture and were returned to England.

1st Lieutenant Arthur H. Allen Jr, the pilot of *Hi Lo Jack* in the 333rd Squadron wrote:

> I can't tell you what force is driving me to write this, because I really

don't know. Perhaps it is the desire to let somebody really know just what is happening around me. So I'm writing down a few impressions this godless war has left upon me. You wonder why I said godless. Well, there doesn't seem to be any rhyme or reason as to how men die. Our good, clean-living ones die while our scum continue to live. The pick of our country's young men and the cream of German youth seek to destroy one another five miles up in the blue ozone. Why does God continue to let this thing go on – why should men die – why should the thousands before us have died – and for what? We still don't know, but these are a few of the reasons why this war seems Godless to me.

We haven't been in England long, about six weeks and in that time we have been on seven raids over German owned and occupied land. And it isn't at all what we expected. Back in the States we read newspaper stories of Flying Fortresses making raids and always at the bottom was the phrase, 'None of our bombers were lost.' Of course we had read of B-17s being all shot up and coming home on two engines, but we really thought that these were isolated cases. We didn't have the slightest idea of the nature of this theatre of operations. We never dreamed that after six weeks of operations, we'd have one squadron with 72 per cent loss of flying personnel, some twenty airplanes completely washed out and more close friends killed than we can count on our fingers and toes. We could see the B-17, which we were told was so sturdily built that it could stand anything, fall apart before our eyes. And there were many more incidents that will be imprinted on our minds forever. We weren't told that we were in the 'Big Leagues' of aerial combat, that this theatre is the toughest, most deadly, most heavily defended area in the world. Compared to this theatre, the African campaign and the war in Japan are in the bush leagues. All of these things and more we are finding out very quickly. Our first two missions were warm ups over targets of minimum military importance with little flak or fighter resistance. But since those first two targets, we've had no picnic. Our first really tough mission was the Lorient run. Our target was the powerhouse and it was our job to knock it out. We did knock it out, but for a time most of us felt that we wouldn't survive the battle.

I suppose every pilot figures he has the best crew in the world, but I am sure that I do. And that, coupled with a lot of luck, is the main reason for returning from our missions safely. It's not right to say that anyone man on the crew is more important than another, because we are a team and as a team every man has a vital job to do. Ken [2nd Lieutenant Harold K. Cahill] is my co-pilot and to me more important than any other man on the crew. For seven months we've flown together and as pilot and co-pilot we've learned to think the same and simultaneously, a combination that really counts in combat. When the going is toughest and fighters are buzzing all over the place, the sky black with flak and the formation whiplashing all over the sky, I don't have to tell Ken what to do – he knows and he does it. We've become such a coordinated team that we even duck in rhythm. It is my honest opinion that Ken is the coolest co-pilot in the business. And if God sees fit to let him get it one of these days, I just pray that I get it with him, because I don't care to face death with any other man on that seat beside me.

Down in the nose are Greg and Carl. You have to speak of them together, because just as Ken and I are a team, so are they. Greg and Ken were the first two men assigned to my crew at Tucson, Arizona, back in the early days of September. Greg is Irish and as a navigator there isn't a better one in the group. He makes mistakes, as we all do, but he has one fine characteristic that most navigators don't have. He will admit when he doesn't know where he is while there is still time for us to work the problem out together. I think we'd follow him to hell if he should plot a course that way. But, even more important to the crew is the fact that he is really the nucleus of the crew. To the officers he's a pal and a companion, but to the enlisted men he is a big brother. He's the type of guy that if we were to lose him, it would be very difficult for the crew to function properly.

Carl of course is the bombardier. He's the guy that drops the bombs. One of the greatest disappointments to us all is the fact that we haven't had the opportunity to drop any bombs with our own bombsight. We are required to toggle them out upon seeing the leader's bombs fall. For six months we practised that particular job and now we have to depend on the leader to hit the target. Carl is awfully proud and he's good. With the .50 calibre guns he is deadly and as long as they work, we don't have to worry much about nose attacks.

The oldest man on the crew is the top turret gunner. He is Albert Herndon, a World War I veteran, forty-four years of age. Most of the guys call him 'Pappy'. I doubt if many crews would accept him for combat because he's so hard of hearing, but we wouldn't part with him at any price. Ken and I have worked out a signal system of letting him know what we want when he doesn't hear. It works perfectly and the old boy can really fire his twin barrelled guns.

Keith Muir is our radio man and if the officers have a favorite, I guess he would be it. He's just a happy, carefree, hard working, sincere man and there isn't a better radio operator anywhere. Perhaps it is humorous when I say that each man is the best, but I've flown with a lot of crews and none of them measure up to my bunch.

Tommy Wagner is the tail gunner – we call him Wag. If the Germans confine their attacks to our tail, we'll come through our twenty-five missions in grand style. Wag is the type of guy who really throws lead in a fight. He didn't have much respect for the German fighters at first, but that was before they started shooting at him in earnest. I noticed that after one raid, he altered the sign painted on the tail of our aircraft. It read, 'Shoot, you're faded,' but with black paint he covered the word 'shoot,' making it read, 'You're faded.'

And there's Brown, our armorer gunner, Miller our engineer and Hobbs the ball turret operator. I could 'blow the breeze' about them too, but suffice to say they are worth their weight in gold. So you can see with a crew like mine you wouldn't be afraid to walk into the very best 'Jerry' has, would you? But even that may not be enough someday. I'll tell you why.

Contrary to what you may believe, or what you've read or been told, Germany has the very best pursuit planes there are and the very best pilots and the best aerial organization and defenses. All in all they are good. This we found out when we went to Lorient. That was the day we lost our first ship. And as I said before, the day we almost lost our ship and our lives. We had a bad engine, acting-up all the way and at one point I considered turning back. But Ken, said, 'Let's go on' and we did. The fighters hit us at the Initial Point. For fifty-five minutes there was hot lead flying everywhere at our altitude, 23,000 feet. I think my heart gave a little flutter when our oil line was hit over the target. I think it was enemy fighter fire that severed the line. Both Ken and I knew that it was only a matter of time until we lost the engine. Being a little inexperienced at that time, we decided not to feather the propeller so we could utilize the power as long as possible. Looking back, it was lucky we did this because it kept the fighters from concentrating on us for another fifteen minutes.

About twenty miles from the Channel we lost our second engine and about that time the first engine prop ran away. As any combat pilot knows, you can't stay in formation at 23,000 feet on two engines. So we fell behind. And then it was a merry time. The enemy fighters flocked in for the kill. We'll never know how we got out of that fight alive or how many fighters were firing at us. At one time there were eight FW 190s (the best fighter this war has produced) diving on our tail and numerous attacks from every direction. They scored many hits, but luckily they didn't hit any vital areas. We limped across the Channel with our gas rapidly disappearing and finally landed at an RAF station in southwest England.

It's true that the B-17 can take a lot of punishment because we proved it on this leg of our flight. We had a total of 169 holes in old *Hi Lo Jack* not counting the BB holes from unknown sources. There were .30 calibre and 20mm holes, large flak holes and even some .50 calibre damage coming from ships in our own formation. One 20mm cannon shell burst between the guns in the tail, bending one gun and rendering the other inoperative. The barrage exploded ammunition, blew a portion of the tail off of the ship and threw Wag up against the tail wheel. One small piece of armor plate was responsible for saving Wag's life. Both of the life rafts were shot out. We wouldn't have had a ghost of a chance in the water. All of our radio equipment was damaged, including our emergency set. The oxygen system was shot out but luckily did not catch fire. The tail elevators and rudder controls were shot away and there were gaping holes all over the ship. The only area that wasn't hit was the cockpit and the hydraulic system. And with this damage, not one man had a scratch. God had to be with us on that day. I believe that after that raid, we were veterans and it had an odd psychological effect upon us.

On the morning of the 17th George Rawlings, a bombardier in the 96th, visited Group Headquarters to ask Colonel Archie Old if he could attend the funeral of his pilot, Captain Derrol W. Rogers who had been killed four days earlier returning from Lorient when the crew had to bail out near Kings Lynn. Rogers had died of overexposure in the North Sea. Rawlings was thrown a curve. The CO told him that he was to get into flying clothes and report immediately to briefing because he was to fly in place of influenza-stricken Bob McGuinnis on 1st Lieutenant Louis Haltom's *Boot Hill* crew who had been grounded by the flight surgeon.

I did not know any of the *Boot Hill* crew personally. However, I had seen the officers around the club. Nor did I know Captain William Carnahan who flying with us as observer took a position between

> the pilot and co-pilot... It is my recollection that when we crossed the French Coast we were tail-end to a long string of aircraft and there were no friendly fighters around. Shortly after entering France we encountered yellow-nosed Focke Wulfs. At one point in firing at them, my gun froze but I was able to become operational again by use of a small bottle of kerosene that a number of bombardiers carried just for that purpose. If I recall properly, we were hit by flak just after we turned onto the IP. Our pilot was determined to remain on course although we were falling behind. As soon as I dropped the bombs, we turned to intercept the main formation, which had already turned for England. As we cut across the circle, we were attacked by a number of fighters.
>
> I remember one engine really brewing up a storm and that another one was out. About the same time, my ammo box was hit and one of the incendiary rounds began to glow. We were surely hit in other places because Haltom rang the bailout-bell. I landed in a tall tree, which collapsed my chute and I fell fifteen feet into a rock fence. Later I found out I had some banged up ribs. Three of us who had bailed out of the nose hatch, navigator Baily Lovin, Captain Carnahan and I landed in a town garrisoned by the Germans and we were captured at once. We were held in a large room in the jail overnight and then taken to St-Brieuc and placed on a train for Frankfurt. The train stopped en route at a Focke Wulf fighter base and we were served lunch in the officer's mess... One of the Germans told us that it was he who had shot us down. Much later in *Stalag Luft* III I was joined by two of my original crew, Norvile Gorse and Joe Hudson. I must say Lou Haltom did one hell of a job of keeping *Boot Hill* in the air and stable until we all got out.[7]

On 18 May 55 B-17s of the 4th Wing were detailed to attack U-boat pens at Flensburg on the Danish coast. There was a two hour delay and Arthur H. Allen and his crew sat on the grass around their Fortress while waiting. Allen wrote:

> That's when it hit me. My thoughts began to wonder about dying and I was, honest to God, afraid. It's a hard thought realizing that those men up there in the sky are really shooting lead with the intention of destroying you and your plane. But it's true, we weren't just playing a game like we Americans do back in the States, where you win or lose and gather around a table in some beer hall or soft drink fountain, laughing and talking about it. Over here they play

> for keeps and when a German bullet hits you in the right place, it's the end. You die and hopefully, you find peace with your maker. I couldn't help thinking of those three enemy fighter pilots that my crew had already shot down. They were confirmed victories and we know that there were several more that we could not legally claim. They died in the game of keeps. Were they afraid too, like I admit I was at the time? And the rest of my crew spread out on the grass, were they thinking the same thing? I don't know, but I believe they were because they were very quiet.

The 305th led sixty-eight Fortresses in the 1st Wing to the turbine engine building at Kiel. The Group, which had lost four aircraft on 17 May, suffered the loss of another four Forts. They included *Yo-Yo* and two others that were originals brought to England by the Group in October. This brought the Group's number of Forts lost since the beginning of the month to ten. Following this mission, fog and rain cloaked East Anglia and the Fens, preventing any missions being flown until 21 May when the 1st Wing target was Wilhelmshaven and the 4th Wing Emden. At Wilhelmshaven weather conditions hampered the formation and it was further disrupted by constant head-on attacks by enemy fighters. The Emden force also encountered heavy fighter opposition despite diversionary ruses at the coast. Twelve B-17s were lost on the two raids, the 1st Wing coming off worst with seven shot down. Four of them, including *Jersey Bounce*, which was ditched in the North Sea and *Desperate Journey* were from the 91st. Three were from the 306th, among them *Dearly Beloved* flown by Lieutenant Robert H. Smith. His seven gunners set a new record, downing eleven fighters before the B-17 was forced to ditch in the North Sea. All the crew was picked up by an ASR launch and returned to Thurleigh. 0There was no such luck for 1st Lieutenant Floyd J. Field's crew who ditched after being knocked out of the sky by fighters. One wing was burning badly and when the plane struck the water it split in half at the radio room. Fields and four of his crew drowned. Five men made it into the one good life raft that had popped from its storage bin. Only the co-pilot was unhurt. The tail gunner had a broken arm and a broken leg and the bombardier, a crushed right elbow. The engineer had a gunshot wound in the groin and the waist gunner was also injured. The men were in the North Sea for seven hours before the five survivors were picked up by a twin-engined German seaplane and flown to Heligoland where all were hospitalized.[8]

Arthur Allen wrote:

The Flensburg raid proved to be another tough one. As usual we were all shot to pieces, but they say we blew hell out of the target. Scotty [2nd Lieutenant Charles B. Scott on 1st Lieutenant Urban S. Adams' crew] got it – killed in action at his post, bending over the bombsight and it was the first time that we realized that death was among us. That night I slept pretty sound but I remember thinking just before I went to sleep that if Scotty had had a flak suit he might still be with us. But, as is the case so many times, we just didn't have enough of this equipment to go around.

The next mission to Germany was to Emden [on 21 May] and they really had a hot reception awaiting us. They tell us our intelligence system is good, but on this day somebody slipped up because the Germans knew exactly where we were going, our check points, climbing points, number of ships and estimated time of arrival. Why do I believe this? Because they met us fifty miles out to sea, fought us all the way to the target and left us five minutes before crossing the flak batteries. After clearing the flak area they met us again and fought us for a hundred miles out to sea, pursuing cripples right down to the water surface. It is obvious that the Germans have a good organization. Their attacks are systematic, starting at the lower flights and working up, but they aren't systematic enough to do what they did today without inside information. The FW 190 can only fight one hour and a half before it must refuel. On this day they fought us one hour and fifteen minutes, which indicates that they did not take off until the deadline and just made it home before running out of fuel.

Emden was a costly raid for us. Fat Mac [Marvin N. McGown] got it. A 20mm cannon burst in his stomach. Three other ships and their crew of ten men were lost also – Ecklund, Wetzel and Wieand. Our ship was badly shot up again. The flight controls in the tail were destroyed, there was a huge hole in the wing and the radio compartment had a hole in it big enough for a man to dive through. Greg got creased by a .30 calibre bullet and Miller became our first casualty when he got a slug in the place he usually uses for sitting. This won him the Purple Heart and a two-month rest in the hospital. This trip revealed several facts to me. The engines of the B-17 are a very vulnerable part and if the Germans can manage to set one on fire at an altitude above 5,000 feet, it is very likely that the crew will have to bail out. If this happens over water it is risky for the crew, because the average life span of a man in the freezing North Sea is around thirty minutes. Another impression was that if a bullet hits a wing brace in the right place it is likely to drop off. I saw it happen before my very eyes. Third, if they get a direct hit in the cockpit, there is about one chance in ten of the crew surviving. It is worthy to note that we don't give a tinker's damn about the ship if we can save the crew.

After this raid, the group's sixth, everybody went on a three-day bender to London. Sometimes I wished I drank – but I can't stand the taste of the stuff, so I had to be content to watch the rest. I remember one night in London during that three-day stand when 'Bank man' Greg, Captain Adams, 'Rondy' and 'Pie' were slowly getting tight and in walked [Lieutenant Charles B.] 'Chic' Harrison, a very close friend of Greg, a swell little bombardier named [Lieutenant Roland C.] McCoy – he'd had two close calls already – and Vanderhook [Max Hecox' co-pilot].

'Come on and get tight with us', urged Greg, who was pretty close to that point already. Chick, Mac and Van laughed and joked with us as we said 'some other time'.

The irony of the whole thing was that there wasn't going to be any other time for those three. The very next mission [29 May] they went hurdling to their death in a spinning bomber.

Can you imagine a more horrible death – a bombardier and a navigator pinned against the sides of their nose compartment, watching the earth come up to meet them, through the Plexiglas nose and powerless to save their lives? A lot of things must have passed through their minds before they made their final contact with the earth below.

Notes

1. According to *Stars & Stripes, Nudes, Names and Numbers,* by Andy Rooney, 5 August 1943, 'The men in one group are known as the "Ball Boys". Every Fortress in the group [sic] bears the name of some "ball" variation and Major Clinton F. Ball is their commanding officer. Back at their home station in El Paso, Texas, he named his Fort *Linda Ball* after his year-old daughter and the rest of the squadron followed in the ball tradition.' The 'Ball Boys' Squadron included *Linda Ball* (I and II), *Lucille Ball* (and *Lucille Ball II*) which were was named after a Hollywood star of the time, *Foul Ball, Crystal Ball, Cannon Ball, Screw Ball* (I and II), *Queen of the Ball, Onda Ball, Belle of the Ball, Silver Ball, Pin Ball, Spit Ball, High Ball, Pistol Ball, High Ball, Fire Ball* (I and II), *Snow Ball, Speed Ball, Victory Ball, Devil's Ball, Cue Ball, Sky Ball, Golden Ball, Bedlam Ball, Archie Ball, Fireball II, Lucky Ball, Slow Ball, Meat Ball/Major Ball* and *Eight Ball,*

which became *No Balls At All*. The second *Spare Ball* was lost on 6 August 1944.

2. All ten men in Captain Ross C. Bales' crew perished.
3. *Scrappy*, piloted by Lt John Y. Reed from Matamoras, Pennsylvania, had been badly damaged over the target but Reed nursed it back to Shipdham, where ten of the crew bailed out. *Scrappy* had to be shot down by RAF Spitfires. Adam Wygonik, the engineer/top-turret gunner, had been hit by 20mm cannon fire on the bomb run and badly wounded in the head, eyes and arms. Sergeant Alan Perry, the radio operator, put a parachute on Wygonik's harness and shoved him out of the aircraft while they were still over the shipyards. As he was bleeding profusely and without his oxygen supply, it is doubtful whether Wygonik would have survived the long flight back to England. German soldiers soon picked him up. Later, his right eye was removed at hospital in Vienna before he was eventually repatriated.
4. *Memories of a Mission – Kiel, Germany, 14 May 1943* by Lt Colonel R.L. Fisher writing in Vol 23 of the *2nd AD Journal*, June 1984. Alexander's crew had joined the 68th Squadron on 16 March 1943. Robert L. Fisher completed his tour on 9 November 1944.
5. Casey Howell – *In Honor of his Uncle, B-17 Combat Crewmen & Wingmen*, Vol 27 2008.
6. Eleven B-26 Marauders of the 322nd BG flew a diversionary mission to Haarlem and Ijmuiden to bomb targets they had completely missed three days before. None returned.
7. Co-pilot Forslund was killed by flak. The evadees were: Louis Holtom, gunners H. Marshall, Roy Martin, Glenn Wells, N. Loudenslager and W.C. Martin. Louis Haltom transferred to the 449th BG, 20th AF and flew B-29s against Japan Bob McGuinnis, whose influenza prevented him from getting shot down with his *Boot Hill* buddies on 17 May, was shot down and captured on 28 July. Post-war George Rawlings became a pilot and pulled tours of duty in Korea and Vietnam.
8. See *First Over Germany: A History of the 306th Bombardment Group* by Russell A. Strong (1982).

CHAPTER 5

To Hell and Back

We were escorted by Spitfires and we met no opposition. Since we flew at 28,000 to 30,000 feet the enemy couldn't have seen us unless we were giving off vapour trails. Bombing was perfect. We hit the ammunition dumps and blew the whole works to hell. The aiming point was a cemetery just south of the ammunition dumps. The best crack I heard about the raid was, 'the dead will rise tonight.'

Claude W. Campbell, raid on the Focke Wulf airfield at Beaumont

Bad weather throughout the latter part of May restricted deep-penetration missions with a layover of nearly a week. The lull gave Arthur H. Allen at Bury St Edmunds time for thought. He wrote:

> ...a few of the men cracked during this time. One flight commander said he just couldn't take any more and was grounded. After two raids he came back to fly again, just as I figured he would. You can't imagine how those men felt until you've been with them and come as close to death as they have. It works on your nerves – nobody wants to die so young – but you have the comfort of knowing that those who go with you feel the same way. Sometimes I feel as though I'd like to quit and get into something safe – anything – as long as I wouldn't have to face those mad men in the head-on attacks by FW 190s and the accurate flak batteries. But you pull yourself together by telling yourself if you quit, somebody else will take your place and he wants to live just as badly as you do. He might die in your place, so you go again and again until one day they may get you.

It was decided that the 94th, 95th and 96th would transfer south to form the nucleus of the new 4th Wing commanded by Brigadier General Fred Anderson, with headquarters at Marks Hall, near Colchester. Anderson had served as Deputy Director of Bombardment at AAF HQ since January 1942. On 23 May the 94th began moving from Thurleigh to Earls Colne in Essex and the 96th began leaving Grafton Underwood for Andrews Field, six miles from Earls Colne.[1] The 95th was also due to move, from Alconbury to Framlingham, Suffolk, but its departure was marred by a tragic accident on 27 May when a B-17 exploded while in the process of being loaded with ten 500lb bombs. Nineteen officers and enlisted men were killed and twenty severely injured; one of whom died later. Four B-17s parked in the vicinity of the explosion were destroyed and eleven others were damaged in the blast.[2] The lull in combat operations delayed the introduction of the new groups such as the 379th commanded by Colonel Maurice 'Mo' Preston, which took over a new base at Kimbolton. On 29 May Preston's group finally 'got its feet wet' when the target for 1st Bomb Wing crews was St-Nazaire. Heavy cloud moving across Western Europe caused several stop-go decisions before the B-17s finally got the green light. Colonel Preston recalls the debut of the 379th Bomb Group (seven YB-40 'gunships' also made their debut this day).

> A diversionary force had been sent out in an effort to induce the German fighters to take off early, thus forcing them to run out of gas as or before, the main force arrived. Well, the tactic worked perfectly. The 'Abbeville Kids' committed themselves early and soon ran out of gas but they got back up in time to intercept us at the tail end of the bomber column just as we passed the IP. The fighters attacked us with a vengeance and then drew off to hit us again as we departed the target and before we were able to reassemble in wing formation. We lost three aircraft and thirty crewmembers, including John Hall, a squadron commander. 'Swede' Carlson, another squadron commander, lost two engines near the target and suffered damage to a third, causing it to be lost later when he had to land in a Brussels sprout patch in England.[3]

In the 305th formation, 1st Lieutenant's James G. Stevenson was forced to ditch *Barrel House Bessie* in the sea about forty-five miles from the English coast after flak disabled the left wing. All of the crew except the tail gunner took to their dinghies and were eventually rescued by a Royal Navy PT boat. Staff Sergeant Hugh G. Erwin failed to get aboard the dinghy and was never found. The British PT boat captain refused to stay and look further because of the great danger of enemy aircraft. Later, another B-17 received the name *Barrel House Bessie from Bessie Street* and was lost on 5 January 1944 when all ten of 2nd Lieutenant Percy H. Hoag's crew were taken prisoner. The 29 May mission proved to be the last for some time for both the 'Flying Eightballs' and the 'Travelling Circus', which had bombed the U-boat pens at La Pallice. Both were taken off operations. They were not, as the B-17 boys thought, being stood down permanently but they were being switched to low-level training flights over East Anglia in preparation for a top-secret mission.

That night the 94th at Bury St Edmunds (Rougham) licked its wounds having lost three more full crews and aircraft. Arthur H. Allen, a pilot in the 33rd Squadron, wrote:

> One crew – [Lieutenant Merle E.] Brown, Woody [2nd Lieutenant Ortho B. Wood], Lieutenant Quentin L.] Sandahl and [Lieutenant William J.] O'Brien – had been with us since we began four-engine training back in the States. And we saw Jack Workman's crew, with funny little Petruzzie, go to pieces in the air.[4] These are things we try to forget. Captain Arthur J. Herbert limped back to England with a crippled airplane and a dead ball turret gunner. He was shot by a .50 calibre slug from one of our own B-17s. This was just one of those 'can't be helped' accidents that happen in war.[5] We came back shot up as usual, with a feathered prop, the bomb bay door locked down and a badly damaged wing.
>
> Tonight, as I write these words, we are again on alert. Tomorrow a raid with 1,000lb bombs means a submarine pen somewhere. Tonight 400 fighting men will go to bed, thinking, dreaming and tossing. Some of them will get very little sleep, of this I am sure. But we go on, as we all know we will, being afraid, but not yellow – not by a damn sight! We may live, we may die – it's God's will.

During a battle in the Kiel area, on the mission to Hannover on 26 July an exploding rocket shattered the forward cockpit area of Allen's aircraft. The windshield was broken and Allen was hit. After the co-pilot got the aircraft under control it was discovered that Allen was dead.

The weather prevented missions being flown until 11 June, when 168 heavies bombed the U-boat yards at Wilhelmshaven after cloud ruled out bombing at Bremen. During the bomb run the leading 'Hell's Angels' formation in the 1st Wing was bracketed by a severe flak barrage. Colonel Chuck Marion, the CO, lost two engines and following aircraft had to manoeuvre violently and reduce speed dramatically to avoid a collision. Just at that moment the *Luftwaffe* took advantage of the now scattered formation to make repeated head-on attacks and one B-17 was rammed by a FW 190 that failed to pull out in time. The 379th, flying only its second mission, bore the brunt of the attacks and lost six aircraft. Eight B-17s were lost in all. Later, a newspaper article dubbed the Kimbolton Group 'The Hard-Luck Kids' due to their many casualties.

On 13 June the 1st Wing was assigned Bremen, while the 4th Wing went to Kiel for another raid on the U-boat yards. The 94th, 95th and 96th took off from their bases at Earls Colne, Framlingham and Andrews Field for the last time. Heavy losses in the Marauder groups prompted their transfer further south to these three B-17 bases so that their fighter cover could be improved. When the B-17 groups returned from the raid, they would touch down at the former B-26 bases at Bury St Edmunds (Rougham), Horham and Snetterton Heath respectively. As it turned out, the three B-17 groups' last mission from their old bases was a disaster. It had been hoped that another twin-pronged attack on the coast would split the German fighter force but it turned out to be a total failure, almost all of the enemy fighters forsaking the 1st Wing to concentrate on the four combat boxes of the 4th. The leading 95th Group was particularly hard hit, losing ten B-17s in combat and an 11th crashed in England. Among the casualties was Brigadier General Nathan B. Forrest, the first American general to be lost in combat in the ETO. Captain John Miller, 412th Bomb Squadron Operations Officer and pilot of the severely damaged Fortress *T'Ain't A Bird*, recalls that the news that 102 flight crewmembers were MIA had a stunning impact on Colonel Alfred A. Kessler his group commander.

> Following a thoroughly depressing and sad debriefing during which he listened to the accounts of the surviving crews in silence, Colonel Kessler, his eyes brimming with tears and very obviously distressed, could only murmur, to no one in particular, 'What's happened to my boys? What's happened to my boys?' Sergeant Arlie Arneson, one of Miller's waist gunners, noted. 'We had taken a beating, a heavy beating. Before the debriefing we received a drink or two of Scotch whiskey instead of coffee and a Spam sandwich. This was a first. All I wanted to do was to go off somewhere quiet to cry or get drunk. I did both.

The 94th lost nine B-17s. Six fell in the combat area and the rest flew back in a semblance of formation, as Sergeant Dick Lewis, the right waist gunner in *Mr Five By Five* (named after the pilot, Captain Kee Harrison, who was short and stocky) recalls.

> Cover from the short-range Spitfires ended as we flew northeast over the North Sea. As we approached the German coast swarms of German fighters rose to defend Kiel. It seemed that most of the *Luftwaffe* was gathered there. The action was intense and I saw many ships going down in flames or exploding in mid-air. I'll never know how *Mr Five By Five* came through it unscathed. It seemed like a

> miracle. Returning, we were flying at low level over the North Sea. German fighters passed to the side of us at very high speed and out of gun range. Several miles ahead of us they turned and came at us head-on. Lieutenant George W. Hendershot's 'plane [*Visiting Fireman*], was on our left wing. I saw cannon fire hit the leading edge of his wing. A section peeled off. Suddenly the ship nosed up, did a complete loop and dove into the sea. It all happened in a few seconds. It was there and then it was gone. The entire crew of ten was lost.[6]

An eighth B-17 was also shot down in the encounter and *Shackeroo!* flown by Major Lewis G. Thorup had its left stabilizer shot away and three engines put out of action. *Shackeroo!* staggered over the sea for a further thirty miles on the one remaining engine before Thorup ditched the crippled Fortress in the water. 'Pappy' Colby's crew dropped a life raft and a radio but both broke up as they hit the sea. ASR finally rescued Thorup's crew after eleven hours in the water. In all, twenty-two of the twenty-six bombers shot down were from the Kiel force. The three 4th Wing groups put down at their new bases in sombre mood. The new 4th Wing CO, Colonel (later Brigadier General) Curtis E. LeMay, moved into the former Third Bomb Wing headquarters at Elveden Hall near Thetford. One of his first tasks was to replace Colonel John 'Dinty' Moore, CO of the 94th and Alfred Kessler with Colonels Fred Castle and John Gerhart respectively. Gerhart had been one of the 8th's original staff officers at its activation in January 1942. Castle, born on 14 October 1908 at Manila in the Philippine Islands, was a soft-spoken man with great intellectual and leadership ability. A graduate of West Point, he had returned to active duty in January 1942, had joined General Eaker's staff and had shared in the responsibility for planning the airbase and depot system in England. From the beginning Castle had a burning desire for combat action and he had flown eight combat missions in his spare time in preparation for such an opportunity.[7]

If anyone needed confirmation of the need to attack the *Luftwaffe* where it would hurt most, the Kiel debacle had proved it beyond doubt. Decisions taken at the Casablanca Conference led to Operation *Pointblank*, which emphasized the need to reduce the German fighter force. Eaker therefore sent a record number of bombers on the first really deep penetration of Germany, on 22 June, to the synthetic rubber plant at Hüls, near Recklinghausen. Hüls, which accounted for approximately 29 per cent of Germany's synthetic rubber and 18 per cent of its total rubber supply, was the most heavily defended target in the *Reich* at this time. Most of the route was to be flown without escort, so three diversionary raids were planned to draw most of the fighters from the main attacking force of almost 300 B-17s. However, the diversionary force aimed at the Ford and General Motors plant at Antwerp failed to materialize. The 100th Bomb Group was delayed by ground mists and the 381st and 384th, which were flying their maiden missions, were behind schedule and failed to make contact with the escorts which were to escort them to Antwerp. This lapse placed another, smaller diversionary force at the mercy of the *Luftwaffe,* which had refuelled after an earlier raid by RAF medium bombers. Head-on attacks succeeded in shooting down four B-17s, while three badly damaged survivors flew their own formation, hugging the waves all the way back to England. Two B-17s in the 384th were so badly damaged that they were later named *Patches* and *Salvage Queen*. The Hüls force also came in for repeated attacks, as 'Pappy' Colby in the 94th flying *Thundermug,* recalls:

> ...We got the works. They hit us at the Dutch coast and it got progressively worse. Colonel Castle rode behind me on the campstool and took notes all through the thick of it, cool as a cucumber. We made a beautiful fifty-five-second run and dropped our pattern square on the buildings alongside of the burning tank, which had exploded. Flak suddenly became very heavy. After dropping, the remains of the lead and low squadrons strung along with us and we caught up with the 95th. At Rotterdam the Spitfires met us and chased off the German fighters but it was a rough mission and we were beginning to wonder about the invincibility of the Flying Fortress. We lost two of our aircraft in the 333rd and the group lost quite a few more.

Mr Five By Five lost an outboard engine and with the propeller feathered it became a sitting duck. Dick Lewis says:

> Captain Harrison came on the intercom, informing us that he intended to try and escape by lowering the landing gear in sign of surrender and then diving the ship. We were told to hold our fire. Enemy fighters closed in to escort us to a landing. Suddenly, the dive began! This manoeuvre had never been covered in my flight training. It was a wild ride and I wondered if the ship would hold together. It did! Captain Harrison pulled her out at about a thousand feet and then dove again to treetop level, frustrating the enemy fighters, who broke off the action and left. He began zigzagging the 'plane back to England. We took a hit from a ground battery and Lieutenant Schaefer, our navigator, was wounded in the leg. Despite his injury

> he stuck to his post, changing course every few minutes. And I'll never forget the sight of Dutch farmers standing in their fields, waving their arms and making the 'V for Victory' sign as we roared overhead. I breathed a sigh of relief as the Channel appeared ahead of us and that mission came safely to a close. The inside of the ship was drenched with condensation from the rapid descent, –40F to +75F. The entire crew was grounded for several missions, recovering from related ear problems. *Mr Five By Five* went into Repair Depot for replacement of several wing spars weakened or bent from pulling out of the dive. I never saw our 'plane again.[8]

Hüls had been well hit, with smoke rising as high as 17,000 feet and the plant was put out of action for a month. Full production was not resumed for another five months after that. Martin Shenk in the 381st put down at Framlingham and *Little Chuck* landed at Manston while *Mary Jane* in the 379th put down at RAF Coltishall. Fifteen B-17s were lost, including a YB-40, which flew with the 92nd and another 170 bombers received varying degrees of damage. Fighters and flak had claimed most of the victims, although ths loss of the YB-40 was something of a mystery, as Howard Hernan relates.

> Two YB-40s flew on the lead ship's wings and another YB-40 flew in the number six slot. Just before the IP the YB-40 in front of us in the No. 2 position suddenly went down. I couldn't understand how come he went down when there was no flak. We had not then been attacked by fighters so it wasn't a fighter. I would think that he had an engine malfunction and just couldn't keep up. The last I saw of him was after he dropped below us and made a big sweeping left turn to the path that we were to take when we came off the target. He probably thought that we could catch up with him after we had completed our bomb-run. I had an opportunity to look over one of the three multi-gunned B-17s assigned to the 303rd shortly before the Hüls raid and concluded later that with all the armour plating around the tail and waist gun positions, the Martin turret over the radio room, and all the extra ammunition, the YB-40 just had to be tail heavy. Of course, it weighed the same when it got off the target as it did when it got there. When we dropped our bombs we were somewhat lighter and it made a lot of difference. I believe it was a mistake to spread the YB-40s around the groups. My opinion was that they should have been left to fly as a squadron and then if they wanted to attract any fighters, to bear out a little and let them come

in. The YB-40s had a tremendous amount of fire-power but if they lost an engine they were in trouble.[9]

Next day, 23 June, 180 Forts were sent to Villacoublay and Bernay-St-Martin airfields in France but all were recalled. It was while the Fortresses of the 381st were being bombed up for this mission at Ridgewell that one exploded at dispersal, killing twenty-three men and damaging *Connie*, another Fort, that had to be salvaged. After a day's rest, 197 Fortresses were dispatched to bomb Hamburg on the 25th but cloudy weather broke up the formations and made formation flying very difficult. The 167 Forts that made it across the enemy coast attacked convoys and targets of opportunity. Fifteen B-17s, including six in the 379th and five in the 91st, were shot down. At Molesworth three Forts in the 360th Squadron in the 'Hell's Angels' were missing also. There was no sign of *The Witche's Tit* and Lieutenant Dave Mack's crew or *The Avenger* and Lieutenant Joseph F. Palmer's crew or *Qui-Nine Bitter Dose*. *The Witche's Tit* was famous for the broom-riding hag with pasty orange flesh, green and black striped stockings and black and white teeth that adorned the nose. *Qui-Nine Bitter Dose* whose name was partly made up with a pair of dice – one showing five and the other four – had sundry patches from earlier trips over the Continent. The pilot, Captain George V. Stallings, was a big man from Rowayton, Connecticut, weighing almost 250lb. He was accustomed to urinating in flight without crawling through the bomb bay to the relief tube, simply opening his side-sliding window and letting go. The resultant steam in the below zero upper air had led to false reports about *Qui-Nine* being on fire over the target. *Qui-Nine* was leading the high squadron but Stallings could see nothing further because of the solid cloud building continuously as the mission went on. At the target *The Witche's Tit* was hit by flak and it went down, smoke streaming from the radio compartment hatch. Stallings could see chutes coming out and knew that his close friend Dave Mack was still alive. Mack and eight of his crew were taken prisoner. Then enemy fighters attacked *The Avenger*. Only four men got out. Seven of the crew including Palmer, who was dead in his seat, were killed.

Qui-Nine was the next victim. Dick Jones, the radio operator, was hit in the chest by a 20mm shell and he died instantly. One of the gunners was hit in the knee and a 20mm that exploded by the nose ripped through the outer skin, popping and spewing out fragments that shredded navigator James Ford Kelly's maps. Then a cannon shell exploded under the table, throwing fragments into his leg. As they crossed the coast near Emden *Qui-Nine* took more flak hits. Down below Stallings could see a smoke screen covering Emden. Perhaps the Germans thought that this was a big raid and not a badly damaged B-17 staggering out to the North Sea. Despite taking more hits from fighters over Emden, Stallings and his co-pilot, Joe Bradbury, kept the shattered Fort in the air. Kelly brought them in right over the Norfolk coast but damage to the B-17 was such that Stallings decided not to risk attempting a crash-landing and he ordered the crew to bail out in the vicinity of RAF Coltishall at 5,000 feet. But as they prepared to bail out the escape door and the bomb bay doors were jammed. Finally the crew jumped on them and out they went. Stallings took *Qui-Nine* back out to sea and just as the plane crossed the shoreline near Waxham, he put on his parachute and bailed out. Hanging in his harness Stallings looked back at the Fortress. All that was left of the tail was about six feet of spars and all along the fuselage were chinks of light coming through holes. *Qui-Nine* circled once and then hit the sea in a cloud of spray and steam.

At 1200 hours the coastguard telephoned Caister life boat station to report that an airman had landed in the sea by parachute 500 yards south-west of Waxham. The Coxswain and several other crewmen were away so ex-Coxswain, seventy-three-year-old Charles Laycock took charge. He put together a scratch crew, which included three soldiers and launched the Caister boat *Jose Neville* at 1220 hours. The Fortress had already sunk and the crew of the lifeboat could see the B-17 under the water and reported its position to a Royal Navy rescue launch. A fresh northwest wind was blowing and the sea was choppy. The wind caught Stallings' chute as he hit the sea and it dragged him about half a mile before he unbuckled the harness and began swimming toward the shore. A few people had gathered to warn him that the beach was mined. Finally Stallings was led to a small cottage where a little old lady took a bottle with about an inch of rum in it from her mantelpiece and offered it to Stallings. He felt that he could not take it and politely declined but the lady insisted. 'I've been saving it for just such an occasion,' she said.[10]

Next day when the Fortresses in the 1st Wing were dispatched to targets in France and the 4th Wing B-17s, fitted with 'Tokyo' extra-range tanks, went to St-Nazaire, it was the 384th at Grafton Underwood that suffered high loss with five aircraft missing. These took their losses to ten on the first four completed missions. Claude Campbell, who flew in the 303rd formation, which went to the Focke Wulf airfield at Beaumont, described it as 'an excellent mission'. The main effort this day was directed by the 4th Wing on St Nazaire, as 'Pappy' Colby recalls.

There was much speculation at the briefing because only ships with the new 'Tokyo' extra range tanks were going. Our target was some kind of new lock at the sub pens. I led the 333rd Squadron with the job of filling in aborts from the 96th Bomb Group. We had a hell of a time trying to pick out the 96th from all the others in the sky because they didn't answer our flare recognition signals for a long time. We finally located them, late as usual and then had trouble following them as their formation was lousy and they were only doing 145mph. We filled in several aborts and, as we approached the IP, I tacked on to the lead element of their high squadron. They made a beautiful bomb run and each ship unloaded two 2,000lb bombs on the target. Very heavy flak came up and a six-inch piece of shell came up through the floor of the radio room and smacked Patrick on the fanny. Luckily, its force was pretty well spent and all he got was a big black and blue spot. It was a long way home and we were down to 300 gallons in the main gas tanks when we turned on our new 'Tokyo' tanks. They brought us home with plenty to spare.

That night after supper I was told to report to Colonel Castle at his quarters. I quickly cleaned up and wondered what had been said to put me in the doghouse again. To my great surprise, he asked me if I could take over command of the 410th Squadron and build it up to where it could become combat operational again. The squadron had lost nine out of its ten original crews and the replacements hadn't had a chance to really learn what combat operations were all about. It had lost both its COs and Ops Officer and had been withdrawn from operations as a squadron, with the new crews being used to fill in aborts. This put their people behind the rest of the group in acquiring the necessary twenty-five raids to complete their tours and made them very unhappy. I told him I would do my very best and the job certainly boosted my morale. Next morning I took command of the 410th and Wally Barker, the Assistant Operations Officer, was sure glad to see me. He was a big help in briefing me on their problems. That afternoon, who should show up unexpectedly but the Bob Hope Special Services Show with Frances Langford, Jerry Colonna and Jack Pepper their guitarist. They put on a terrific show that did us all a world of good. Unfortunately, the group had gone on a raid to Le Mans and didn't get to see the show. But when the tired crews from the raid came into the mess hall for debriefing, who was standing just inside the door shaking hands with each one, but Bob Hope and his entire cast. Some of the lads were so overwhelmed they had tears in their eyes and personally, I'll never forget it.

Officers on the Control Tower roof at Chelveston on 14 May 1943. (USAF)

Major General George E. Stratemeyer talks with 44th Bomb Group CO, Colonel Leon Johnson a 39-year old West Pointer (centre) and Major Howard "Pappy" Moore and Lieutenant Bob Brown of the 67th Bomb Squadron by the nose of B-24D-5-CO 41-23817 *Suzy Q* at Shipdham on 21 April 1943. In the background is B-24D-25-CO 41-24278 *Miss Delores,* which FTR with Lieutenant 'Bob' Brown and his crew on the disastrous mission to Kiel on 14 May 1943. Brown was among the survivors who became PoWs. Johnson, who led the Flying Eightballs in *Suzy Q* on the low-level mission on 1 August 1943 to "White V" Columbia Aquila at Ploesti, was awarded the Medal of Honor for his leadership on the raid. The medal was presented to him in a ceremony at Shipdham on 22 November 1943, by which time he commanded the 14th Combat Bombardment Wing. (USAF)

B-24Ds over Kiel, 14 May 1943. The B-17 groups flew behind and above the B-24s for the fi time in the ETO and this resulted in heavy losses for the Liberators. The 44th's cargo incendiaries had required a shorter trajectory and a two-mile longer bomb run than the B-17 Flying a scattered formation, the B-24s were exposed to fighter attack. Altogether, five Liberatc were lost, including three in the 67th Bomb Squadron, which brought up the rear of the formatic The first to go down was Lieutenant William Roach and his replacement crew flying in B-24I 30-CO 42-40126 *Annie Oakley.* There were only two survivors. The 44th Bomb Group w awarded a Distinguished Unit Citation for its part in the Kiel raid; the first made to an 8th Air For Group. (USAF)

B-17F 42-5243 *F.D.R's Potato Peeler Kids* in the 303rd Bomb Group which was lost with Capta Ross C. Bales and crew in the North Sea on 14 May 1943. There were no survivors. (USAF)

3-17 42-3085 *Helno Gal* in the 94th Bomb Group which crashed at North Weald on 21 May 1943 on the return from Emden. It became a hangar queen. (USAF)

3-17F 42-3053 *Desperate Journey* in the 91st Bomb Group, which was lost with Lieutenant Norbert D. Koll and crew on 21 May 1943. The aircraft was shot down by fighters and crashed at Wilhelmshaven killing eight crew. Two men survived to be taken prisoner. (USAF)

With No 3 feathered and No 4 throwing oil, B-17F 229793/BO: P of the 368th Bomb Squadron nursed home across the North Sea by 1st Lieutenant George E. Paris and his co-pilot. At 12 hours, during the bomb run at Wilhelmshaven on 21 May 1943, the seventeen Fortresses of t 306th Bomb Group formation were attacked by FW 190s. Flying left on the leading B-17, Pari aircraft sustained 20mm cannon shell hits on the right wing and engines. Another hit, on the l side of the radio room, wounded the operator. Three 306th B-17s were lost as a result of ener fighter attacks, one ditching and its crew being rescued by a Royal Navy minesweeper. V Bomber Command lost 11 per cent of its force bombing Wilhelmshaven that day- no wonder th during the first half of 1943, a bomber crewman had less than a one-in-three chance of completi his tour of 25 missions (USAF)

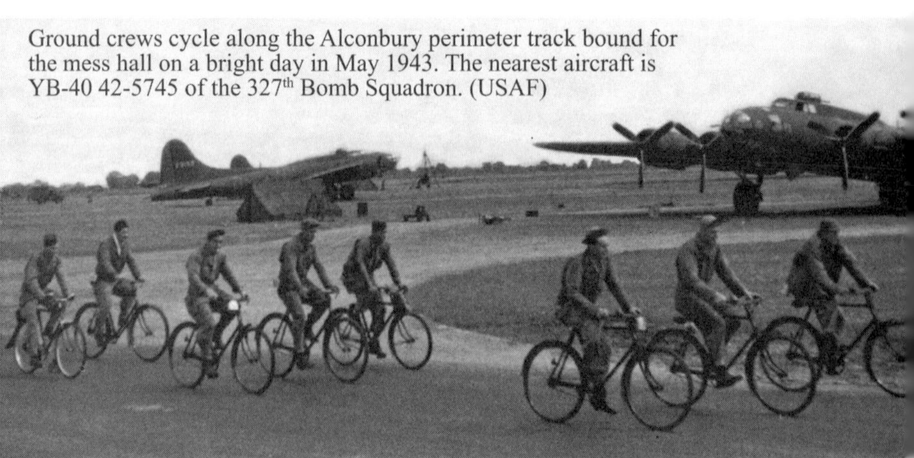

Ground crews cycle along the Alconbury perimeter track bound for the mess hall on a bright day in May 1943. The nearest aircraft is YB-40 42-5745 of the 327th Bomb Squadron. (USAF)

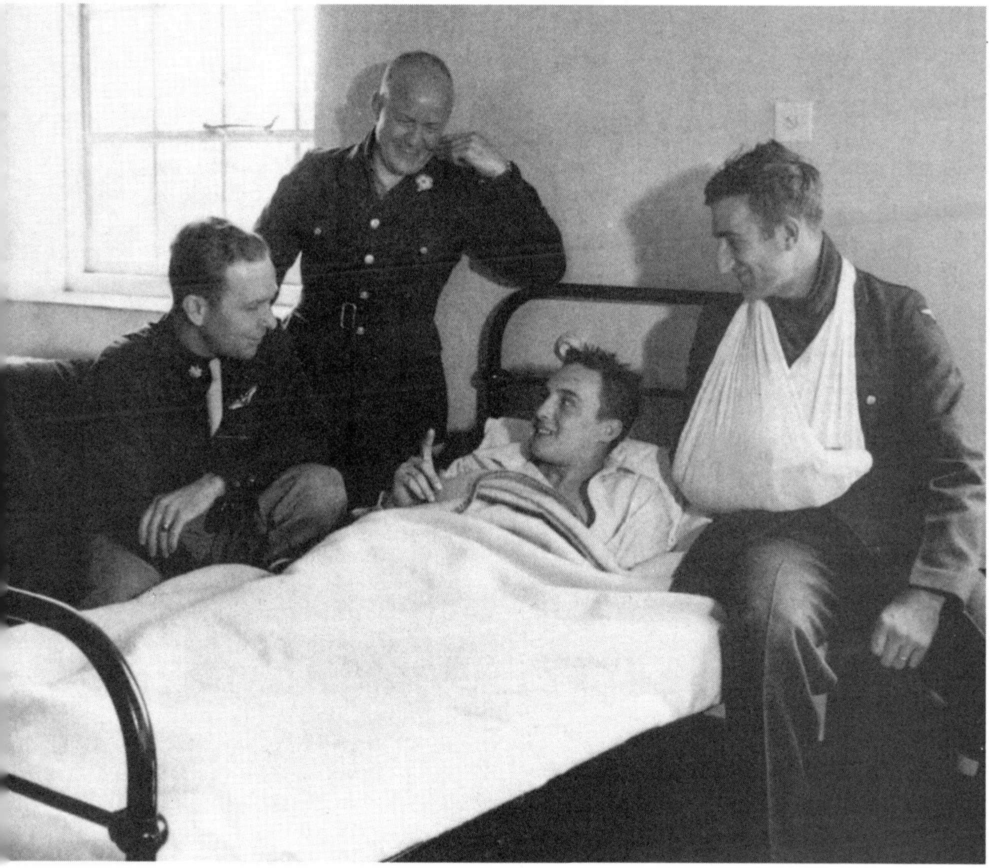

At Hüls the leading 91st Bomb Group took the brunt of an enemy fighter assault with many frontal attacks, five of its Fortresses failing to return. Lieutenant Buster Peek and his crew in 42-297971 *Old Ironsides* made it to the Channel and ditched. The tail gunner disappeared after ditching and an RAF air-sea rescue craft picked up the nine survivors within half an hour and gave emergency dressings to three who had been wounded in the air battle. Their wet clothing was temporarily replaced with RAF uniforms, which were still being worn by the wounded men when they were visited in hospital by the Group CO, Lieutenant Colonel Baskin Lawrence. Standing behind Lawrence is the bombardier, Lieutenant Chauncy Hicks; in bed is T/Sgt James F. Osborne, radio operator; and sitting on the bed is Staff Sergeant William G. Zeigler, a gunner. (USAF)

B-17F 42-30107 *Black Magic* in the 379th Bomb Group which was shot down on 25 June 1943. Two of Lieutenant Weldon Homes' crew were killed and 8 were taken into captivity. (USAF)

General Ira C. Eaker (second from left) Lieutenant Colonel Donald K. Fargo the 305th Bomb grou CO (with his back to the camera) and Mr Anthony Eden the British Secretary of State for Foreig Affairs at Chelveston on 25 June 1943. Far right is General Frank Armstrong Jr. (USAF)

B-17F 42-5382 *The Witche's Tit* in the 303rd Bomb Group which was lost with Lieutenant D. W Mack and crew on 25 June 1943. One man was killed and nine taken were taken into captivit (USAF)

Lieutenant Fred R. Gilbert with crew members and crew chief in the 305th Bomb Group after their 25th mission on 5 July 1943. Gilbert was co-pilot to Lieutenant Fred Rabbo and later got his own crew. (USAF)

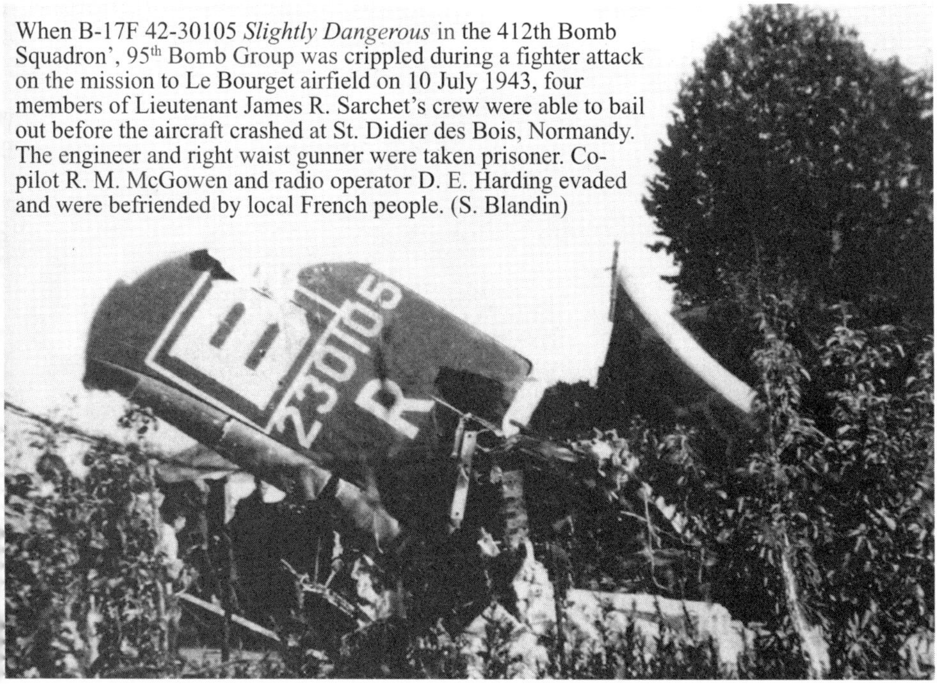

When B-17F 42-30105 *Slightly Dangerous* in the 412th Bomb Squadron', 95th Bomb Group was crippled during a fighter attack on the mission to Le Bourget airfield on 10 July 1943, four members of Lieutenant James R. Sarchet's crew were able to bail out before the aircraft crashed at St. Didier des Bois, Normandy. The engineer and right waist gunner were taken prisoner. Co-pilot R. M. McGowen and radio operator D. E. Harding evaded and were befriended by local French people. (S. Blandin)

Henry Stimson, US Secretary of War, reads the citation before decorating S/Sgt Maynard Smi with the Medal of Honor, the highest US award of gallantry. 'Snuffy' Smith was the first Eight Air Force recipient and the first to wear it. A total of fourteen Medal of Honor awards were mad to Eighth Air Force fliers and those participating in its operations by the end of hostilities, half all to members of the USAAF. Smith was ball turret gunner on a 306th Bomb Group which caug fire in the radio room after being shot up on the St-Nazaire mission of 1 May 1943. After oth crew members in the rear of the aircraft bailed out, Smith fought the fire, eventually extinguishin it and enabling a safe landing to be made in Cornwall. The ceremony took place at Thurleigh o 15 July 1943. (USAF)

ACM Sir Arthur Harris, C-in-C RAF Bomber Command, and Major General Ira Eaker, Eighth Air Force Commanding General, take the salute at an awards ceremony at Bushy Park, Teddington, 17 July 1943. Despite different views on the execution of the strategic bombing campaign, they remained lifelong friends. (USAF)

B-17F 42-29606 *Toots-Butch* in the 303rd Bomb Group, which failed to return with Captain John A. Van Wie and crew on the mission to Hamburg on 25 July 1943. Four of the crew were killed and six were taken prisoner. (USAF)

B-17F-20-BO 41-24539 *Jersey Bounce* in the 358th Bomb Squadron, 303rd Bomb Group at Molesworth after returning from Rouen-Sotteville with a cannon shell in the fuselage on 12 December 1942. Three months later on 18 March 1943 *Jersey Bounce* had two engines and a tire shot out over Vegesack but still managed to return safely. The Fortress had been assigned overseas on 16 September 1942 passed to the CCRC at Bovingdon on 27 July 1943. (USAF)

B-17F 42-5813 *Jackie Ellen* in the 379th Bomb Group which on 30 July 1943 2nd Lieutenant William C. Breiner crashed at Alconbury, 2 miles from its base at Kimbolton returning battle damaged from a mission. (USAF)

British mechanics in a Burtonwood hangar work on B-17F 41-24502 of the 368th Bomb Squadr in the 306th Bomb Group at Thurleigh which was crash-landed at Sudbourne, Suffolk on retu from the 28 July 1943 mission to Kassel. Burtonwood became a Base Air Depot with more th 11,000 British and US personnel working on a range of aircraft repair, servicing and modificatio (USAF)

On the 6 September 1943 mission to bomb industrial targets at Stuttgart over 100 B-17s returne with battle damage and there were nine write-offs in crash-landings. The crashes and at least dozen of the losses were caused by many of the older aircraft running out of fuel. Captain Jaco James in the 303rd Bomb Group got 42-29944 *Winning Run* of the 427th Bomb Squadron, in sig of the small RAF airfield at Deanland near the South Coast cliffs, only to have the engines fa on approach. All walked away from the crash-landing. Previously known as *Buzzin' Bronco,* th aircraft was used on the secret mission to North Africa in August 1943. (USAF)

B-17F-15-VE 42-5763 *Bomb-Boogie* in the 401st Bomb Squadron, 91st Bomb Group, which was lost with Lt Elwood D. Arp's crew on 6 September 1943. Four men evaded and six were captured. (USAF)

Hollywood movie star Major Clark Gable poses with *Delta Rebel II*. (USAF)

Traditional 'smoking' of the ceiling of the 306th Bomb Group Officers' Club at Thurleigh with missions. (USAF)

B-17F 41-24505 *"Quitchurbitchin"* in the 91st Bomb Group which suffered battle damage on t mission to St. Nazaire on 22 November 1942 and became a hangar queen at Bassingbourn befc being returned to flying condition and transferred at the end of 1943 as a training aircraft in t USA. USAF)

Crew of B-24D 41-23717 *Exterminator* in the 93rd Bomb Group suiting up for a mission at Hardwick. *Exterminator* was lost in a mid air collision on 1 August 1943 in North Africa. (USAF)

Enlisted members in Lieutenant John H. Murphy's crew in *Shoot Luke* in the 328th Bomb Squadron, 93rd Bomb Group at Hardwick preparing to go on leave. (USAF)

Feathered prop. (USAF)

Captain Robert K. Morgan, pilot of all 25 missions in the *Memphis Belle* in the 91st Bomb Group. His girlfriend, Miss Margaret Polk of Memphis, Tennessee, was the inspiration for the name. (USAF)

B-17F 41-9121 *The Big Bitch* which in 1942 operated in the 303rd, 97th and 92nd Bomb Groups and in 1943 with the CCRC. .It was salvaged in May 1945. (USAF)

Robert Morgan shakes hands with the ground crew of *Memphis Belle* as Jim Verinis and Chuck Leighton look on. M/Sgt Joe Giambrone the crew chief is far right. (USAF)

T/Sgt Harold P. Loch, Green Bay, Wisconsin, top turret gunner/engineer on the *Memphis Belle*. (USAF)

B-17F 41-244 53 *The Bearded Beauty Mizpah* in the 91st Bomb Group which was lost with 2nd Lieutenant Everett L. Kenner and crew on 17 August 1943. Five men were killed. Five survived to be taken prisoner. (USAF)

Pilot and co-pilot of a B-17 ready for take-off. (USAF)

To end the month the 351st lost four Forts from the five that went missing on the raid to St-Nazaire and Beaumont-le-Roger airfield on 28 June. Next day 148 Forts were sent to attack airfields and other aviation targets in Northern France but 10/10ths cloud was encountered and all returned without bombing.

At early morning breakfast at Chelveston on 4 July Barry Urdang, a navigator in the 422nd Squadron, sat between Frank Scott the pilot of *Black Swan* and his co-pilot Robert Brazeal. The *Black Swan* had been named after a Maureen O'Hara and Tyrone Power movie. Despite a fine combat record, three days earlier the Frank Scott crew had been disbanded by Major Jerald Price, the Commanding Officer of the 422nd, because he felt that the officers were excessively 'fraternizing' with the enlisted men and the ground crew. They shared the air crew's booze and they gathered ration cards from the ground crew and bought rations at Oxford, London or any other place for those that seldom got off the base. They had heat in their barracks and the higher ups could not get coal and they did not like it, so the crew was broken up. Only Scott, Brazeal and Marvin Williams, engineer, from the original crew flew the mission on 4 July when 192 Fortresses of the 1st Wing were assigned the Gnôme et Rhône Aero engine factory at Le Mans and an aircraft factory at Nantes. Meanwhile, eighty-three of the longer-range B-17s in the 4th Wing went to the U-boat pens at La Pallice.

Shortly after noon the two 1st Wing formations, flying parallel courses, crossed the French coast just east of the Cherbourg Peninsula, while the 4th Wing headed for La Pallice on the Bay of Biscay coast. At 1230 the 1st Wing formations crossed Laval, eighty miles inland and then split into two formations, one heading for Nantes and the other for Le Mans. The Nantes force was attacked by hordes of German fighters all the way from the IP and they did not break off until thirty-five miles after the target. When the fighter attacks had subsided slightly some crews suddenly became aware that a B-17 had already eased out of formation and was swinging wide right with the burning flames from the No. 3 engine shooting as far back as the tail. It was the *Black Swan*. The ship momentarily hung on a wing tip, rolled over on its back and headed straight down engulfed in flames. Seven crewmen exited but only six of the chutes billowed, for someone yanked his ripcord too soon, resulting in nothing but a plume of fire. The ship plunged earthwards on fire and appeared to explode before it crashed into the sea. A German fighter flew through the parachutes but did not fire at them. About six miles south of Belle Isle six open chutes went into the water but none of them survived a savage sea. The last transmission of the plane was simply, 'One B-17 going down.'

Captain Roland 'Rollie' L. Sargent, pilot of one of the B-17s in the 92nd formation, recalls:

> Enemy planes made their attack after we left the target. As they drew closer the ships on our left opened fire with their tail and ball turret guns. We could see the bursts of smoke stream back from the muzzles of their 50 calibre machine guns and the empty shell casings falling away. I felt the vibrations of our own bomber's guns as they commenced firing. We continued our evasive action. In front and below us 20mm cannon shells exploded in a line of white flashes and puffs of white smoke. That occurred two or three times while we droned steadily on, seeming to crawl toward the English Channel and the distant white blur that were the White Cliffs of Dover, England and safety. The fighter engagement lasted about fifteen minutes before Spitfires came streaking down out of the sky ahead of us, their guns literally spitting fire at the German fighters behind us as they flashed past overhead; a heart warming sight to our bomber crews.
>
> At last we reached the coast and crossed out over the Channel – Dover chalk cliffs now a clear dividing line between the blue Channel waters and the green English countryside beyond. Though the sky around us was spotted with fighters, mostly Spitfires, and I no longer felt the pounding of our plane's guns, a good indication they'd done a good job of driving off enemy fighters. One Spitfire, obviously in trouble, was flying an erratic course toward England with a long plume of white vapour trailing out behind.
>
> We reached the English coast and began letting down. We lost altitude over the Thames and up around London. At about 10,000 feet I let Jim have the plane's controls and I leaned back, removed my tight-fitting oxygen mask and relaxed a little. At these low altitudes, when oxygen wasn't in use, we could smoke and those not needed at their stations – like gunners when we were over England – could move around. Sergeant Roberts, our tail gunner, came up into the cockpit all excited about this initial contact with the enemy. For the first time in his life, he'd experienced the fearful sensation of being shot at by cannon and machine gun fire with the intent to kill or maim and of himself, retaliating in kind and like intent, with his twin 50 calibre guns. The excitement showed in the slight trembling of the hand holding his cigarette and in his voice and gestures. He

> looked around the cockpit at Jim and me and shook his head in wonder. 'I don't know how you fellers could just sit here and flying this thing while all the shooting was going on.'
>
> Sergeant Pearson, from his position in the lower ball turret, joined the group in the cockpit (now five in number), including the flight engineer, (whose combat station was the top turret located between the cockpit and the bomb bay) and we kidded him about his remarks on the intercom while the flak had been tracking after us. He grinned sheepishly, then, as if suddenly remembering something urgent blurted out, 'did you see that bomber [the *Black Swan*] on fire back there – one of ours? There was flame a mile long shooting out behind it. I thought sure it was a goner, but it stayed close behind us and the fire gradually went out. It's still with us.'
>
> We hadn't seen it from the cockpit, but the other gunners there nodded their heads. Our view was primarily to the front and side. My attention was riveted on the B-17 to my left and little ahead in the formation. So we saw only a little of what had evidently been some pretty spectacular action behind us. We found out later that one of our bombers did go down just before we reached the French coast.

Joe Chely's co-pilot, Lew Hart, who was on his first mission, could not believe what was happening. 'It was nothing like the romance or the glory of the World War I flicks like *Lilac Time* or *Wings*, which we doted upon as kids. It was more like one weird, hopeless dream.' From his ball turret position, Joe Kocher remembered the burning chute but no other details, because he regarded the matter '...as a done deal and turned to the immediate problem of tracking the lurking German fighters.'[11] Many witnessed the end of the drama but few knew at the time whose ship it was or what had precipitated all its problems. The most likely explanation of what happened to the *Black Swan* crew was offered by Barry Urdang.

> My tail gunner Buster B. Copp probably had the best view. A lone Ju 88 that came in from the rear largely unnoticed, attacked from 6 o'clock low. It practically stood on its tail, lobbing and arcing its 20mm in the general direction of the leading 306th Group, unluckily damaging the third engine of the Black Swan flying opposite to us. Scott carefully lowered and pulled off to the right in order not to endanger other aircraft. For about ten seconds or so, he seemed to have doused the flames with the help of the wing extinguishers but then both three and four broke out in rampant fire as far back as the radio room. My gunners reported seeing five chutes with one afire

> but they could have easily missed seeing the other two chutes from where they released. The plane nosed straight down and exploded before it hit the water.

The 92nd formation of sixteen B-17s and three YB-40s also came under heavy attack and Lieutenant John J. Campbell's B-17 was believed to have hit the sea and burned. Six parachutes were seen to open and another partially opened. Lieutenant Robert L. Campbell brought *Ruthie*, named in honour of his wife, home to Alconbury and ground looped with a flat tyre after repeated attacks by enemy fighters had seriously damaged the bomber. The Le Mans force encountered intense fighter opposition fifteen minutes from the target but the B-17s were able to pick up their fighter escort at Argentan and reach safety. For once the multiplicity of bomber attacks seemed to break up the *Luftwaffe* concentrations and they were able to account for only 3 per cent of the attacking force.

Rollie Sargent recalls:

> Soon our field came into view and circling around its perimeter, we broke formation, coming in to land one at a time. I taxied around to our hard stand, turning in to it in a 180-degree circle till we were faced outward again, ready for the next mission.
>
> We brought back two jagged holes in the metal skin, souvenirs of the flak batteries north of St-Omer – the plane's first battle scars. The men, still encumbered with their heavy fur-lined flying suits, piled out of our plane and gathered around the tail talking excitedly. On the ride back to the Interrogation Room the voices still edged with the effects of this day's events – the first experience in combat for all of us. In marked contrast to this almost joyous releasing of tension, Bob White, whose failure to release the bombs we'd carried weighed heavily on him, sat quietly staring at the floor, seemingly unaware of the boisterous banter around him.
>
> Climbing out of the truck at the Interrogation Room, Bob again voiced his regret and frustration over the failure to drop. I tried to reassure him and cheer him up, along with a friendly pat on the back, but after we'd turned in our flying equipment and been given coffee and sandwiches, he remained glum and unsmiling all through the questions the S-2 (Intelligence) personnel subjected us to, taking each returning crew separately in turn. Roberts, the tail gunner, surprised me by putting in a claim for the destruction of a FW 190, which Pearson corroborated. He'd said nothing about it when he was with

> us in the cockpit on the way back. (Later he received official confirmation of his claim and was awarded the Air Medal for it.)
>
> When the questioning was finally over, all information had been given and noted, the men had given vent to their keyed-up tensions and exhausted their stories of what they'd seen and done and were ready to repeat them to anyone who'd listen, we left the debriefing and made our way-back to our quarters on foot, a walk of nearly one mile. We walked in a almost dream-like euphoria filled with an intoxicating sense of well-being – a feeling of being on top of the world – the next stage in the emotional 'high' of returning home safely from a combat mission. The final stage for me came later after a quiet afternoon in my quarters and writing a short letter to Dorrie (my wife) – to bed and blessed, deep, recuperative sleep.[12]

The weather continued cloudy and VIII Bomber Command flew several more missions to France in the hope of spotting its targets. On 14 July, Bastille Day, over 100 B-17s attacked the FW 190 repair facility at Villacoublay. Another 100 aircraft headed for airfields at Amiens-Glisy and Le Bourget. All three targets were well hit – at Villacoublay, hangars and seventy FW 190s were destroyed – but over 150 Forts were damaged by the German defences and five had failed to return from the raids on the two airfields. Le Bourget was covered with clouds, and ships in the 94th could not drop their sixteen 300lb bombs. Dick Lewis, right waist gunner in Captain Kee Harrison's B-17, a replacement for *Mr Five By Five,* which was still under repair following the Hüls mission:[13]

> ...felt the ship take a forward hit. Smoke filtered back through to the rear. 'What the Hell is going on up front?' I yelled to Earl Porath, back-to-back with me at his left waist gun position. Through my own open gun port I could see German fighters continuing the attack on the front of the ship, diving from above or zooming up from below like a swarm of angry hornets.
>
> The ship began to fall out of formation. I squeezed off a couple of ineffective bursts from my .50 calibre Browning gun as the fighters flashed by at such speed that it was nearly impossible to track them through my gunsight for more than a fraction of a second. Those German pilots were smart veterans. I could hear and feel Porath's .50 firing behind me and Jeff Polk's twin .50s blazing away from his ball turret below me. In the tail of the ship, Ossie Asiala's guns added to the racket. But I couldn't hear firing from any of our forward guns. The smoke was getting heavier. The ship went into an abrupt dive,

> then levelled again and seemed to move erratically as if the pilot was taking evasive action. I realized that the German fighter attack had ended. I listened on the intercom for some word from the cockpit. Silence! We were in deep trouble. A horrible thought came to me. Had they all been killed up front?

Lieutenant David H. Turner, the co-pilot, explained what happened:

> Because of the lack of oxygen and the fact that we were blinded by smoke, we had to get down in a hurry. While I was getting rid of the fire by stamping and beating the flames, Harrison was getting downstairs as quickly as he could. Those fighters were chipping us to pieces, but none of the crew was hurt. It looked hopeless though and Harrison gave the orders to jump.

Four men in the nose of the ship bailed out before Sergeant James H. Curtis, the top turret gunner, who had helped Turner extinguish the fire by damping it down with his parachute pack, discovered that it was now unusable. Turner, who burned his hands badly, concluded: 'We sure couldn't jump and leave Curtis in the ship, so Harrison decided to land her, bombs and all'.

Dick Lewis continues:

> The ship went into a shallow dive and it was hard for me to hold my footing. Porath yelled: 'Here they come, Looie!' German fighters were closing on us – not head-on or diving, but rather parallel to us, as if in escort. I could even see the pilot of one fighter looking at us. I was amazed by this tactic, but didn't stop to think about it. My enemy was out there at practically point-blank range. Instinct took over and I began firing. So did Porath, Polk and Asiala. Parallel to us, with their fixed wing guns at right angles to us, they were totally defenceless. I saw two fighters in flames and one of them exploded as it fell. Others may have been hit, but I wasn't sure. Then all hell broke loose! Other German fighters raked the ship. Wires and control cables dangled like spaghetti. I listened for the bail out order. Silence – again.

The gunners in the rear never heard the order because the intercom was shot away. They did not know that Harrison had lowered the landing gear to indicate surrender, and that was why the fighters presented such an easy target; they were literally 'sitting ducks'. Harrison had taken evasive action, hoping to reach the safety of a cloud bank, but the German fighters kept heading him off. Lewis continues:

> She went into a steep dive. I was torn loose from my gun and flipped against the bulkhead. Porath slammed against me. Polk had gotten out of the ball turret and then he, too, fell against the bulkhead. As I lay pinned there, I couldn't see out of the ship, and thought: 'Oh my God, we're going straight into the ground!' I lost all hope. 'This is it,' I said to myself.
>
> Unbelievably, the steep dive angle was lessening and I dimly wondered if the ship was still airworthy and who was at the controls. Harrison, I hoped. She began to pull out and levelled off. We staggered to our feet, heading for the door to jump. I struggled to hook my 'chute buckles as I got to the door. Porath was shaking his head 'No!' and pointing out the window. The ground was rushing up to meet us. We braced ourselves. We were going in!
>
> She nosed up gently and bellied into a wheatfield. The tail touched first and we heard a tearing, crunching sound. Someone yelled: 'The bombs!' We looked toward the bulkhead. The ball turret had torn loose and was pushed up through the floor. It seemed an eternity before we slid to a halt. There was no fire. Almost no sound. We had ridden her in!

Incredibly, Harrison had got away with it. The crew scattered in all directions. Harrison was assisted by the French Underground and barefoot, he later crossed the Pyrenees into Spain. Lewis and Ossie Asiala, also aided by the Underground, managed to evade capture until October before being betrayed and sent to a PoW camp after some uncomfortable *Gestapo* interrogations. At *Stalag Luft* VII they were reunited with Jim Curtis and Earl Porath. Later, they heard that Turner, Polk, Charlie McNemar, the radio operator, navigator and bombardier, had travelled through the Underground and returned safely to England.

The Memphis Blues failed to return to Molesworth when twenty-two-year-old Lieutenant Calvin A. Swaffer, who came from Memphis, Tennessee, and was once in the RAF, was forced to ditch in the North Sea on his last mission. Air Sea Rescue picked up all ten crew thirty miles off Shoreham. At Grafton Underwood they waited in vain for Lieutenant James S. Munday's crew.

Jim Munday was shot down in the vicinity of Versailles.

> Plunging into a chestnut forest marginally walking-wounded and with the help of the French Maquis, I eventually arrived at a not-so-safe-house in Paris. Slowly recovering from my multiple wounds, I was programmed by the French Underground for evasion by way of

> Spain over the Pyrenees Mountains via the Brandy Line and Andorra to Barcelona. In the foothills of the Pyrenees: early into my second evening of my so called 'gruelling' trek to freedom, an incompletely healed bullet wound back of my left knee began to bleed copiously. I could not continue. I was running out of blood. My most capable and sympathetic Basque guide, with his small group of fellow escapees, no Americans, stoically advised me that he could not turn back. Hence with an abrupt *au revoir* and *bon chance* and a large one cycle handshake, I was abruptly left sitting in a towering, lonely niche, between two large rocks, pondering a bleak future.
>
> My salvation turned out to be a band of roving, sympathetic, outlawed gypsies. Once again, regaining my health within their austere clan, I later continued my crossing solo. I was one of a very few American evadees (if any) to accomplish this, shall we say, 'solo feat'. Eventually arriving Madrid via Barcelona, I was ferried by the British Embassy limousine to Gibraltar then via British air back to Scotland to England and thence to the remnants of my 384th Bomb Group. I had been gone over four months and had covered 3,000 miles. My greatest thrill was receiving almost five months' back pay. My cup runneth over. Never again would I be so rich and yes, so thankful to Him my Guide and Benefactor.

At Chelveston sixteen of the twenty Forts in the 305th that had taken off returned damaged and one – *Windy City Challenger* – was missing.

Joe Chely's crew had been scheduled to fly the mission in *Big Moose*. But as Ed Burford, navigator recalls:

> ...he could not start the animal's second engine so we hurriedly switched to '803', which had four guns inoperative because crew chief 'Junior' Grimm and his men had been unable to complete their work. The Chely crew liked '803' even though she had no nose art, was dressed in dull olive green and had a few unseemly patches and oil-stain streaks but she seemed sturdy, dependable and unflappable. Bombardier Jim Miller and I liked jumping, swinging big band music and one of the favourite records which we took overseas was *Flat Foot Floogie with a floyjoy – yeah!* We liked the idea of *Flat Foot Floogie* for a name but unfortunately we never knew of Bruce Bairnsfather nor did we have time to supervise any nose art. Nevertheless, we affectionately called her by that name and more often than not, merely *Floogie.*
>
> Shortly after some very bad flak over the target and bombs away,

I first caught sight of a lone yellow-nosed bastard giving us one fantastic flying exhibition at 12 o'clock high for the benefit of our entire 40th Combat Wing. That hot rock did it all – figure eight, chandelle. Corkscrew – all that good stuff that pilots really enjoy. It could have been *Kommodore* Pips Priller, Wutz Galland, Karl Borris or any one of a host of their aces.[14] Either the fighters had arrived late or the German controllers could not decide how deep we were going for their ideal plan was to whack us at the IP and just beyond in order to distract the bombing But there was going to be a dance, no doubt about it. My bombardier roommate, Jim Miller, who was on his first raid, had washed out of primary pilot training and was especially entranced by the show but I was eyeballing the star's playmates pulling up left getting in position for Act II. After the solo, everybody knew what would follow. Finally, the leader levelled off at 12 o'clock with his wingman very close behind and barrel rolled and kept firing at the group lead with his plane lit up like a Christmas tree. The tracers were unbelievable. Every gun from our wing that could bear on those two targets let loose in a tremendous tracer cone of red but it did not seem to deter them one iota.

Although everyone knew what was going down, someone sang out on the intercom, 'Fighter 12 o'clock level!' Miller had his hands on those twin fifties long before and watched intently. He quickly answered with a 'Roger'. I could not bring my gun to bear on the targets, so I stupidly decided to watch the show out the Plexiglas nose. By this time the whole sky was lit up. Now our pilot Joe Chely was getting nervous in the service and screamed, 'Get that son of a bitch, Miller!' My heart was in my mouth as I kept sinking towards the floor yelling, 'Get him; get him, Jim.' Those two FW 190s practically split our squadrons by mere feet and knifed downwards. I couldn't tell you exactly how many feet away, for by that time my eyes were closed and I was flat on the floor of the airplane for it was too brutal to watch. Believe it or not, our Walter Mitty bombardier had not fired one shot!

Man, after I got my nerve back, I was hopping mad, dumbfounded and not in the least amused by Miller's performance. I barked at him. 'What in the hell was the matter with you? Did you freeze?'

He turned with a blanched face and answered, 'I have seen good flying before but nothing like that.'

Ouch, what a guy. Instead of hanging on those triggers, he sat quietly and admired them.

Afterwards, at the briefing, Joe Chely remarked to the intelligence officer:

'The very first FW 190 came in at 12 o'clock dead level Jim never even got his guns on him but Balsley in the top turret got in a short burst that did no damage. He went into a neat half roll about two hundred yards from our nose and still firing dove into the 422nd Squadron below us. He hit the ship directly below us with 20mm and set the #3 engine on fire. The *Windy City Challenger* was seen to explode shortly afterwards and only two chutes were observed.'[15]

The fighters followed us for about twenty minutes and we ran into more heavy and accurate flak about ten minutes before we left the coast at Le Havre, *Floogie* was hit three times by flak. One piece penetrated the fuselage just above the left waist gun, which had Joe Showalter shaking his head. Another burst exploded directly beneath the bomb bay tearing a jagged whole in one door. The other piece hit the #2 engine penetrating the lower part of the cowling and lodging in a rocker box. Chely was sure we had lost an engine but all we lost was a little oil. Our ball turret gunner, Larry Ashcraft, said that pieces of flak bounced off his turret twice.

Crew chief Junior Grimm and his men had some work to do.

On 17 July a record 332 bombers, including the 385th and 388th Bomb Groups, which were flying their first missions as part of the 4th Wing, were dispatched early in the morning to Hannover. At 0955 after the bombers had crossed the Dutch coast the mission was recalled owing to bad weather, which had prevented the combat wings from forming up properly. Twenty-one heavies bombed Amsterdam with poor results and thirty-four others bombed targets of opportunity. Fortunately for the unescorted bombers the widely dispersed formations prevented the German fighter controllers from concentrating their fighters in any one area and encounters were few. *Luftwaffe* pilots claimed thirteen bombers shot down. One of these was *Snowball* in the famed 'Ball Boys' Squadron in the 351st Bomb Group, which caught the brunt of a head-on attack. After a twenty minute air battle, 1st Lieutenant William Peters, who was flying his thirteenth mission, ditched the plane in the North Sea, midway between Amsterdam and England:

The nine of us who survived to climb into life rafts were later found by the pilot of an Anson, picked up by the crews of two Walruses and transferred to two naval launches. Three hours and several bottles of Johnnie Walker later, we staggered happily onto the wharf at Great

Yarmouth, more inebriated than hurt. Ambulances took us to a Roman Catholic hospital in town where we spent the night. The last thing we wanted to see the next morning was fish but at breakfast we were confronted by kippers![16]

The 385th had moved to Great Ashfield, Suffolk, during the first week of July and the 388th landed at Knettishall nearby. On 18 July the seventh and final group to join the 4th Wing – the 390th – flew south from Prestwick to its permanent base at Parham, near Framlingham in Suffolk. General Eaker now had the means to launch an all-out air offensive. All the commanders needed was a week of fine weather for 'Blitz Week' (after the German word for 'lightning') to succeed. On 23 July Eaker was informed that clear skies could be expected over Europe for a few days; long enough to mount the long-awaited succession of attacks, which would become known as 'Blitz Week'. It began in the early hours of 24 July and at briefing crews learned that this would be no ordinary mission to an ordinary target. For the first time the 8th Air Force would bomb targets in Norway. The 1st Wing would bomb the aluminium, magnesium and nitrate plant of Nordisk Lettmetal at Heroya, which was still nearing completion. A smaller force of 4th Wing bombers equipped with 'Tokyo tanks' would bomb the dock areas at Bergen and Trondheim, the Trondheim mission necessitating a 2,000-mile round trip, the longest American mission over Europe. To save fuel there would be no assembly; the lead B-17s would go on course immediately after take-off and would cruise at reduced power and at low altitude to allow the following aircraft to take their positions in the formation as they flew out over the North Sea.

The bomb groups began taking off in overcast but the formation proceeded on course. Well off the coast of northern Denmark the 1st Wing flew northeast up the Skagerrak and climbed to bombing altitude at 16,000 feet, while the 4th Wing groups continued up the West Coast of Norway to their targets at Bergen and Trondheim, not far south of the Arctic Circle. Each wing flew with a gap of ten minutes, or about thirty miles, to allow time for the smoke from exploding bombs to clear and give the following strike forces a more precise aiming point for their bombardiers. The planners had considered this feasible because flak defences were believed to be poor that far north. When the bombers reached their relatively low bombing altitude of 16,000 feet over the Skagerrak they began flying above overcast that lay below them at about 10,000 feet. The cloud blotted out the countryside and was probably instrumental in keeping the *Luftwaffe* grounded at their bases in northern

Denmark. The bomb bay doors swung open beneath the B-17s and still there appeared no break in the cloud. It began to look as though the crews would have to return to England carrying their bombs but Colonel William M. Reid, the 92nd CO and the air commander, took the formation around for a second time and bombed through a sudden break in the cloud. (This feat earned him the Silver Star.) The groups following had difficulty in picking out the mean point of impact, so they were instructed to bomb the centre of the smoke pall, which by now hung almost stationary over the entire target area.

Colonel Budd J. Peaslee, CO of the 384th, was flying the mission. Peaslee was born in upper New York State and grew up in California's Salinas Valley. He had attended the Salinas schools at the same time as John Steinbeck, had studied at the University of Nevada and enlisted in the US Army Air Corps as a Flying Cadet. He received his regular commission in 1928. Peaslee flew with the Roosevelt Flying Service carrying the *New York Times* to Montreal with the 18th and 8th Pursuit Groups and the Army air mail service before he was assigned, in 1940, to command the first bomber squadron to Alaska. During the early days of the war, he served with the Fourth Bomber Command, charged with the air defences of the West Coast and later he was reassigned to the 2nd Air Force and the training of the combat bomber crews. On 1 January 1943 Peaslee began training the 384th, accompanied them to England in June and for the next twenty months was engaged with them in combat.

> On the second bombing run the flak gunners had ample opportunity to perfect their aim and as the formation approached the target the bursts became accurate and intense. This time the bombs went away and the navigator gave the return flight course. As the bombers withdrew it was possible to see that the island was in a shambles… destruction had been heaped on destruction. Great fires were burning and ships at the docks were in flames. An awesome sight and one to remember for a lifetime.

Altogether, 167 bombers bombed Heroya and completely devastated the great industrial complex. The attack, so far from England, caught the enemy unaware and many German dignitaries and Norwegian quislings attending a dedication ceremony were killed in the raid. No bombers were lost, but *Georgia Rebel*, flown by 1st Lieutenant O.V. Jones in the 381st, was damaged severely by flak over the target and managed to drop its bombs was seen leaving the formation at about 1418 hours with No. 2 engine feathered. The prop was bent and a hole was seen in the port wing near the fuel tanks with petrol leaking out. No. 3 engine was smoking and losing oil. *Georgia Rebel* was then seen to make a 180-degree turn and fly in the general direction of neutral Sweden. At 1500 hours Jones belly-landed the ailing B-17 at Vännacka ninety kilometres south-east of Oslo in Sweden. The crew was not willing to give any information about their mission to the Swedish authorities. Soon after the B-17F's emergency landing the aircraft was dismantled and taken to SAAB in Linköping, where it was later used for spare parts for rebuilding other B-17s as commercial airliners for ABA, the Swedish airline. The crew was interned at Camp I at Främby (Falun). Jones and 1st Lieutenant G. McIntosh the co-pilot returned to England via Bromma airport in Stockholm on 22 November and the other eight crew members returned on 12 March 1944 in a BOAC C-47 Dakota.[17]

Colonel Peaslee concludes:

> The bombing of Heroya has passed into history and is rarely recalled, except by those who made the trip and who still survive. To them it was the most successful and shrewdly planned and executed mission of the entire war.

Forty-one B-17s of the 4th Wing bombed Trondheim from 20,000 feet and testimony to their accuracy was provided later by a RAF photo-reconnaissance Spitfire, which brought back photos of a sunken U-boat, a damaged destroyer and gutted workshops in the harbour area. The other 4th Wing groups crossed Bergen harbour at 16,000 feet but the target was completely covered with clouds and eighty-four aircraft had to return to England and land with full bomb loads – something crews were never happy about. About fifteen Junkers Ju 88s put in an appearance on the return leg but caused no damage to the B-17 formations. Crews were upset about the failure to bomb Bergen; none more so than 'Pappy' Colby, who was flying with the 94th.

> It was 8 hours 45 minutes of flying for nothing but we did see some of the mountains of Norway and one peak was covered with snow. The country appeared rugged, as all the towns and small farms were located in fords on the west coast. One of my memories of the mission was coming home down the North Sea all relaxed and listening to beautiful German opera music on our radio.

The following day, 25 July, the Fortresses were again out in force, this time to targets in north-western Germany. One combat wing from the 1st Bomb Wing was dispatched to Kiel; the remaining groups going to Hamburg to bomb the Blohm und Voss shipyards. As they neared the city crews could see a towering 15,000 feet column of smoke; a result of fires still burning after a raid by RAF Bomber Command the previous night. Crews in the first elements managed to bomb before thick cloud added to the smoke and the shipyards were well hit. However, Hamburg's notorious flak and fighter defences accounted for nineteen Fortresses, including seven in the 'unlucky' 384th.

Meanwhile, 4th Bomb Wing Fortresses headed for Warnemünde on the north German coast. Clouds obscured the target and they were forced to head for the submarine construction yards at Kiel. About thirty fighters attacked the 94th near the target. Lieutenant John P. Keelan, pilot of *Happy Daze*, recalls:

> When the fighters hit us, the wing swelled up like a balloon and then burst into flames and we went into a dive. I didn't give the order to bail out because I thought we might pull out of it. I got it under control only 150 feet from the water, just in time to ditch, about 60 miles off the coast. [Getting into a life raft one of the gunners fell into the water, breaking the strap on his Mae West and he could not swim! He was never seen again.] We tied our dinghies together and then started worrying. We were a long way from home and closer to Germany than any other land. We were afraid that the Germans might pick us up. We not only watched Kiel burning that night but we actually sat out there in the water and had a grandstand view of the RAF bombing the German coast. We could see the flak bursting and the fires started by the RAF blockbusters. About noon the next day a British plane [a Halifax] spotted us. He dropped three big dinghies and then hung around to protect us from possible attack by a Ju 88 that hovered in the distance. Soon another RAF plane [a Lockheed Hudson] joined him, then three more, then three Forts showed up. It looked like the combined Allied air force above us. One of the RAF planes [a Warwick] dropped a launch by parachute. It was a sight to see that boat come parachuting down, settling right beside us. It was all closed with hatches sealed, we opened it up and there were sleeping bags, food, water, gasoline and directions for running the thing. I had an idea that I might get the boys to head for New York...

They sailed the boat 120 miles, at which point a Danish fishing boat picked them up. The Danes agreed to take the crew to England and instead of returning to Denmark, decided to join the Free Danish Navy operating from the British Isles.

There was no let-up in the American offensive and 'Blitz Week' gained momentum. On 26 July more than 300 heavies were dispatched to Hannover and Hamburg. Thick cloud over East Anglia hampered assembly and despite the recent introduction of 'Splasher' beacons for forming up, many groups became scattered and so they were recalled. Only two combat wings won through to their targets. Other elements bombed targets of opportunity along the German coast. Among the ninety-two Fortresses that successfully attacked Hannover were seventeen Forts and two YB-40s of the 92nd. Shortly before they crossed the coast the formation came under frontal attack by FW 190s. *Yo' Brother* flown by Lieutenant Alan E. Hermance was seen to hit the water about ten minutes from the island of Nordeney with one engine on fire and the tail badly damaged. Lieutenant Paul S. Casey Jr and the crew of *Hell-Lena* also ditched in the sea and all the crew were rescued. Captain Blair G. Belongia's aircraft, after sustaining an attack by seven FW 190s just after entering the enemy coast, suffered the loss of two engines and lagged behind the formation. Bombs were salvoed south of Hannover and the ship was put into a slow, shallow dive and the shortest route taken for home, with every possible care taken to avoid the heavily defended areas. However, flak was encountered at Ashendorf and to avoid it, the aircraft dropped down to 50 feet, narrowly missing some of the buildings of the town. Over Emden Bay, heavy fire was encountered but the enemy smoke screen helped immeasurably. Limping along over the sea at about 200 feet, the aircraft was attacked by a Bf 109. Belongia dropped down to about 25 feet and the fighter, unable to dive under the ship, nosed up to the right, where Staff Sergeant Joseph M. Walsh, the tail gunner, fired a burst into its belly. The enemy crashed into the sea. With fuel running low Belongia ordered everything removable to be jettisoned. Over the English coast, the No. 1 engine went dry. When no suitable landing field was sighted, Belongia turned the aircraft back out to sea and ordered the crew to take their positions in the radio room for ditching. The plane was brought down on the water about two miles from shore near Sheringham; the crew abandoned ship safely and piled into one dinghy. An hour later they were picked up by a fishing boat and landed on the coast.

Other 92nd aircraft suffered in the attack. They included *Ruthie II*, piloted by Lieutenant Robert L. Campbell, who had brought the first *Ruthie* home from Nantes on 4 July and his co-pilot, Flight Officer John Morgan, a six-foot red-haired Texan who had flown with the RCAF. For seven months before transferring to the 8th Air Force. The navigator, Keith J. Koske, later wrote:

We were on our way into the enemy coast when we were attacked by a group of FW 190s. On the first pass I felt sure they had got us for there was a terrific explosion overhead and the ship rocked badly. A second later the top turret gunner, Staff Sergeant Tyre C. Weaver, fell through the hatch and slumped to the floor at the rear of my nose compartment. When I got to him his left arm had been blown off at the shoulder and he was a mass of blood. I first tried to inject some morphine but the needle was bad and I could not get it in. As things turned out it was best I didn't give him any morphine. My first thought was to try and stop his loss of blood. I tried to apply a tourniquet but it was impossible as the arm was off too close to shoulder. I knew he had to have the right kind of medical treatment as soon as possible and we had almost four hours flying time ahead of us so there was no alternative. I opened the escape hatch, adjusted his 'chute for him and placed the ripcord ring firmly in his right hand. He must have become excited and pulled the cord, opening the pilot 'chute in the up draught. I managed to gather it together and tuck it under his right arm, got him into a crouched position with legs through the hatch, made certain again that his good arm was holding the 'chute folds together and toppled him out into space. I learned somewhat later from our ball turret gunner, James L. Ford, that the chute opened OK. We were at 24,500 feet and 25 miles due west of Hannover and our only hope was that he was found and given medical attention immediately.

The bombardier, Asa J. Irwin, had been busy with the nose guns and when I got back up in the nose he was getting ready to toggle his bombs. The target area was one mass of smoke and we added our contribution. After we dropped our bombs we were kept busy with the nose guns. However, all our attacks were from the tail and we could do very little good. I had tried to use my interphone several times but could get no answer. The last I remember hearing over it was shortly after the first attack, when someone was complaining about not getting oxygen. Except for what I thought to be some violent evasive action we seemed to be flying OK. It was two hours later, when we were fifteen minutes out from the enemy coast, that I decided to go up and check with the pilot and have a look around. I found Lieutenant Campbell slumped down in his seat and a mass of blood, the back of his head blown off. This had happened 'two hours' before, on the first attack. A shell had entered from the right side, crossed in front of John Morgan and had hit Campbell in the head.

> Morgan was flying the 'plane with one hand, holding the half-dead pilot off with the other hand and he had been doing it for over two hours!' [It was no mean feat; Campbell was a six-footer and weighed 185lb.] Morgan told me we had to get Campbell out of his seat, as the 'plane couldn't be landed from the co-pilot's seat as the glass on that side was shattered so badly you could barely see out. We struggled for thirty minutes getting the fatally injured pilot out of his seat and down into the rear of the navigator's compartment, where the bombardier held him from slipping out the open hatch. Morgan was operating the controls with one hand and helping me handle the pilot with the other.

The radio operator, waist and tail gunners were unable to lend assistance because they were unconscious through lack of oxygen, the lines having been shattered several hours earlier. Morgan's action was nothing short of miraculous. Not only had he flown the aircraft to the target and out again with no radio, no interphone and no hydraulic fluid but he had maintained formation the whole time. It was an incredible feat for a pilot flying one handed. Morgan brought *Ruthie II* in to land at RAF Foulsham, a few miles from the Norfolk coast and put down safely. Campbell died 1½ hours after they reached England. The other crew members survived, including Weaver, who had been put in a PoW camp after hospitalization.[18]

On Tuesday 27 July the 8th was stood down for a badly needed rest while the forecasters waited for the weather to improve over Europe. Aircraft were patched up and others were pensioned off. *Jersey Bounce* in the 'Hell's Angels' took no further part in the fighting war. It was transferred to the 11th CCRC[19] at Bovingdon following repairs to battle damage sustained a few days before. The radio operator, who before the war had been a store manager in Salt Lake City, recalled:

> We were getting along all right until the flak caught up with us and a fragment sliced through the fuselage into the ankle of our navigator. The pilot called me on the interphone to come and administer first aid to the navigator but I was too busy fighting off enemy planes that were attacking from the rear. As soon as I had a chance, I crawled forward to the nose and found the navigator sitting on an ammunition box cheerfully spotting fighters for the bombardier, who was leaping from one side of the nose to the other, manning both guns. I applied a tourniquet to the navigator's leg, gave him some sulpha pills and sprinkled the wound with sulpha

> powder. Three times I had to stop to take a gun and help the bombardier ward off attacks from dead ahead. Then the lead ship of our element was hit in the No. 1 engine and began to fall back. We dropped back too, holding our position on our leader's wing. Just then a FW flashed in like a barracuda, came right between the two Fortresses and raked our ship with cannon fire. I could feel the hits slamming into us. Word came through that the tail gunner was hit and then just afterward the interphone went dead. The wounded navigator seemed all right, so I crawled back to the tail gunner. He was intact but he told me that the ball turret had received a direct hit. I went back to take a look and found that it was completely wrecked. The gunner was crumpled in the wreckage. I tried to do what I could for him but it was no use. I don't think he ever knew what hit him. I reached into the turret and fixed the broken connection of the interphone and then I went back to the nose and gave the navigator a shot of morphine to ease his pain. Then I went back to the radio compartment to man my own gun again.
>
> That's all there is to it.[20]

'Blitz Week' was resumed on the morning of Wednesday 28 July, when the 1st Wing made an ambitious attack on the Fieseler Works at Kassel and the 4th Wing had the dubious honour of flying the deepest penetration so far, to the FW 190 assembly plant at Oschersleben about eighty miles from Berlin.

Captain Caroll Joe Bender, pilot of *Tarfu* (Things are really fucked up) in the 'Snetterton Falcons' who earned a reputation for getting damaged ships back to base ... fifteen maybe ... recalls:

> After forming up, the mission started out from the UK coast and went over the North Sea, north of Germany. Where it appeared we should turn right and enter, we actually turned left and continued north, the idea being to use the additional spare fuel we carried to perform a feint to attract the German fighters and let them use up some of their fuel, then go into Germany to the target. We made the turn west but by then were in an awful battle. We made the turn again to the left, now aligned south to penetrate. We had considerable weather and all kinds of clouds. The lead group took us through it and the 96th was ambushed by squadrons of fighters, with large flak-charged cannons on their Me 109s and FW 190s that shot hell out of us. The 337th Squadron's lead plane, *Liberty Bell*, flown by Captain Milton C. Fulton, the flight leader, was shot out of formation. All

hands were lost except bombardier Lawrence Wolford who survived only because he was rescued from the North Sea by a German air-sea rescue plane.

I took the lead but nobody but Nance stayed with me. My ship had a tremendous hole in the right wing. We'd lost our Tokyo gas (extra fuel) and oxygen. We'd never have got out of Germany if we hadn't aborted. I signalled Nance to leave me and go into a group. I dove into a cloud and came out of it with six fighters on our tail and one on the right wing. There were two flights of three attacks on our nose. We got six of the bastards and the one on the right wing. A single fighter tried to get a left turn, come in at an angle and rake us, a dark aircraft that must have been a night fighter. He must have looked at his fuel and it was now or never. I moved closer to him; then when he finally made a pass, I skidded and slipped to make him tighten his turn, which must have made him black out. He came very close under us, never to be seen again. I think he must have cut the antenna on the belly of our aircraft. As for three fighters that came in on the nose from above, bombardier Bill Henry fired the 50 cal' and luckily hit the lead fighter, so the other two broke left and right. I never saw the flight that came in on the nose from under, but the ball turret gunner did, prior to getting the bombs out. The top turret engineer, Zack Brooks, followed a fighter through clouds he was using to obscure his attack and got this one as he came out of the clouds to fire. Outmanoeuvred the knockout blow. God, what a fight alone!

And then we flew home. As we had come in over the sea, we circled a picket boat quietly riding the waves. Maybe it was the one that let the Germans know we were coming and what time. I couldn't see anyone aboard though, and told the gunners not to fire. We could probably have put a few holes in that boat if we had.

I had to land the crippled ship on one wheel. Back at the base, I steered off the runway into the ploughed area in order to keep the runway clear for the others coming in after me. We got out of the plane promptly, the crew ready for possible fire. Lew Fluelling, the navigator, looked at Lew Feldstein, the co-pilot and said, 'Ah, Lew, ya' left the flaps down!' Lew clambered back onto the plane and put them down.

At that point, I yelled, 'Lew, get out a' there!' The only casualty was that Loughery, the radio operator, got a chip off his nose, but not bad. I walked around to the tail end of the airplane, tears in my eyes and frustrated as hell, wishing I had another plane and could

> instantly return to flight. Then I realized I was looking into the eastern sky for the damaged planes to come in. There weren't any. (Some of the aborted planes had landed at other bases.) Major Emerson went down with Fulton. Seven of the Fortresses which left Snetterton Heath at 0545 did not make it back to base and that evening there were seventy empty cots in quarters. It was hell to be in empty barracks. Losing Fulton's crew broke us up badly. Lost Nance too. There were three original crews out of twelve and three replacement crews of our squadron. I hoped to get in twelve more missions okay, and then go home. Twenty-five missions in this theatre were too much. By God, I wanted to win this war.[21]

Fifteen Fortresses in the 4th Wing were lost[22] but strike photos showed that the Forts had knocked out 50 per cent of the plant. Cloud interfered with the mission to Kassel and only a fraction of the 182 B-17s managed to hit the Fieseler works. JG 1 and II, some of which attacked firing rocket projectiles, 8 inches in diameter from beneath their wings, were credited with shooting down most of the total of twenty-two bombers that were lost. Bomber losses would have been greater had it not been for the Thunderbolts of the 4th Fighter Group who engaged an estimated forty-five enemy fighters over northern Holland and claimed nine destroyed.[23] One of the worst hit groups was the 95th, which lost three B-17s[24] while in the 1st Wing seven Forts went down and four more were written off in crash landings at Framlingham, Foulsham, and southwest of Oxford.[25]

On 29 July the 8th set out for the fourth time in five days, the 168 Forts in the 1st Wing setting out for the shipyards at Kiel and the 4th Wing heading for the Heinkel assembly plant at Warnemünde, which had escaped the attention of the B-17s four days before. Many of the same crews who had gone to Kassel were in the air for this mission. At Thurleigh the CQs were in the barracks at 0430 to get the crews out for the long haul to Kiel with take-off scheduled for 0700. The grousing was a loud rumble since crews were being called on for their third tough mission in five days. Little did they know that the fighter attacks at Kiel would be just as vicious and almost as prolonged as they had been the day before. It was this kind of mission that produced the nightmares, the tears and the extreme fatigue among the flyers. Captain George E. Paris Jr, a 369th 'Fightin' Bitin' lead pilot with a new set of double bars on his shoulders was leading the 306th. Eighteen planes left Thurleigh but by 0845 five ships had aborted for a variety of reasons. One crew could not catch the group after a late plane change before take-off, another had crew 'problems'; others reported mechanical failures.[26]

At the Heinkel plant the bombing was described as 'excellent' and FW 190 production was severely curtailed. At 1st Wing bases eight Forts were missing.[27] Four of them were in the 306th and all were claimed by pilots of JG 26. 1st Lieutenant Keith Conley, a twenty-two-mission veteran and his crew had been the first to go down when fighters swept through the depleted low squadron. Ten chutes were counted out of the aircraft but two crew died. Next down was 1st Lieutenant Donald R. Winter's crew from the same low squadron. A wing came off and Winter and three crew were killed. A few minutes later all of Flight Officer Carl D. Brown's crew, the entire crew in the 'Clay Pigeons' Squadron, died when the aircraft exploded. Eight chutes came out of Flight Officer Berryman H. Brown's plane in the same squadron after it lost two engines and could not be controlled.

Next day, 30 July, VIII Bomber Command brought down the curtain on 'Blitz Week' when 186 Fortresses in the 1st and 4th Wings went to the aircraft factories at Kassel – a round trip of some 600 miles. The weather was fine and P-47 Thunderbolts equipped with long-range fuel tanks escorted the heavies almost to the target and back again. Without the 'Jugs' B-17 losses would have been on an alarming scale because the Fortress formations were hit by a ferocious onslaught of enemy fighters as Howard E. Hernan, flying as top turret gunner aboard *The Old Squaw* in the 303rd formation, remembers:

> We were hit by more enemy fighters than ever before. The estimate was well in excess of 300. At one time I counted 157 flying off to our right. A fighter came down through our formation and then a whole *Gruppe* of them got ahead of us and started making pass after pass. Most of them we fought off and turned away at 7–800 yards. They would flip over on their backs and down they would go to get more latitude and then they would try again. Of course, the *Luftwaffe* painted their aircraft various colours and some were quite pretty. A snow-white Bf 109 dived on us. He had a beautiful Iron Cross painted on the wings and fuselage. He was coming so fast, with a strong tail wind behind him, that he came right through the formation and began making a turn to the right. So help me God he came between us and our wing man on the left, upside down, went between our wings and never touched either of us!

The B-17 crews flew four of the six-hour round trip on oxygen and over enemy territory Hernan's supply ran out. Arthur W. Miller, the co-pilot, had to feed him oxygen from walk-around bottles while he tried to shoot at incoming fighters. Hernan and Quick were each credited with one fighter apiece. On the way to the target the Fortresses had been aided by a strong wind that had given them 160mph indicated airspeed. Now, on the homeward trip, they had to buck this wind. Howard Hernan picked out a landmark and looked down on it. Ten minutes later it was still there! Altogether, twelve Fortresses were lost as a result of enemy action and others came home low on gas. No. 4 engine quit, out of fuel just as *The Old Squaw* finally reached the coast of England and Claude Campbell glided down on to an airfield before the No. 2 began to splutter. *Upstairs Maid* failed to make it home to Molesworth. Lieutenant Cogswell ditched twenty-two miles off Felixstowe and all the crew were rescued by ASR. One by one, others ran low on fuel and put down where they could. *Old Jackson* crash-landed at Woodbridge. *Patches* in the 384th crash-landed at another fighter airfield, at Boxted, the salvaged parts being used later for other B-17s in the group. In the 379th, which had lost *Flying Jenny* and another Fort over the continent, Lieutenant Melton D. Wallace crashed and burned at Framlingham, killing all ten crew while *Jackie Ellen* crash-landed near Alconbury. *Hell's Belle* overshot the runway on return to Bassingbourn and was written off, adding to the two others shot down over the continent. *Man-O-War* and eight members of 2nd Lieutenant Keene C. McCammon's crew were killed. Two survived to be taken prisoner. Eight men survived in Lieutenant Robert M. Miles' crew flying *Yankee Dandy*.

The crew of *Poisonality* in the 351st had seen a few fighters and a little flak as they crossed the coast going in and things had gone well until forty minutes from the target when the manifold pressure of No. 4 engine suddenly dropped to twelve and stayed there. James J. Maginnis, the pilot, recalls:

> We manipulated turbo control, throttle, mixture, rpm and cowl flaps but could get no rise from the turbo. It was quite evident that either the turbo regulator or the turbo itself was gone. The engine was left running since it wasn't holding us back too much and a feathered engine is always an invitation to enemy fighters. We determined to reach the target so long as they didn't cause us to lose the formation.
>
> At this time [twenty-three-year-old Jimmy E.] McCurdy, the left waist gunner, reported that the flaps had crept down four to five inches. This was indicated in the cockpit but the flaps would not retract electrically. The waist gunner was ordered to crank them up and bind the handle in place. This was done, though the flaps remained slightly down. We stayed with the formation on three

> engines until about ten minutes before the target when No. 4 engine began to throw oil and smoke very badly. At this point, we feathered it. The target was reached OK and our bombs were dropped from close formation. With the help of William J. Holloway, the navigator, the turns from the target and rally point were anticipated and utilized to keep us close to the formation.
>
> Right after the target we began totalling the gas and found the greatest amount was 95 gallons in No. 4 tank. It was evident we would have entirely too little gas to complete the mission as scheduled. William A. Glenn, the engineer, was ordered to transfer fuel from No. 4 to No. 1 tank since No. 1 was the lowest. He set the fuel transfer valves and pump, but after fifteen minutes it was evident that no gas was leaving No. 4 tank. The pump fuse was checked and found OK. No hand transfer pump was installed. It was necessary to use full power all the way out to stay with the formation in its evasive action against flak. When possible we climbed up into the high squadron on the inside of turns and when necessary we dropped down into the lead or low squadron on the outside of turns. Then as we approached the coast, No. 1 began cutting out for lack of gas causing us to drop behind the formation. We dove to try to catch the low squadron and at this time I first heard the plane being peppered with bullets and shells. We could not catch the low squadron so I dove for the group below us.
>
> An explosive shell hit the oxygen, throwing splinters into the pilot and co-pilot, filling the cockpit with smoke and dust and starting a fire. Although not wounded, Holloway and Edward C. Piech, the bombardier, were knocked down and stunned.

William A. Glenn, the radio operator, adds:

> When the shell hit *Poisonality*'s oxygen system, the concussion made our ears nearly useless and started a fire in the cabin. Peterson handed me a fire extinguisher and the fire was put out quickly. I saw Peterson reach behind him, grab a chest chute and put it on. I thought we were getting ready to bail out. I looked for mine and couldn't find it anywhere. I thought it had fallen out of the hole the 20mm had made in the floor of the cabin. The hole (between my turret and the pilot's seat) was as large as a No. 2 washtub. I resolved to myself that nobody was going to bail out without having me go with them, piggyback. On the ground later, I found that the chute Peterson had put on was mine. He was really embarrassed about that, even though

> he got it by mistake. It was his chute that had gone through the hole in the floor. (After that experience I went to the armament shop and had a hook made. From then on, I kept my chute in the corner of the cabin, where no one could get it).

Maginnis continues:

> The co-pilot [Roy H. Peterson] put the fire out with a fire extinguisher. Simultaneously, the bomb bay doors swung open, the flaps went down one-third and No. 1 engine stopped putting out and was feathered. I started diving at 250–300 mph and over 6,000 feet per minute, taking evasive action, while heading for a layer of stratocumulus clouds at 5,000 feet. Near the cloud layer, with No. 1 and No. 4 engines feathered, orders were given to prepare for ditching. In the cloud layer a course of 275 degrees was taken and soon No. 3 engine ran out of gas and was feathered. Altitude was lost to 3,000 feet, where we broke out below the cloud. The fighters had left us. No. 4 engine was unfeathered and was found to put out full power but no turbo boost. Airspeed was kept at 110–120 to maintain 3,000 feet altitude. All preparations had been made for ditching. SOSs and QDMs were going out OK. McCurdy, badly wounded, was in the radio room being treated. We sighted the English coast about ten miles ahead. As we crossed the coast at 3,000 feet, No. 2 engine began to falter and soon thereafter was feathered. That left No. 4 doing all the work.
>
> A few miles inland we spotted an airfield [Leiston] under construction. We examined the control cables and surfaces and found them satisfactory for any landing. The wheels were put down and we stayed between the coast and the airport so a ditching or a beach landing could be made if the wheels [failed to extend fully]. Two of the three runways had large obstructions on them, but the third had only minor obstructions such as barrels and bales of wire. The wheels and tyres were down and checked, so an approach was made with the crew in position for a crash-landing. The landing was made and immediately the right tire began to go flat. The ship was kept on the runway with the left brake and No. 4 engine, the only un-feathered engine. About thirty gallons of gas were left in No. 4.
>
> Perfect co-operation was achieved by the whole crew. Every man did his assigned job throughout and all obeyed orders quickly and accurately. In the few minutes of running fight, Daniel L. Reeder, the tail gunner, shot down two enemy fighters; Verl P. Long, the ball

> turret gunner, shot down another; and McCurdy a fourth after he had received his mortal wound.[28]

Four other members of the crew, including Maginnis, were struck by 20mm shell fragments and were treated in hospital. *Poisonality* was so badly shot up by enemy fighters that it could not be repaired.

In a week of sustained combat operations VIII Bomber Command had lost about 100 aircraft and 90 combat crews. This reduced its combat strength to fewer than 200 heavies ready for combat. On 31 July groups were told to stand down after a week of exhausting raids. Crews had flown themselves almost to a standstill and were glad of the rest, however brief, as 'Pappy' Colby recalls.

> Some of the boys were developing the equivalent of shell shock, in spite of all our doctor's efforts. The nervous strain of continuous raids had been more than some of them could take. It raised the very rough command problem as to how long these lads would still be fit to fly a combat mission, especially the pilots whose nine-man crews trusted them with their lives. I finally had to go to Colonel Castle about one pilot who was rapidly coming unstuck, as the British say and they sent him to the rest home in southern England. He didn't like it and I felt real sorry for him, but Colonel Castle agreed that it was no longer safe to send him on combat raids.

Notes

1. Andrews Field was so-named for Lt General Frank Maxwell Andrews, Commanding General of the ETO. He was killed on 4 May 1943 when the Liberator in which he was flying, piloted by Captain Robert 'Shine' Shannon of the 93rd BG, crashed into a bleak Icelandic mountain on the way home to the USA. Only Sgt George Eisel, tail gunner, survived after being trapped in the wreckage for fourteen hours. Shannon, son of the editor of a small daily paper in Washington, Iowa, and the crew of *Hot Stuff* was the first crew at Hardwick to complete a tour.
2. The 96th BG's former base at Grafton Underwood was taken over by the 384th BG commanded by Colonel Budd J. Peaslee, which arrived in England during late May. The 351st BG remained at Polebrook. The 1st BW received additional 'teeth' with the arrival of the 381st BG, commanded by Colonel Joe J. Nazzaro, which flew into Ridgewell on 31 May and the 379th BG.
3. Six men in Captain John O. Hall's crew were KIA and four were taken prisoner after their B-17 crashed in France. All ten men in Lt Arthur P. Hale's crew survived and were taken prisoner. Eight of Lt Theodore M. Peterson's crew in *Lady Godiva* were captured and two evaded. Major 'Swede' Carlson

crash-landed at Little Staughton. On 1 May Carlson had been at the controls of another ship that was wrecked at Prestwick at the end of a ferry flight from the USA.

4 2nd Lt William A. Petruzzi of Elyria, Ohio, was one of two men KIA. Jack Workman of Newbury, South Carolina, and seven others PoW. The other two B-17s that were lost were *Hell Below* flown by Lt Max Hecox, which ditched in the English Channel. Nine of the crew including Lt Charles B. 'Chic' Harrison, Lt Roland C. McCoy and 2nd Lt Rolland V. Vanderhook were KIA (two PoW). On Lt Merle E. Brown's B-17, eight men including Brown, 2nd Lt Ortho B. Wood, Lt Quentin L. Sandahl and Lt William J. O'Brien were KIA (one PoW).

5. Herbert was shot down flying *Klo Kay* on 13 June and had to ditch in the English Channel (nine KIA, one PoW).

6. Hendershot had been Harrison's original co-pilot until he had been given his own crew.

7. *Lingering Contrails of The Big Square A: A History of the 94th Bomb Group (H) 1942–1945* by Harry E. Slater (1980). Also, the 4th Wing was strengthened by the arrival, in early June, of the 100th BG (first to Podington, then to Thorpe Abbotts, Suffolk) and the imminent arrival of two more, the 385th and 388th, which would increase the 4th Wing to six groups.

8. On 14 July Captain Kee Harrison in a replacement B-17, as *Mr Five By Five*, was still under repair following the Hüls mission was hit repeatedly by German fighters. He crash-landed in a wheat field and the crew scattered in all directions. Harrison was assisted by the French Underground and barefoot he later crossed the Pyrenees into Spain. Lewis and another crewmember evaded capture until October before being betrayed and sent to a PoW camp after some uncomfortable *Gestapo* interrogations. At *Stalag Luft* VII they were reunited with two of the crew and later they heard that the five other crew had been returned safely to England.

9. The first weeks of YB-40 operations indicated that the idea of multi-gunned B-17s flying in bomber formations would not work. The additional machine guns on each YB-40 did not add materially to the combined firepower a group formation could provide. Only stragglers were regularly attacked by the *Luftwaffe* and the YB-40s were unable to protect these from concentrated attacks. Losses were not made good although the YB-40s continued flying missions until the end of July 1943.

10. Captain Stallings was awarded both the British and US DFC. 1st Lt James Ford Kelly, waist gunner S/Sgt Joseph S. Klasnick and engineer, T/Sgt James A. Watson received the Silver Star for their actions during the mission.

11. As told to Edgar 'Ed' C. Burford. *John Burn One-Zero-Five* (by William Donald, GMS 2005)

12. Captain Rollie Sargent's crew were shot down on the mission to Schweinfurt on 17 August. Three evaded and seven were taken into captivity.
13. Later *Mr Five By Five* flew in the 384th BG and was lost on the 25 February 1944 mission to Stuttgart when it was flown by Lt Kack K. Larsen.
14. It was *Staffelkapitän* Georg Peter 'Schorch' Eder of 7./JG 2, who singled out *Windy City Challenger* south of Paris. (In November 1942 *Oberleutnant* Georg-Peter Eder, *Staffelkapitän,* 12./JG2 and *Oberstleutnant* Egon Mayer, *Kommandeur,* III./JG2 were credited with developing the head-on attack, where the bomber armament was weakest. In Russia Eder destroyed ten Soviet aircraft before being badly wounded on 24 July 1941. In 1942 he had returned to operations with 7/JG2.) Eder recalls: 'I pushed the black button on the right of the panel and the three yellow rings and cross flicked on in the sight glass. We were doing about 450km/h now and were coming down slightly, aiming for the noses of the B-17s. There were about 200 of us attacking the 200 bombers but there was also the fighter escort above them. We were going for the bombers. When we made our move, the P-47s began to dive on us and it was a race to get to the bombers before being intercepted. I was already close and about 600ft above and coming straight on: I opened fire with the twenties at 500 yards. At 300 yards I opened fire with the thirties. It was a short burst, maybe ten shells from each cannon but I saw the bomber explode and begin to burn. I flashed over him at about 50ft and then did a chandelle.'
15. Johnny Perkins' and six of his crew were killed. Three other crew and a photographer aboard survived and were taken prisoner. Before *Windy City Challenger* went down she and Johnny Perkins had a plan to send the plane home to Chicago like the *Memphis Belle* did. At Chelveston meanwhile, a Fortress was christened *Windy City Avenger* in the crew's honour.
16. The victory was one of four claimed by pilots in the Third *Gruppe* JG 26 at Nordholz who attacked the incoming bombers west of Heligoland. Finally, the *Abschuss* was awarded to *Unteroffizier* Rudolf David. The three other claims were not upheld. See *The JG 26 War Diary Vol 2* by Donald Caldwell (Grub Street, London 1998). Fifty-two bombers were damaged. *Luftwaffe* losses were twenty fighters damaged or destroyed.
17. *See Making For Sweden... Part 2– The USAAF* by Bo Widfeldt and Rolp Wegmann (ARP 1998).
18. On 18 December 1943 listeners to the BBC's evening news learned that Flight Officer (later 2nd Lt) John C. Morgan (now with the 482nd BG) had received the MoH from General Ira C. Eaker in a special ceremony at 8th AF HQ. And they heard him relive the events of 26 July.
19. Combat Crew Replacement Center.
20. *Target Germany*; The US Army Air Forces official story of the VIII Bomber Command's first year over Europe. 1944.

21. Joe made it home before Christmas in 1944. *The Battle Within the Clouds Oschersleben, Germany, July 28, 1943* by Joe Bender.
22. A crippled ship in the 385th BG crashed into two others off Heligoland, bringing down all three. Eight men died aboard *Roundtrip Ticket* and all ten were killed on board *Betty Boom* while only two parachuted to safety from *Lady Susie II*. The Group's fourth loss was *Grim Reaper*, which was shot down by flak.
23. I and II *Jagdgeschwadern* lost twenty FW 190s and Bf 109s with three pilots killed and eight injured.
24. On the return leg over Holland *Leutnant* Eberhard Burath of 1./JG1 singled out *Spook III*, flown by Lt Francis J. Reagen, which was finished off by *Gruppenkommandeur* Hauptmann Emil-Rudolf Schnoor, his third victory. *Spook III* ditched in the North Sea with the loss of all ten crew. Lt James F. Rivers' crashed at Hoehausen and all the crew were taken prisoner. *Exterminator* flown by Lt Fred D. Hughes crashed at Lathen, Germany, and all the crew were made PoW.
25. The 92nd BG lost two of the Forts. 42-3116 in the 407th BS flown by 2nd Lt Harold W. Porter crashed at Wageningen (two KIA, eight PoW). 42-29798 in the 326th BS flown by 1st Lt Benjamin Smotherman crashed at Schelluinen (10 PoW) and *Feldwebel* Erich Ahrens of 3./JG 26 claimed one of them shot out of formation near Dordrecht. During the morning JG 26 claimed a total of four B-17s. See *The JG 26 War Diary Vol 2* by Donald Caldwell. (Grub Street, London. 1998.) At Thurleigh there was no sign of *Peck's Bad Boys* flown by 2nd Lt Stephen W. Peck (all ten PoW) and the Fort flown by 2nd Lt Jack Harris. He and five of his crew were KIA. The 306th BG was also missing another three Forts in crash landings on the return. One, which crashed at Framlingham, hit and damaged a parked B-17F of the 390th BG and was demolished. A 379th ship landed at Foulsham in Norfolk with four injured crewmembers.
26. *First Over Germany: A History of the 306th Bombardment Group* by Russell A. Strong. (1982).
27. *Whale Tail* in the 381st BG landed near Snetterton on return and a damaged 305th B-17 that put down at Oulton was written off.
28. November 1943 issue of *Air Force* magazine.

Index

Stackpole Military History Series

Real battles. Real soldiers. Real stories.

Stackpole Military History Series

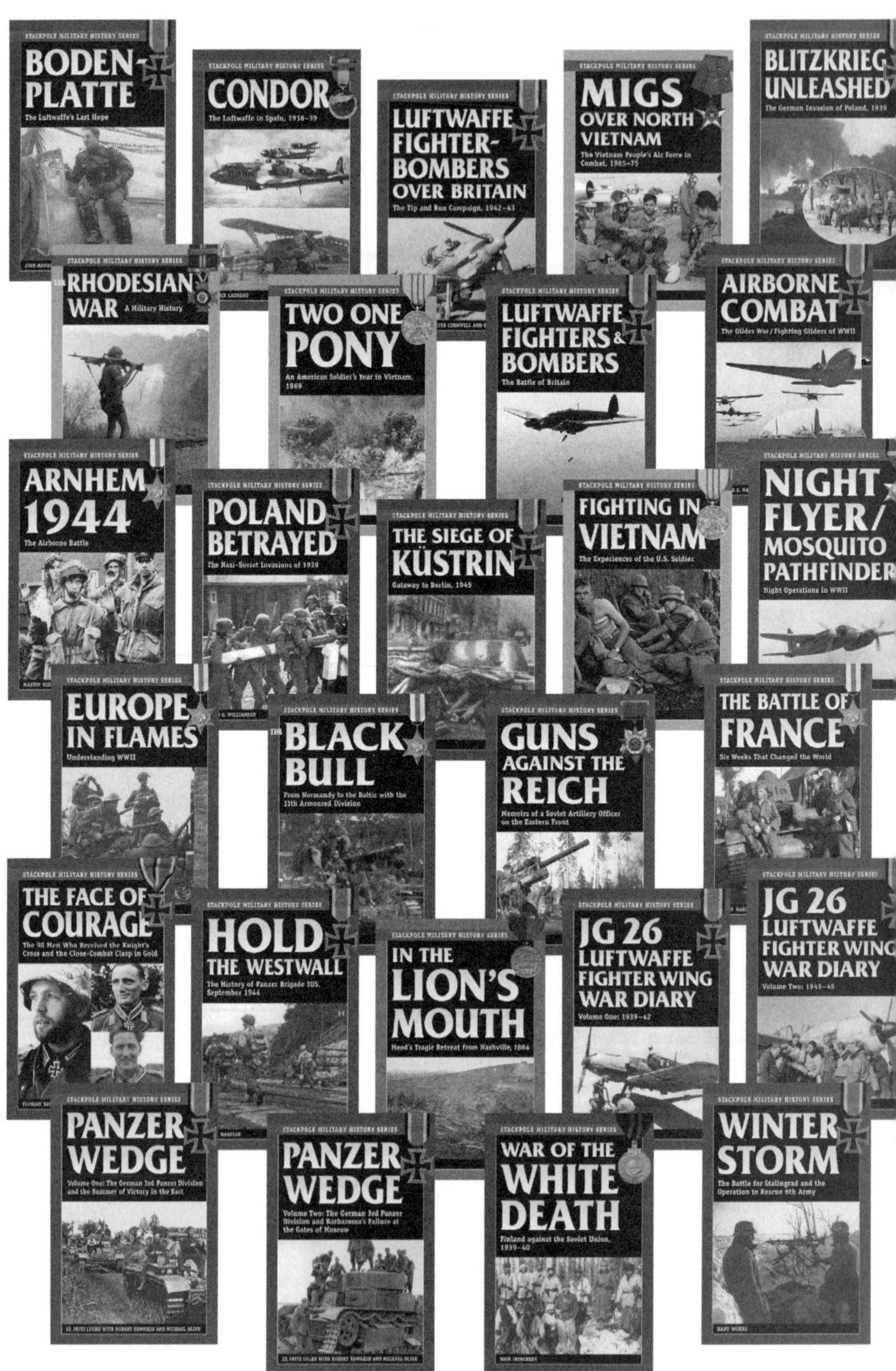

Stackpole Military History Series